Supporting people with alcohol and drug problems

Making a difference

Sarah Galvani

LEARNING
RESOURCES
CENTRE

First published in Great Britain in 2012 by

The Policy Press
University of Bristol
Fourth Floor
Beacon House
Queen's Road
Bristol BS8 1QU
UK

tel +44 (0)117 331 4054
fax +44 (0)117 331 4093
e-mail tpp-info@bristol.ac.uk
www.policypress.co.uk

North American office:
The Policy Press
c/o The University of Chicago Press
1427 East 60th Street
Chicago, IL 60637, USA
t: +1 773 702 7700
f: +1 773 702 9756
sales@press.uchicago.edu
www.press.uchicago.edu

© The Policy Press 2012

British Library Cataloguing in Publication Data
A catalogue record for this book is available from the British Library.

Library of Congress Cataloging-in-Publication Data
A catalog record for this book has been requested.

ISBN 978 1 84742 116 6 paperback
ISBN 978 1 84742 117 3 hardcover

Cover design by The Policy Press.
Front cover: image kindly supplied by www.istock.com
Printed and bound in Great Britain by Hobbs, Southampton.
The Policy Press uses environmentally responsible print partners.

Contents

List of tables, figures and boxes

Tables

Figures

Boxes

Acknowledgements

A number of social work friends and colleagues have contributed to the production of this book. Their advice and experience has been invaluable. These people include: Trevor McCarthy, Kate Holliday, Rachel Hek, Pete Hoey, Melody Treasure, Isfharn Khan, Jo Utting, Nicki Walker, Richard McVey, Linda Sole, Russell Norton.

Thanks go to Larry Harrison and Dr Katy Cigno – friends and former lecturers who encouraged my confidence, passion and interest in substance use issues.

I very much appreciate all the social workers and students who have emailed their interest in, and support for, this book and all those who responded to my requests for advice or help via the jiscmail list on social work–alcohol–drugs. I was only able to follow up some of the offers but they were all greatly appreciated. Particular thanks to regular responders including Jane Elliot, Lynne Froud, Dan Caruana, Alan Laurie, Gwen Moncrieff.

A number of specialist alcohol and drug agencies have also been very supportive of their staff contributing to this book. Those who have given their permission include Dash NHS North West, Project 6 Drug and Alcohol Agency, Aquarius, Angus Council Social Work & Health, Harbour Drug & Alcohol Services.

Finally, my love and thanks go to my parents for their unconditional support and, most of all, to my partner for his endless patience, love and support.

List of abbreviations

AA	Alcoholics Anonymous
ADHD	Attention Deficit/Hyperactivity Disorder
AMHP	Approved Mental Health Professional
BASW	British Association of Social Work
BI	Brief Interventions
BMI	Brief Motivational Intervention
CAF	Common Assessment Framework
CBT	Cognitive Behavioural Therapy
CCETSW	Central Council for Education and Training in Social Work
CM	Contingency Management
CNS	Central Nervous System
CRA	Community Reinforcement Approach
CSIP	Care Services Improvement Partnership
DAAT	Drug and Alcohol Action Team
DCSF	Department for Children, Schools and Families
DfE	Department for Education
DfEE	Department for Education and Employment
DfES	Department for Education and Schools
DH	Department of Health
DSM-IV	*Diagnostic and Statistical Manual of Mental Disorders, 4th edition* (APA 2000)
EMCDDA	European Monitoring Centre for Drugs and Drug Addiction
FASD	Foetal Alcohol Spectrum Disorder
GSCC	General Social Care Council
IAS	Institute of Alcohol Studies
MET	Motivational Enhancement Therapy
MI	Motivational Interviewing
NA/CA	Narcotics/Cocaine Anonymous
NAS	Neonatal Abstinence Syndrome
NATMS	National Alcohol Treatment Monitoring System
NDTMS	National Drug Treatment Monitoring System
NIAAA	National Institute on Alcohol Abuse and Alcoholism
NICE	National Institute for Health and Clinical Excellence
NIMHE	National Institute for Mental Health (England)
NOS	National Occupational Standards
NTA	National Treatment Agency for Substance Misuse
ONS	Office for National Statistics
SCARS	Six Cornered Addiction Rescue System
SCR	Serious Case Review
SDS	Severity of Dependence Scale

TBI   Traumatic Brain Injury
TSF   12-step Facilitation [Therapy]
UKDPC   UK Drugs Policy Commission
YOT   Youth Offending Team

Setting the scene: alcohol and drugs in social work practice

1

Introduction

Social work is a helping profession. While the organisational and policy context in which it sits changes and evolves, at its core remains a profession that seeks to help other people in need of support or at risk of harm. Among these people are those whose use of alcohol and drugs causes, or contributes to, problems to themselves or others.

It is rare that people with alcohol and drug problems are presented as vulnerable and worthy of our support and help. More often the image is of a sickly looking youth hooked on drugs and stealing to fund his habit, or the woman who is prostituted to fund her own and her boyfriend's/pimp's drug use. Alternatively there is the unemployed, red-faced, middle-aged man whose heavy drinking and associated embarrassing behaviour have alienated him from his family and friends. None of these images engenders an empathic or caring response without some reflection on what got people to that point in their lives. More often, the response is unsympathetic and intolerant.

These narrow, stereotypical images serve only to perpetuate the marginalisation of people with substance (alcohol or other drugs) problems and maintain the stigma and shame that prevents people from seeking or receiving help. These images may fit some people with alcohol or drug problems, but they are not an accurate picture of the people who use, or have problems with, alcohol or other drugs. There is no easy stereotype defined by age, level of education, employment status, class, income or gender.

This book provides social work students, social care practitioners and managers with information on alcohol and drug use and guidance on how to engage with, and respond to, people whose use is problematic. It moves away from defining alcohol and drug use as a medical or criminal justice issue, identifying social model perspectives and linking the use of substances to social issues and to potential social harms.

It is an introductory text with chapters that address issues relevant to all areas of social work practice and those areas that, while relevant to all social workers, address substance use within particular service user groups. It covers a range of topics, starting with an overview of why substance use is an issue that deserves social work attention and a summary of the history of social work's relationship to the subject. It makes clear links between engaging with substance use and social work ethics, principles and values, and reviews the conceptual and theoretical framework that marries social work practice and substance use interventions, including the similarities and differences between the theoretical and philosophical frameworks that underpin practice in these areas. It outlines the key approaches to substance use interventions, and good practice in making referrals to substance use services. It also points out the key relevant policy frameworks from both social work practice and substance use that are relevant to working with substance use issues.

This book can be read from start to finish for a comprehensive overview of the topic; however, it can also be used as a resource for information on a particular service user group, bearing in mind that most service users don't fit into one group alone. The first three chapters and the concluding chapter are relevant to all areas of social work practice.

The focus of the text is on alcohol and illicit drugs, with some reference to prescribed drug use where appropriate. While smoking tobacco remains a major public health concern in the UK and often accompanies drinking alcohol and drug use, smoking is a huge subject area and beyond the scope of this book. Similarly, because the focus is sharply on social work and social issues and substance use it will not be possible to address criminal justice responses to substance use in any depth.

Prevalence of alcohol and other drug use

Before focusing on social work practice it is important to understand the broader context of substance use. History provides a clear evidence trail of how substance use has played a greater or lesser role in the customs and traditions of British society. It is this history and the envelopment of substance use within traditional British culture that has perpetuated substance use even when evidence begins to show the negative impact it can have and the problems it can cause for individuals, families and communities.

The extent of substance use is hard to establish, as people's substance use will vary greatly over time. It is also expected that people underestimate the amount of substances they use, particularly in relation to alcohol, where home measures are often much larger than pub measures (Robinson and Harris 2011). This underestimation is worthy of a mental note for any social worker asking about substance use; it is important to accept that people, through ignorance, shame or fear of the consequences, may underestimate or not fully disclose their substance use.

The UK's annual surveys of drinking, smoking and drug use provide the most recent estimates on prevalence in the population. Further, they allow analysis of patterns of substance use, changes in consumption by particular drug type or within a particular group of people or geographical region. These data in turn feed in to decisions about where specialist support and services need to be targeted.

For drinking and smoking the annual General Lifestyle Survey (formerly the General Household Survey) provides data on the frequency and extent of alcohol consumption, as well as individual characteristics associated with it. Alcohol consumption is measured in terms of alcohol units, and reported as such.

> **Box 1.1: Alcohol units[1] (NHS Choices 2011)**
>
> - An alcohol unit is defined as 10ml or 8g of pure alcohol.
> - The body takes about one hour to process one unit of alcohol (although this will vary from person to person).
> - Daily guidelines for the number of units of alcohol that men and women should not regularly exceed are **2–3 units for women** and **3–4 units for men.**
> - The number of units in a drink can be calculated multiplying its strength by the amount in litres and dividing by 1000: For example, to work out the number of units in a pint (568ml) of strong lager (ABV 5.2%): 5.2 (%) x 568 (ml) ÷ 1,000 = **2.95** units; a litre of 13% ABV wine has 13 units; a 500ml – ½ litre – bottle of 4.8% ABV beer = 2.4 units (half of 4.8).
>
> NB. To help you calculate your own or somebody else's units, there are 'unit calculators' freely available online or contact your local alcohol service. Currently in the UK many – but not all – drinks have unit information on the label.

The following data are drawn from the most recent survey on alcohol consumption (Robinson and Harris 2011). Overall alcohol consumption has fallen for both men and women since 2000–02 and more people are reporting abstinence than in previous years. Nevertheless, 37% of men and 29% of women reported drinking more than the recommended daily number of units on one day in the seven days prior to the survey, with 20% of men and 13% of women reporting drinking heavily on more than one day in the previous seven days. These are large proportions of the population.

Men remain far heavier drinkers than women, and this is particularly evident in the over-65 age group, where men's average weekly unit consumption far outweighs women's (12.7 units compared to 4.6 units). Those in higher socioeconomic groups also drink more, on average, than those in lower classes. The same pattern holds for household income: those in higher-paid or managerial roles drink, on average, more than those in lower-income or manual roles (Robinson and Harris 2011). People in lower-income groups experience higher levels of alcohol-related harm in relation to their consumption (National Institute for Health and Clinical Excellence (NICE) 2010). This suggests that higher class and income confers a level of protection or access to support or resources.

Figures for people in alcohol treatment in 2009/10 show more than 111,000 people reporting alcohol as their primary drug of choice, with a further 31,000 stating it to be one of a number of drugs they had problems with (DH/National Treatment Agency (NTA) 2011). The average age of people in treatment services was 41 years and the vast majority were ethnically White British (88%) and male (65%).

Annual drug misuse figures are even harder to estimate, given the illegal nature of most drug use. Unsurprisingly, it is the Home Office that is responsible for the annual reports of drug misuse, as part of the British Crime Survey in England and Wales. The survey only covers 16- to 59-year-olds, with separate survey data exploring the drug use of those aged 11–15 years (see Chapter Eight). The survey records drug use within the last year and whether survey subjects have 'ever' used. In 2009/10, as with alcohol, overall drug use had fallen; 8.8% of adults stated that they had used drugs in the previous 12 months, although the use of Class A drugs (3%) has remained stable (Millard 2011).

Box 1.2: Classification of drugs

Drugs are classified under the Misuse of Drugs Act 1971 according to the degree of harm they are thought to cause when 'misused'. There are three categories or classes: A, B and C, with Class A containing the drugs thought to be the most harmful and Class C the least harmful. Examples of drugs and classes are as follows:

- Class A – heroin, ecstasy, magic mushrooms, morphine
- Class B – amphetamines (speed), cannabis, mephedrone
- Class C – ketamine, tranquilisers, GHB.

Criminal justice sanctions for drug offences, for example, possession, trafficking, are harsher for the drugs with higher classifications.

In relation to particular drugs, use of powder cocaine decreased slightly. As in previous years, cannabis remained the most popular drug, followed by powder cocaine and ecstasy. Despite falling levels of young people's use overall, one in five of the younger cohort (16–24 years) had used drugs once or more in the previous 12 months. An important finding for social workers, is that the home – either their own or someone else's – was the most common place to have bought or been given drugs (Millard 2011).

In relation to treatment, there was an increase in methadone use and more than 206,000 adults were in touch with treatment services, with 50% being treated for heroin or crack-cocaine use (Davies et al 2010). The UK Drugs Policy Commission (UKDPC) estimates that over 1.4 million adult family members live with a problematic drug user (Davies et al 2010).

Research on the prevalence of alcohol and drug use among social work caseloads in the UK is even more limited, given the lack of a consistent social work approach to identification, assessment or intervention of substance use. However, the following figures relating to specific service user groups provide some indication of the potential scale of the problem:

- In a review of the evidence, Manning et al (2009) found that for children under 16 years of age, 6% were living with a 'dependent drinker' and 2.8% of children were living with a 'dependent drug user'.
- In relation to social work caseloads, evidence suggests 40–70% of child protection cases involve parental substance use, depending on the stage that child protection proceedings have reached (Hayden 2004; Galvani et al 2011).
- For young people, UK figures show alcohol and drug consumption is decreasing; however, UK youth remain near the top of the alcohol and cannabis use tables when compared to other countries within Europe (Hibell et al 2009). Evidence from social workers in England suggests that almost one-third of young people in touch with social services included concerns about their substance use, and similar levels were reported for a cohort of looked-after children (Galvani et al 2011).
- For people suffering mental distress, there are wide-ranging estimates; from 15% to over 50% for the prevalence of substance use (see Chapter Nine for review). In one recent study of social workers in England, they estimated that almost one-third of their service users (32%) had coexisting substance problems (Galvani et al 2011).
- Anecdotal evidence from social workers suggests that older people's substance use, particularly use of alcohol, is noticeably increasing, as is problematic prescription drug use. The lack of prevalence data about substance problems among older people is a major gap in the research, however. Galvani et al (2011) reported social workers' estimates that 5% of their caseloads involved concerns about an older person's substance

use. However these social workers also reported difficulty in identifying substance use and few asked routine questions, suggesting that this figure is almost certainly an underestimate.

■ Two other areas that are minimally researched in relation to substance use in the UK are learning disabilities and physical disabilities. There are difficulties in the data that do exist, as they often focus on a particular learning or physical disability, for example, low IQ, or hearing impairment, while other data include all disabilities without differentiation. For people with learning disabilities, the prevalence of substance use appears to be quite low, although it is higher among those with mild learning disabilities. One study of social workers reported that 9% of their caseloads of people with learning disabilities involved concerns about their substance use (Galvani et al 2011). For people with physical disabilities, US data suggest prevalence is far higher than among the general population and some UK data appears to support this (Hoare and Moon 2010), but again, caution is needed and the research to date is not conclusive.

Added to this, social workers are also working with a number of substance-related issues that fall less neatly into particular groups. For example, domestic abuse and substance use are highly correlated (Galvani 2010a), even though the relationship between the two is not a direct causal one. Childhood abuse is a common precursor to problems with alcohol or drugs in adolescence and adult life (Simpson and Miller 2002; Jonas et al 2011), and research suggests that family members of people with alcohol or drug problems have poorer physical and mental health outcomes, although this improves with interventions for family members in their own right even if the family member does not engage in treatment (Copello et al 2000a; Orford et al 2007).

When people have problems using substances, these rarely affect them alone – they have wider ramifications for partners, children, friends, colleagues and the social acceptance of the individual within non-using social circles. There are no clear estimates of the number of people affected by a person's problematic substance use, but it is known that children avoid bringing friends home for fear of embarrassment and will not accept invitations from others because they are unable or unwilling to reciprocate. Adults can stop social contact with friends who use drugs or drink heavily because they are always the last to leave, behave badly or put pressure on others to use substances to the same extent. The social isolation that ensues for the individual and their family is one consequence of problematic substance use that is often overlooked, yet evidence repeatedly shows its importance, along with a stable home environment, in helping people to overcome drug and alcohol problems (Azrin 1976; Costello 1980; Powell et al 1998; Dobkin et al 2002). Social workers are perfectly placed to support individuals and families to overcome their problems with alcohol or drugs when working in partnership with others to provide specialist substance use interventions.

As noted earlier, there is a need for better research evidence on the prevalence of substance use in a number of areas of social work practice. However, we can make some observations based on the evidence that we have. The obvious one is that these are not small numbers of people, and evidence suggests that these numbers are often reflected within social work caseloads. If social workers are prepared – in both senses of the term – to engage appropriately with these issues when they arise, they are likely to provide a better quality of service to service users. Such preparation will also help social workers to unpick the often overlapping issues they are presented with in complex cases. However, history suggests that the preparation of social workers for this work has been found wanting, with social workers receiving low levels of education in relation in supporting people with alcohol and other drug problems.

History and relevance to social work practice

While most social workers do not specialise in substance use, it is often one of the most challenging issues they face in the course of their work. As the evidence suggests, many areas of social work practice, particularly in children and family social work contexts, encounter high levels of substance use alongside domestic violence and mental ill-health (Galvani and Forrester 2008; Ofsted 2008; Brandon et al 2010; Galvani et al 2011). Substance use may not always be evident at the first meeting or initial assessment; alternately, it may be one of a number of overlapping and complex issues that have triggered the involvement of social care. Wherever and whenever it arises, social workers need to be able to know what to ask, how to ask it and how to intervene when they or the people they are working with are concerned about substance use.

The National Occupational Standards (NOS) for Social Work mention alcohol and drug users as one of several 'main groups of people using services' and for whom social workers must learn appropriate 'theories, models and methods' of working (TOPSS 2002).[2] While this recognition is important, it has failed to address the need for social workers to have an underpinning knowledge of the subject and confidence in recognising and identifying the issues before being able to apply theories, models and methods. Research shows that many social workers lack both training and confidence in addressing these issues (Galvani and Forrester 2011a; Galvani et al 2011). Theories, models and methods are helpful, but only once the underpinning knowledge is in place that allows people to identify and begin to engage in conversation about alcohol and drug use.

Historically, social workers have not been well trained or supported to work with alcohol or other drug use among their service user groups (Harrison 1992; Lawson 1994; Davies et al 1995; Kent 1995; Corby and Millar 1998; Adams 1999; Forrester 2000; Harwin and Forrester 2002; Foster et al 2003; Guy and Harrison 2003; McCarthy and Galvani 2004; Galvani 2007). This is not the fault of individual social workers; it is more to do with a lack of recognition by policy makers and social work educators that alcohol and drug issues are something social workers encounter and for which they need at least basic preparation (see Galvani 2007 for a review). Combined with traditional notions of substance problems as the remit of health and/ or criminal justice professionals, this has resulted in the people working with the social consequences of substance use not receiving the substance use education and support that they need. This lack of understanding about social work roles is reflected in the national drug and alcohol strategies in England, where there is no mention of social workers in responses to substance use (Home Office 2002a; Cabinet Office 2004; DH et al 2007; HM Government 2010a). Social work has not been seen as having a front-line role in working with people using alcohol and drugs. This has resulted in social work education that has not routinely incorporated substance use components in qualifying and post-qualifying programmes, and social work practice that frequently fails to engage with these issues.

For more than three decades there have been attempts to influence social work education, training and practice in terms of their engagement with substance use issues (see Galvani 2007 for a review); however, evidence suggests that little has changed (Galvani et al 2011). Guidance for social work education on substance use issues has been noticeably absent since the publication of *Substance misuse: Guidance notes for the Diploma in Social Work* by the Central Council for Education and Training in Social Work (CCETSW) for England in 1992. This publication resulted from curriculum development work led by Larry Harrison at the University of Hull, following concern expressed by the Department of Health and the Inter-Ministerial Group on Alcohol Misuse. They noted the 'inadequate' professional education for social workers on this subject (Harrison 1992: 7). Since then, concerns about other drug use, in addition to alcohol, have increased, and polydrug use is common, yet social work education has failed to respond. The lack of engagement with substance use by social work education means that social workers often feel ill equipped to perform this element of their job with confidence. Other social care professionals fare even worse, with very few ever having received education or training in substance use (Galvani et al 2011).

However, it is possible that the tide is turning a little. The final reports from the Social Work Task Force (2009) and the Munro review of child care social work practice (Munro 2011) highlight alcohol and other drug problems as being among the issues having a negative impact on service users and for which people may need social work support. The Curriculum Development Group of the Social Work Reform Board has stated that substance use is one area of social work education for which there will be guidance (personal communication, Burgess 2011). The Coalition government's drug strategy (HM Government 2010a) emphasises the need to better support families and communities affected by substance problems. It references the work of the Munro review and the Social Work Reform Board as vehicles to engage social workers in issues around the impact of parental substance use on children and families. Clearly, social workers are well placed to provide this type of support and are suitably experienced in working within these contexts. In addition, the government wants communities' needs to be assessed and commissioned at a local level, with input from all key statutory and voluntary sector providers of health and social care. This provides a timely opportunity for social care providers to advocate for greater support and services for families and communities and to join forces with specialists to support the social work and social care workforce in improving its practice in the area of substance use.

One of the defining characteristics of the social work profession is its commitment to viewing people within their environment with all its constituent parts. The theoretical frameworks that underpin our professional training include both environmental theories, for example, ecological theory (Bronfenbrenner 1979 cited in Jack and Jack 2000) and individual theories, for example, attachment theory (Bowlby 1951 cited in Misca 2009). The importance of this range of theory is in its recognition of the interplay in people's lives between the individual and the environmental. It is about looking not just at the individual but also at their partners, family, home and work environments. It is about recognising the negative impact that social exclusion and disadvantage have on a person's ability to cope with the problems they encounter, including difficulties with substance use. Too often, social workers face hugely important decisions about people's lives where alcohol or drug use is just part of a bigger more complex picture. Thus, underpinning knowledge of substances, patterns of use and their impact on individuals, families and friendships can help us to better understand how alcohol and drugs relate to some of the issues and decisions we are faced with in practice. If this knowledge is coupled with support on how best to approach, assess and respond to a person's substance use, it is likely that we will be better equipped to intervene at different points in a person's substance use, rather than be faced with problematic use at the point of crisis intervention.

Substance use and social work ethics and values

At the core of social work practice is a particular set of ethics and values. Social work education at all levels stresses the need to explore and critically reflect on our personal ethics and values, the extent to which these are similar to or different from professional ethics and values, and how they can have an impact on our attitudes and social work practice. All social workers must be prepared to abide by a particular ethical code of practice, as determined by the General Social Care Council (GSCC) (2010) (Box 1.3).

Box 1.3: Code of Practice

Social care workers must:

1. Protect the rights and promote the interests of service users and carers;
2. Strive to establish and maintain the trust and confidence of service users and carers;
3. Promote the independence of service users while protecting them as far as possible from danger or harm;
4. Respect the rights of service users whilst seeking to ensure that their behaviour does not harm themselves or other people;
5. Uphold public trust and confidence in social care services; and
6. Be accountable for the quality of their work and take responsibility for maintaining and improving their knowledge and skills.

On the surface, this is easy to sign up to. However, applying such principles to particular issues or particular groups of service users whose actions or behaviour make them less popular or sympathetic requires maturity and a commitment to the Code of Practice without exception. People who have problems with alcohol and drugs are often presented in a negative and unfavourable light, particularly if their substance use is related to harmful or abusive behaviour towards others.

Consider how easy it is to show respect for the rights of a young person with a drug problem who is verbally abusive towards you and your colleagues and repeatedly lies about their substance use. Consider how easy it is to maintain the trust and confidence of a mother whose children are at risk of accommodation, due to neglect stemming from her substance problems. Consider how easy it is to promote the independence of a man with serious mental health problems who wants to live alone but whose history of substance use is linked to non-compliance with medication and deterioration in mental and physical health. While these examples may not be representative of the range of people presenting to social workers for support, it is these extremes that push our adherence to the codes of practice to the limit.

Further, where personal beliefs, for example religious prohibition of alcohol or other drug use, conflicts with people's right to choose and use substances, how do you ensure that your body language and attitude remain respectful and do not appear judgemental? If you have grown up in a family where parental or grandparental substance use had a negative impact on your life, how do you overcome the urge to judge others' use of substances harshly?

What will help is remembering the basic mantra – *nobody starts using drugs or alcohol with the intention to develop a problem* – as well as remembering the reasons why people start and continue using alcohol and drugs (see Chapter Two). People with alcohol and drug problems can be vulnerable too, and starting from a point of listening and understanding, rather than rushing to judgement, is vital and key to good social work practice. Empowering practice is about working in a way that enables individuals to make informed choices. Some people with substance problems will feel both powerless and lacking in choices, however confidently they may present. It is part of the social worker's role to understand this and to work with people in a way that demonstrates their commitment to the Code of Practice and their commitment to supporting, not punishing, the service user.

It is also part of the Code that social workers must take responsibility for 'improving their knowledge and skills'. Not knowing enough about substance use to make an informed decision affecting the lives and liberties of service users is a breach of the Code of Practice. Assuming that any heroin use means bad parenting or that alcohol use is to blame for domestic abuse is ignorant and bad practice. No one is asking all social workers to become substance use specialists. All social workers should have good enough knowledge to prevent basic errors of judgement and the awareness not to impose value judgements on people without any understanding of what got them to the point of problematic alcohol or other drug use. Only then can they best support them to overcome it.

Summary

Given the scale of alcohol and other drug use, it is hard to believe that social work as a profession has failed to fully grasp its important role in supporting people with alcohol and other drug problems. However, history provides some insight into why this may be, and history in the making suggests that the tide may well be turning. Responding to substance use is part of a social worker's job, whatever their specialist area of practice. The social worker needs enough knowledge to intervene appropriately (prior to referring to specialists if required), and the social work manager needs the knowledge to support and supervise their staff well. It is the job of both to work in partnership with specialist services and a range of other resources to ensure that the person's needs are met and that important social and psychological support is in place to help those who want to change their drinking or drug-using behaviour.

Notes

[1] Alcohol units and related guidance are under review by the Department of Health at the time of writing.

[2] At the time of writing the NOS for Social Work are under review.

Working with people using substances

Practice examples

1. Dawn (38), single mum of Amy (5)

Dawn and Amy have been referred to the children and families team by Amy's school teacher, who was concerned that Dawn had been drinking on several occasions when she arrived in the car to collect Amy from school. When you visit Dawn for an initial assessment, she thanks you for coming, states that she wasn't drinking that day, that she does have a drink occasionally but not during the day, and she would not drink and drive. She states that she has been drinking more since her partner left two months ago, just to help herself to relax, and that while she's 'not an alcoholic or anything' she would be prepared to speak to someone if you think they could help her to relax.

2. Andy (24), living in a hostel

Andy has been referred to your team because of concerns about his mental health and related behaviour. The hostel staff understand that he has a history of drug use which coincides with a rapid deterioration in his mental health, as he increasingly forgets to take his medication. When you speak to him, he denies using drugs and says he just needs to get his medication sorted out.

3. Gary (72) retired, husband of Helen (66)

Gary is an active man who is a keen gardener and is a season-ticket holder for West Bromwich Albion FC. In recent years he has developed some mobility problems and has become increasingly frustrated at his inability to do the things he normally does. You have been assessing Gary's support needs and Helen's ability to care for him. Helen tells you that he had not been drinking for 20 years since she threatened to leave him if he didn't get help, but that recently he has started to drink spirits heavily in the evening for 'medicinal' purposes and gets angry with her when she raises the issue. In the last month she has found him asleep on the floor in front of the fire on many occasions during the night, and when she wakes him he is verbally abusive to her. When you speak to

Gary in private, he becomes tearful and says he doesn't want Helen to leave him, but he's not coping and has started drinking heavily again.

Why people use alcohol and drugs

Nobody starts using alcohol or drugs intending to develop a problem. When children think about what they want to be when they grow up, or adults think about what their future holds, nobody plans to become reliant on substances just to feel normal, or to spend years battling alcohol or drug problems. This seems obvious, but the importance of a social worker's ability to understand the unintended nature of substance problems is paramount to their ability to empathise and begin to cut through unhelpful stereotypes. The next step is thinking about people's motivations for using alcohol or drugs. This helps to broaden our understanding of why people start using, stop using, continue using, and develop problems with it.

There are a range of theories that have sought to explain why and how people develop substance problems, ranging from moral weakness, through psychological and social learning theories to genetic models of addiction (Peele and Alexander 1998). However, the starting-point of alcohol or other drug use could be a result of many factors: individual, interpersonal, environmental and socio-cultural, or a combination of all of these. For some cultures, particularly those underpinned by strong religious adherence, alcohol and drug use is not acceptable, but for others the use of alcohol, in particular, has played a traditional role in the history of celebrations, commiserations and religious and social events. Thus, the reasons why people start using alcohol or drugs range from cultural norms and learned behaviour to rebellion against cultural or societal constraints, and many points in between. The following list identifies some of the reasons why people begin using substances:

- to experience something new
- to have fun
- to feel more confident
- to fit in with peers or respond to peer pressure
- to take a risk
- to rebel
- to feel better or feel relaxed
- to forget work/home problems
- to escape emotional and/or psychological pain, including past or current abuse
- to celebrate or commiserate

- to conform with cultural norms
- for medical purposes.

Adolescence and early adulthood is the time when many people start trying substances and, while some people will continue to use drugs and/or drink, many people will stop or only use drugs or drink socially. It is mistaken to think of substance use as a simple journey along a continuum, with people starting at one end and taking the inevitable path to ruin at the other. Substance use is complex and people are creative. Patterns of substance use change according to many factors, often to do with life events, peer pressure, availability, affordability, accessibility and so on. For example, new responsibilities, such as parenting or employment, can lead to a change in people's patterns of substance use. People may use less to ensure that they are able to respond to the children in the night or to get up for work and function well during the day. Similarly trauma, bereavement or stress in a person's life may lead to increased use, either temporarily or over a longer term.

However, there will be people who continue to use, or find it difficult to stop or reduce their alcohol or drug consumption. Some of the reasons for this are the same as why people start using, but additional reasons might include:

- to avoid feeling ill when they try to cut down (physical and psychological withdrawal symptoms)
- to avoid painful memories coming back
- to avoid feeling ashamed and guilty
- not knowing how to fill the time that discontinuing substance use might leave them with
- all their friends drink/use – fear of loneliness
- drinking and/or using drugs makes them feel 'normal'
- not knowing how to relax or enjoy themselves without it
- not believing they have a reason or need to cut down or stop.

As social workers, we are working with people at all stages of substance use. Understanding the reasons why people use and continue using, in spite of problems, gives us a clue about what intervention might be appropriate and what support the person might need when we start to work with them. This will be explored further in the next chapter.

Critical reflection

Effective working with people with substance problems requires honest, critical reflection on the part of the social worker. Understanding our own attitudes towards working with people with substance problems has to come first. If we fail to recognise our own potentially prejudicial attitudes towards people with alcohol or drug problems, it is certain that the service user will. On the one hand there are clear codes of practice (GSCC 2010) that registered social workers must adhere to and that seek to define and promote social workers' approach and attitudes to the services they provide. These are further supported by codes of ethics (BASW 2002) from key social work associations. On the other hand, there are the powerful messages that we are exposed to from family, peers, media, personal and professional experience. Consider the potentially different views about how to respond to Dawn and Amy's situation if a practitioner has personal negative experience of living with a parent with alcohol or drug problems, compared to a practitioner without those experiences? Similarly, how might a practitioner's religious beliefs, which forbid and condemn the use of alcohol or drugs, potentially be affected in their work with Andy or Gary?

People with alcohol and drug problems are used to being judged, looked down upon and having negative assumptions made about their honesty and abilities. They will easily detect any of these through both the non-verbal and the verbal communication of the professionals they meet. The starting-point for working with anyone, regardless of their particular needs or problems, is the same. It is about genuine respect, warmth and honesty. It is about being prepared to ask the questions and engage with the issues, not about having an encyclopaedic knowledge of alcohol and other drugs, their effects and street names. Most social workers do not specialise in substance use (although there are an increasing number who do), and for those who do not, critical reflection is also about knowing what you know and don't know.

Knowing enough

A social worker's knowledge about drugs and alcohol does not have to be comprehensive, but they do have to know enough to feel confident to ask the right questions and offer some basic advice or brief intervention. The NOS for Social Work mention alcohol and drug users as one of several 'main groups of people using services' and for whom social workers must learn appropriate 'theories, models and methods' of working (TOPSS 2002).[1] While this is important, social workers must first have a basic knowledge of alcohol and drugs to enable them to identify the alcohol or other drug problem. They will then be able to apply the theories, models and methods where appropriate.

A basic knowledge comprises:

1. an understanding of why people use alcohol or drugs and may develop problems;

2. an awareness of the range of effects alcohol and/or drugs might have on a person or others around them;

3. an understanding of the challenges people face in trying to change their problematic use;

4. the ability to communicate sensitively and effectively with people about their substance use, for example, knowing what to ask, how, and when to ask it;

5. a broad understanding of the range and types of intervention and support available;

6. some knowledge of local services (or at least how to find out quickly).

The examples at the beginning of the chapter briefly outline three different scenarios. If you were going to talk to Dawn it would be helpful to know about:

1. *alcohol effects*: to understand why she uses alcohol to relax, but also to discuss with her the downside of using it to relax when/if it seemed appropriate to do so;

2. *units of alcohol*: to be able to help her work out how much she is drinking and compare that with recommended levels. People often won't realise how much they are drinking – particularly 'home' measures – and just knowing the facts can help to change behaviour;

3. *local services*: Dawn is open to getting some support, so it would be important for you to offer support quickly by explaining the types of service available and giving her information or making a referral for her.

It might be helpful to look at the other two examples in the same way. For example, with Gary and Helen it would help to know about relapse, as well as to know what support specialist agencies offer to family members in case Helen wants support. In Andy's case, you need to think about why he might deny any drug use and to understand the ways substance use and mental health are related (or whom to ask).

 Evidence suggests that when people have training on this subject and a basic knowledge they feel more confident about asking questions and discussing substance use issues. They also feel more supported to do so (Galvani and Hughes 2010; Galvani and Forrester 2011a). Research shows that the outcomes that people achieve can be highly influenced by the relationship they develop with their 'therapist' or professional (Project MATCH Research Group 1998; Baird et al 2007). Knowing enough is therefore a two-way process. The social worker will feel more supported by their knowledge base and confident enough to raise the issue with both the service user and their supervisor when it arises. They will also be able to offer more informed choices and support to the service user, resulting in a better service.

Recognising substance use

There is no 'one size fits all' effect of any substance. Effects will depend on an individual's biological and psychological make-up, their mood, physical tolerance, what other substances have been taken, their beliefs about the effects of the substance and many other factors.

One of the challenges in recognising substance use is working out how to differentiate between somebody who is experiencing the effects of substance use and someone who is experiencing similar effects for other reasons.

Consider the potential difficulties in recognising the difference between someone who is suffering mental illness and experiencing visual or auditory hallucinations and somebody who is hallucinating through drug use. People withdrawing from chronic, heavy drinking may also experience hallucinations. How would you differentiate between someone who has worked double shifts for the past three days and is so tired they can hardly keep their eyes open or speak coherently, and someone who might have taken tranquillisers and/or alcohol?

 The important thing to remember is that the client is the expert on the effects of their substance use. You cannot be an expert in someone else's substance use. It is helpful to have an understanding of the main effects of substances, but ultimately you will need to ASK them to tell you what effect(s) their substance use has on them. This is also a good way to start a conversation, as it puts the person in control and acknowledges their expertise on their own experiences. It allows you to show that you are prepared to learn and to listen to them, and are not just there to tell them what to do.

> ### Box 2.1: Alcohol and drugs information websites
>
> Detailed information on alcohol, drugs and their effects can be found on the following specialist websites:
>
> - Alcohol Concern – www.alcoholconcern.org.uk
> - Drugscope – www.drugscope.org.uk
> - Frank – www.talktofrank.com
> - Re-Solv (solvents and gas use) – www.re-solv.org

Alcohol and drugs, whether legal or illegal, affect many different parts of a person's physiology as the body breaks down and processes the substance(s). The short-term effects are felt by a person as a result of their impact on the body's central nervous system (CNS).

Substances are often put into groups depending on their similar physiological effects on the CNS. These groups are:

- drugs that *depress* the CNS, for example, alcohol, tranquilisers, solvents and gases
- drugs that *stimulate* the CNS, for example, speed, cocaine, crack–cocaine, ecstasy, khat, caffeine, tobacco
- drugs that *alter perceptual function* (hallucinogens), for example, LSD/Acid, magic mushrooms, cannabis
- drugs that *reduce pain*, for example, heroin, opium, methadone, codeine.

People use substances in a variety of ways (Box 2.2). The chosen route of administration will also have an impact on how an individual experiences the effects. For example, injecting into the blood-stream will have more immediate and intense effects than smoking a substance because it is a quicker route to the CNS.

Box 2.2: Ways of using substances

- Orally (chewing, eating, drinking, rubbing into gums)
- Smoking
- Snorting (powders)
- Sniffing (inhaling fumes)
- IV injection (into the veins)
- IM injection (into the muscle)
- Subcutaneous injection ('skin popping' – injecting just underneath the surface of the skin)
- Anally

Some routes of administration are obvious and recognising them will be much easier. In some cases drug paraphernalia used for the preparation and use of the substance will be visible, for example, needles, tinfoil, burnt spoons, bottles or tins of alcohol. Others won't be so obvious to see.

As a non-substance specialist, you will not be expected to know everything there is to know about the preparation and use of all drugs, or the appearance of every type of tablet, capsule, plant and potion in front of you. In addition, it would be wrong and potentially dangerous to make judgements about use and problematic use based on one sign of substance use alone. Consider the person with tins of booze all over the place. They may have a problem with alcohol or they may have had a party and not cleared up. Consider the person who has needles on a table or a 'sharps bin' in the bathroom. They could be injecting drugs and doing so safely and without problems, they could have substance problems or they could be diabetic. It is equally dangerous to make assumptions in the opposite direction. The absence of physical or environmental signs of alcohol or drug use does not mean that the person is not using or drinking to problematic levels. The questions about substance use still need to be asked.

As with all good social work judgements, recognising substance use and, particularly, substance problems needs to take account of a range of indicators, including the service user's view. It is not about jumping to conclusions on the basis of one indicator alone.

Engagement

Building a good relationship with any service user is vital to maintaining engagement and trust. It is particularly important with people who may have a substance problem, because it is perceived to be a shameful and stigmatising behaviour and people may be reluctant to disclose it to you. However, the empathic and non-judgemental approach that underpins social work practice should go some way to building a relationship, provided that you are skilled in communicating it.

How you talk to someone about their substance use will vary according to the context. What you ask and how you ask it depends on a number of issues, including what your role is (therapeutic role or assessment and investigation), the characteristics of the person or people you're working with (for example, the person's age or level of communication), what has already been discussed or disclosed and the impact the substance use is having on them or others, to list just a few. Talking to a young person who is experimenting with alcohol or drugs is likely to be different to talking to a parent whose substance problems, in your opinion, may be negatively affecting their ability to care for their children.

There is no one-size-fits-all question or set of questions, although there are principles for good practice and evidence-based techniques, such as Motivational Interviewing (MI) (Miller and Rollnick 2002), that can be used in a range of contexts. Communication skills are transferable from one subject to the next. Because of the stigma, people with substance problems may expect you to jump to negative conclusions about them and their use. Therefore you need to have clearly thought through how you are going to ask any questions relating to a person's use and communicate from the start why you are asking about it and what will be done with the information.

Box 2.3: Before you start

Consider the following questions:

- What helps you to talk to someone you don't know? What is it about how they look or what they say that would make you want to have a conversation with them?
- What would help you to tell them something you were ashamed about? What would they need to say or do?
- What would stop you from telling them? What type of verbal response or body language would indicate that you should not say any more?

Consider the examples at the start of this chapter. Discussion with Dawn and Gary on the subject of their substance use might be easier than with Andy. However, for all three of them, ask yourself why should they talk to you? What are you able to offer them? What do their responses so far tell you about how you should proceed? If your communication skills are good you will know to take a lead from the verbal and non-verbal signals the other person gives. What would be the point of arguing with Andy about whether or not he is taking drugs? What would that achieve? Working with people who deny or resist discussing their substance use is addressed further later, but it should be evident that pressing the issue when the signals are telling you otherwise is likely to lead to mistrust, resentment, defensiveness and possibly anger and future avoidance: all of which will likely achieve 'disengagement' – the opposite of your desired outcome.

People who have problems with substance use will often have a range of pre-existing or related problems. As a non-substance use specialist, it is likely that you are meeting the person for reasons other than their substance use. Supporting people with their other problems or offering to do something and delivering on it will begin to indicate that you are someone who can be trusted. In most cases, you can return to the subject of substance use later. Even where there are serious child-safeguarding concerns, you can still remain empathic about the challenges of parenting and wanting an escape from the responsibility every now and again, while focusing on the concerns about the child and how to help the parents to do things differently. Stating that you have concerns about their substance use and need to discuss it with them can include reassurances that doing so does not automatically mean that their children will be removed, as some people think. Remind them that there are as many myths about social workers as there are about people who use drugs and alcohol!

Engaging with people about their substance use will be made more difficult for both you and the service user if you are not confident in asking about it. If you hesitate or adopt an apologetic tone, as opposed to a matter-of-fact tone, the person is more likely to become defensive. Be clear that it is part of your role to ask, and be clear why you're asking. You may want to state clearly that you are not there to judge the person, only to ensure that their alcohol or drug use doesn't mean that they, or somebody else, are at risk of harm. (See the following section on assessment for further information.)

Assessment and intervention

According to the Department of Health (DH) and National Treatment Agency (NTA) (DH/NTA 2006; NTA 2006[2]), social workers should be able to:

■ give drug and alcohol advice and information
■ undertake screening and assessment
■ conduct brief interventions where appropriate
■ make referrals to specialist alcohol or drug services
■ carry out partnership or 'shared care' working with specialist alcohol or drug services.

Further, the assessment process includes:

■ identifying a drug or alcohol problem
■ identifying related or coexisting problems (for example, physical, psychological, social)
■ identifying any immediate risks
■ assessing the urgency of a referral.

Additional policy documents have reinforced the need for closer working between substance use services and social care or for greater involvement of social care staff. Much of their focus has been on parental substance problems and the affected children and young people (DfES/HO/DH 2005; DCSF/HO/DH 2008; DCSF/NTA/DH 2009). There has been far less policy attention to other specialist areas of social work practice that do not focus on children, young people and families.

Assessment is one of the key functions of a social worker's role. This is not new. What is new for many social workers is integrating their knowledge and skills in relation to good assessment practice with some knowledge of drugs and alcohol. In addition, social workers need to accept that it is their job to explore alcohol or drug use among their service users and to feel supported and confident to do so.

You also need to be familiar with your organisation's policy on working with alcohol and drug use among service users where it exists, for example in the local authority's child protection procedures manual.

Box 2.4: Pre-assessment considerations

Before asking someone questions about their substance use it is important that you have clear answers to the following questions:

1. What is the purpose of your assessment?
2. Are you knowledgeable enough to carry out the assessment, given its purpose?
3. What are the implications of this assessment for the service user?
4. If you 'assess', can you meet the assessed needs, that is, do you have or know of available resources, what they offer and how to make a referral to them? What are their policies on working with families, children, young people?
5. Can/have you communicate/d what the assessment is about and what will be done with the information?

Asking about substance use should be a routine part of a social worker's assessment, whatever the service user group. It is important not to assume that because someone is elderly or has disabilities or doesn't 'look like they have a problem', it doesn't exist. Identifying the problematic nature of any alcohol or drug use will require exploration and sensitive questioning that conveys support and empathy. (Examples of questions are provided in the next section.)

To be clear, a social worker is not expected to conduct an in-depth specialist substance use assessment, in the same way that a substance use specialist is not expected to conduct an in-depth assessment of someone's mental health or child protection issues. However, each would expect the other to have some knowledge and undertake a preliminary assessment that would, where necessary, lead to joint working and coordinated intervention and support.

The recommended model of assessment with which many social workers will be familiar is the 'exchange' model of assessment, which is geared towards the professional being a provider of resources and the service user being the expert in their own needs (Smale et al 2000). When used properly, this is the ideal model of assessment for people who are experiencing problems with their drug or alcohol use – ensuring that the individual is able to say what their use is and its impact on them and others, and what their support needs are. It is a model that also acknowledges and respects each other's expertise.

Consider applying the exchange model of assessment to the practice examples identified at the beginning of the chapter:

■ Gary has successfully stopped drinking for a long period of time and is best placed to say what helped him and what has contributed to his recent drinking. The social worker's role is to use the assessment process to help Gary identify his achievement to date, and to glean what worked, as well as what has contributed to his recent drinking. Gary has the expertise on his history with alcohol and alcohol interventions, while the social worker will have access to resources and the ability to respond quickly in terms of referrals for intervention.

■ In Andy's situation, the exchange model would suggest that the social work intervention needs to focus on what Andy believes his needs are, in the first instance. Andy may be using drugs because his medication is not helping or is making him feel ill, or because he's run out of medication.

■ Dawn has provided a clue as to why she might be drinking that should be picked up by the social worker and explored further. Dawn is open to being offered a sympathetic response about how she is feeling and support to help her through it. Discussing her alcohol use as a response to her feelings, and concerns about the alleged drink–driving, may need to wait until after alternative support and coping mechanisms have been explored.

The outcome of any of these assessments should be agreement on what needs to happen and who is to do what next. You may need to refer the person to a specialist service with an appropriate degree of urgency. You may also need to determine if there are any risks to them or to others that need to be addressed immediately, and to inform them of your decision (unless there is a very good reason not to).

How to assess

Assessment has to be appropriate to the context in which it takes place. There are a plethora of tools available for assessing problematic substance use, but many of them are far too detailed for social work purposes and/or are geared to specialist substance professionals. There have been a number of attempts to offer guidance for social workers. More than a decade ago, BASW published guidance (undated) on practice and policy for assessing and working with substance use. Since then, the *Framework for the Assessment of Children in Need and their Families* (DH/DfEE/HO 2000) has included one short assessment tool for assessing serious adult alcohol use, but nothing has been provided for illicit drug use. In 2010 BASW's Special Interest Group in Alcohol and other Drugs published a pocket guide to essential information for social workers encountering drug and alcohol use, including some basic information on substance use (McCarthy and Galvani 2010).

Much of a social worker's role is about assessment, care planning and intervention. However, just as is the case with questions about other issues – for example, someone's health, income or family status – there is no one way of asking about substance use, as this will vary depending on what you already know or how urgent your concerns are. What will help you to approach your assessment with some confidence will be to ensure you are clear about what your options are for asking about substance use and what the available local resources can offer by way of support.

Start by asking yourself what you want to know, and why

When you are clear about why you want to discuss the person's substance use and what you want to know, openness and honesty is the best policy. This does not preclude sensitive and empathic communication, of course. Some examples:

> "I can see you want to be the best parent you can be but I am a bit concerned that your drug use is not helping you to look after James and Laura as best as you could. I want to be honest with you about what I'm thinking."

> "I know that you have a number of aches and pains which must be awful for you. However, I am worried that your drinking is not mixing well with your medication. I think it might have a bad effect on your health."

People may well be defensive when you first raise the issue, because of the shame and stigma attached to alcohol and other drug problems – 'Are you calling me a junkie/alcoholic!?'. Alternatively, they may be glad that you've given them the chance to talk about something that's been bothering them. The tone and manner in which you ask questions can make the difference between the person's defensiveness and disclosure, so make sure that you are conscious of the way you're asking and be ready to reassure the person that you are not judging them or jumping to conclusions.

Explore further with a follow-up question

After raising the issue of substance use with the service user you are then able to follow up with either an open or a closed question. Examples include:

- **Closed**: "Can we talk about this for a bit?" or "Do you mind if I ask you some questions to help me understand better?" or "Can you tell me about how your drinking/drug use makes you feel?"
- **Open**: "How does your drug use/drinking make you feel?" or "What are the advantages and disadvantages about drinking/using drugs?" or "When are you drinking/using drugs most?"

If you ask a closed question, you may get a closed response that may appear negative and dismissive of your concerns. Unless there is an immediate crisis, you may want to leave it on this occasion and return to it on the next meeting/visit; or you could say that you remain worried and ask the person to think about talking to you about it next time. Use your judgement.

In a *crisis*, you may have to state that not talking about it means you have to make decisions based on guesswork and limited information about what's happening. Pointing out that guesswork is probably worse than the reality may facilitate some discussion. You may want, or need, to try again and ask an open question.

Whether it is a crisis or not, it will probably be helpful to make it explicit that you are not making any judgements about the person or the rights or wrongs of their drinking or drug use. Emphasise that you need to understand their situation better.

Establishing willingness to change

The Stages of Change model (Prochaska et al 1992) is used by many substance use services to facilitate discussion between staff and service users about their substance use. It is not an intervention; it is an explanatory model to help people understand the processes involved in changing any type of behaviour that has become habitual. The model can be explicitly used in assessment processes to help the worker and service user reflect on which stage they are at in terms of changing the substance use and therefore how to proceed in their work together. This model can help us to understand the change process as well as give us a tool on which to base our thinking and discussion when talking to clients.

There are five stages to the model:

1. Pre-contemplation
2. Contemplation

3. Preparation
4. Action
5. Maintenance.

In addition, relapse is considered within the model, but it not part of the original five stages.

At the 'pre-contemplation' stage someone is not even thinking about changing their substance use. They may deny problems or not be aware of them. At the 'contemplation' stage, as it suggests, people are beginning to contemplate change and the advantages and disadvantages of doing so. At the 'preparation' stage they may start to plan for the action stage, for example, they may think of excuses they can give to substance-using friends to avoid using or drinking, or they may change the shops they go to or the routes they use for walking home from work, to break their substance-using routines. When someone starts to make changes, they enter the 'action' stage. They may contact an agency for an appointment or change their social behaviour to try to make changes on their own. Maintaining the change is often described by service users as the most difficult phase, particularly once the initial change happens and the professional and social support wanes. Further, so much time and energy is taken up by thinking about or using substances that absence of the activity leaves a gaping hole in people's lives that they need to fill. This is where social workers can rally support, help people to re-establish social networks, provide information in relation to employment and activities to fill people's time, provide information on community resources and so on. It is important not to underestimate the crucial role of supporting someone in the maintenance stage of their change process.

As with any change people make, or attempt to make, it is often not successful the first time. Change is hard, and people changing their substance use may go round this cycle many times, or go back and forth between various stages of it. Consider the example of someone whose substance use was exacerbated by their experiences of domestic abuse or is linked to trying to cope with childhood trauma. Changing substance-using behaviour when it is a coping mechanism may be extremely scary, and therefore it is unsurprising that people may need to make several attempts to change.

Exercise 2.1

Think about some aspect of your personal or professional life that you have changed or have considered changing. Perhaps someone else wants you to change something and you do not want to. Examples include changing jobs, starting a social work course (!), losing weight, getting more exercise, giving

▶

up smoking, or even sorting out that junk cupboard that you keep putting off. Go back to the stages of change outlined above and work out which stage of change you are in. Reflect on what it might take for you to move to a different stage in the change process. What would be helpful or unhelpful responses from those around you? What might motivate you to make that change?

One stage in the change process that is recognised (but is not obligatory) is relapse. In people's attempts to change substance-using behaviours they are likely to make a number of attempts before reaching their desired goals (Witkiewitz and Marlatt 2004). This has been recognised and addressed by the growth of interventions specifically targeting relapse prevention – particularly the use of cognitive behavioural models and building social and interpersonal support (Witkiewitz and Marlatt 2004).

Relapse prevention often comprises group or individual work where service users and staff discuss risk situations for returning to problematic levels of use, and how to avoid them. It also explores individual short- and long-term alternatives to using or drinking, as well as identifying people, places and things that are supportive of the person's goal, and those they need to avoid.

The Department of Health and NTA (2006: 72) state that relapse prevention could include the following:

- 'psychosocial therapies'
- 'social support to make lifestyle changes', for example housing, employment, relationships
- 'pharmacological therapies', albeit alongside psychosocial therapies
- 'a structured programme of activities'.

This is a very important stage of the intervention process, so any support that social workers can offer at this stage should not be underestimated. Ultimately, relapse prevention can empower the person with the skills, techniques and information that will maximise their chances of maintaining their desired substance use goals once they have completed their formal treatment process.

Box 2.5: Relapse and lapse

Relapse and lapse are different. Relapse is about returning to *problematic* levels of substance use, often similar to the levels the person was using before attempting to change, or experiencing similar problems or impairments at different levels of substance use. A lapse is also known as a 'slip'. It refers to a momentary or short-term return to alcohol or drug use or, if reduced consumption is the goal, a return to higher levels than intended. Both experiences should be used positively by specialists and social workers working with the person in order to identify what they have learned from the lapse or relapse that could help them to do something different next time. People who lapse or relapse will often feel ashamed of it, so turning it into as positive an experience as possible will help to keep people motivated and focused on the future rather than feeling guilty about their use.

Tailor assessment appropriately

Establishing which stage of change a person is at can help you to determine (a) the purpose of your questions and (b) what type of questions you should ask. Social work interventions often involve effective questioning and strive to put the service user at the centre of the assessment process, harnessing their expertise on their needs as well as working with other social and healthcare partners. Assessing and intervening in substance use requires the same skills, and therefore social workers are well placed to respond.

Pre-contemplation/not thinking about it/denying there's a problem (Andy)

Even when someone is denying that they have a problem or they are not aware of it, it is important to raise the issue with them and state your concerns. Take care not to sound accusatory or back people into a corner, as this may make things worse. Present your concerns, and any other evidence as supporting your concerns. Give people a chance to take in what's been said and to respond. You can also offer reassurance and support; or offer to discuss it again later if you meet resistance. If there is other evidence of problems relating to their substance use (for example, GP or health visitor concerns, related criminal justice involvement) you may want to be open about it at this point.

If you meet resistance, do not become argumentative, but back off, consider what you're saying and how you're saying it and move on or change direction. If someone is refusing help or denying the problem, arguing about it will achieve nothing. In Andy's case you would be best placed to ask how else you can help him and establish a relationship first. You can come back to the substance use later on.

If there is a need for crisis intervention, and immediate safeguarding action has to be taken, then you may not have the luxury of discussion. In this context you may simply need to state your concerns about the person's substance use and its impact on them or those around them, be clear and honest about the decisions you have to make and clarify any choices the person has at that point. If this is done well, when faced with the awareness of your and their choices, the person may still agree to work with you. If not, you have to take whatever steps are needed, but you still need to keep people informed and try not to let your frustration show in your tone or manner.

It is important not to end contact with the crisis intervention. Follow-up contact once the immediate crisis is over should support the person and set out their choices, including those relating to their substance use. Crises may be turning-points for people, particularly where children are involved, so such opportunities to help people change their substance use should not be lost.

Contemplation/thinking about change (Dawn)

At this stage people are thinking about changing their substance use. Motivational questions should be asked in order to increase the chance that they will decide to take action and make some changes. Miller and Rollnick (2002) refer to the 'decisional balance', where ambivalence is assumed and normal, not seen as a negative thing. Asking questions that highlight the positive side of change include: 'Why are you considering changing at this time?' or, alternatively, 'What will you lose and gain by making some changes?'. Avoid doing a 'hard sell' of specialist substance use help, as this is likely to meet with resistance.

When people are contemplating change it is worth leaving information about local services or other relevant material with them. Also, asking about their fears or concerns about seeking help will help to overcome any barriers they may have to seeking specialist substance use support.

Preparing for change

The preparation stage sits between the contemplation and the action stages. To some extent they overlap; however, preparation tends to stop short of action but moves beyond thinking about change. It involves the mental or physical preparation for making changes. The task of the social worker here is to ask questions that help someone move from contemplation towards action. For example, asking someone 'If you were to make a change in your using/drinking, what aspects of your daily routine might need to change?' or 'Who among your family and friends would support you if you decided to make changes to your substance use?'.

Action/doing or nearly doing something

The action stage is evident when the person has begun to make changes, for example, by contacting a specialist agency, talking to their GP about their use or even looking for information on the internet. It does not necessarily mean that their use will have reduced or stopped; rather, it will be evident that they are working towards doing so. Reducing or stopping their substance use is also the main goal in the action stage, and taking action to reach their particular goals is an important part of this stage. Therefore, asking questions at this stage which enhance motivation and offering practical support is the best strategy. Questions might include whether they would like help or support to make an appointment, or whether they want you to refer them to services. Is there information about the service or some other aspect of their substance use that you can provide – for example, about alcohol and prescribed drugs, parenting and substance use, waiting times? Other questions may focus on practical support, for example helping them to think through how they will get to any appointments in terms of transport and the financial implications, or whether they can take someone with them for support and whom that might be. Are there children or dependent adults who will need looking after? Your job will be to ask these questions and help them to find solutions and look ahead.

Where someone is already receiving services or has had some success in making changes, motivating questions can include how they've succeeded so far, what has helped most and who is there to support them. You may also want to ask for permission to get in touch with any specialist support if there are good reasons for doing so.

If their experience of services has not been a positive one, it is important not to avoid discussing this. Exploring it will help both you and them to learn what worked and what didn't and will inform the next steps. Ensuring that you can support the person when they may feel like giving up trying – for whatever reason – is vital.

Maintenance/maintaining the change – reduction in/abstinence from substance use

As anyone knows who has ever given anything up, it is the 'staying stopped' or maintaining the new habit that can be the hardest thing to do. Substance use is no different. Services users report that, once the initial changes are made, they can feel bored, lonely and fearful about the future without the substance use. Questions here need to focus on what they are doing to help themselves maintain the change and if there's any way you can help. How are they filling the void that the reduction or cessation of substance use has left? What are their risk factors for relapse and what strategies do they have in place to cope with those risks? Changing substance-using patterns, particularly after a long period of use, often means a complete, and sudden, change of life-style and social networks. Supporting people to explore their options and interests is vital in helping them to maintain the change.

Consider Gary's situation at the beginning of this chapter. He had successfully changed his drinking for many years, but nevertheless has found it hard to maintain this during a period of change in his life. Maintenance strategies need to be short-, medium- and long-term.

Relapse/reverting to problematic substance use after stopping or cutting down (Gary)

Avoiding relapse has been likened to having an itch and trying not to give in to the urge to scratch it. It is not uncommon, when people make big changes in their behaviour, for them to return to previous patterns of behaviour, in this case, substance use (Marlatt and Gordon 1985; Witkiewitz and Marlatt 2004). There may be a specific trigger, such as the death of a loved one, the loss of a job or another unforeseen stress, or it could simply be a change of heart or a feeling that 'one won't harm'. For many people, 'one' will not harm, it will not signal a return to problematic use – but for some people it may.

Importantly, relapses and lapses need to be used positively as an opportunity for individuals and professionals to learn from the experience, particularly where the person is keen to try again. What were the circumstances surrounding the relapse? What could the person do differently next time? What made them stop/cut down before, what worked, what didn't work? What would it take for them to be willing to try again? Emphasising their previous success is far more motivating than consoling them over their return to substance use and/or punishing them for it. People will often feel like failures when they relapse, so it is important to acknowledge the strength that was needed to make those changes.

Positive support

Research shows that positive social support of people trying to change their alcohol or drug use can contribute significantly to their chances of success (Azrin 1976; Copello et al 2002, 2006; Dobkin et al 2002; Tracy et al 2005). Many people with substance problems have lost contact with the people who could provide such support, as a result of their substance use. They may have chosen to withdraw from family and friendship circles out of shame and embarrassment, they may have been isolated by family and friends whom they have upset by their behaviour, or family and friends may have become frustrated at their loved one's unsuccessful attempts to change their substance use and have given up on them. Some people with substance problems will have had only their drinking or drug-using networks for support. Changing their substance-using behaviour will usually mean breaking away from these networks. The fear of losing these drinking and using friends and the prospect of loneliness is an incredibly difficult psychological and emotional hurdle at a time of significant change in life-style.

Part of the social worker's task is to recognise these anxieties and isolation. Helping the person think about what support they have, want or could have and the practical steps they can take to develop new networks is important in helping the person to sustain their behaviour change over the long term. This may be through new social activities or it may be through discussing with them whom they would like to re-establish contact with, who has been supportive in the past and who may be prepared to be supportive again. If they are worried about the response they will get, then you can provide help by suggesting what words the person can use when they talk to their family member or friend, or support the person to write to them. You could also role-play the situation to help the person gain confidence.

In the absence of positive social support, the social worker and other health and social care professionals may be among the few supports the person has. Ideally, professional support needs to be provided before, during and after the referral and intervention process. There is a great deal of pressure on social workers to 'close cases', but advocating for them to remain open until the person has attained an appropriate intervention and support network is likely to maximise the chances of longer-term success and minimise the chances of seeing the same person back in the system in the future.

One model for thinking about support is in terms of a safety net. McCarthy and Galvani (2004) outlined a model with the acronym SCARS – the Six Cornered Addiction Rescue System (Figure 2.1). This model visually demonstrates the fact that seeking formal intervention or 'treatment' for alcohol or drug problems is only one element of helping someone to address their substance problems. In the SCARS model, treatment is represented as only one corner of the person's safety net. The model refers to an 'Addiction Rescue System'. Simply stated, 'rescuing' someone, or helping them to help themselves, is part of a much wider package of support, and social workers may be involved in any aspect of it. Indeed, social workers may be picking up any of the six corners, depending on the nature of their role. For example, a social worker working with homeless people with mental ill-health might approach this model from the accommodation corner or the psychological health corner. Similarly, a social worker in a Youth Offending Team might approach from the employment corner, or a Child and Families social worker from the significant relationships corner. It doesn't matter where the involvement starts, but it matters most that the social worker recognises

Figure 2.1: The Six Cornered Addiction Rescue System (SCARS)

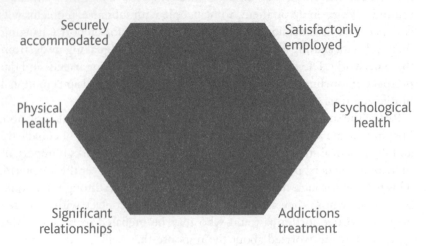

the need for a package of care, identifies where there are gaps and does something to address them. (For full details of the model see McCarthy and Galvani 2004.)

Summary

The reasons why people use alcohol and other drugs are many. Some get into trouble with their use of substances, finding it difficult to cut down or stop. As front-line professionals, social workers are well placed to respond to people who struggle with changing their substance use behaviour or fail to see the negative impact that it has on those around them. Yet, given the stigma associated with substance problems, social workers have to tread carefully and ensure that they know enough about alcohol and other drugs, have reflected on their own views and value base in relation to both substances and are prepared to assess the substance use of service users.

Working with substance use is the remit of all social workers, given that it frequently stems from and leads to social harms. Importantly, ensuring that the person has support in place is vital. The question you need to ask is: 'Who is offering this person support apart from me?' If the answer is no one, then your role is to work alongside the person to get some more support in place. Consider Dawn, Andy and Gary in the practice examples at the start of the chapter. What type of support would benefit them most? In each case, it is clear that their support needs are likely to be very different. The needs may be about joint working with other professionals, or about helping the person to make or re-establish contact with a friend or family member who they think is most likely to support them. Chapter 3 will provide information about the theories, models and methods that underpin specialist substance use services and will help you to gain a better understanding of how these services work, which, in turn, will support better partnership working with specialist substance use professionals.

Notes
[1] The NOS are being revised at the time of writing.
[2] Both under review at the time of writing.

Discussion questions/exercises

1   What are the four groups into which drugs are classified according to their effects?
2   What are the five stages in the Stages of Change model?
3   Using the SCARS model identify what might be the gaps in Dawn's, Andy's and Gary's safety nets.

Further learning resources

■   Barber, J.G. (2002) *Social work with addictions* (2nd edn). Basingstoke: Palgrave. Focuses on the Stages of Change model.

■   Department of Health (2011) *A summary of the health harms of drugs*. London: Department of Health. Available online at: www.nta.nhs.uk/uploads/healthharmsfinal-v1.pdf.

■   Motivational Interviewing website: www.motivationalinterview.org/

■   Specialist websites for information on alcohol and other drugs – see Box 2.1.

3

Working with specialist substance use services

Practice examples

1. Aquarius

Aquarius is a Midlands-based charity providing community and residential alcohol and drug services across the region. It uses a social model approach to substance use and works in a way that supports people to set their own goals for their substance use, that is, reducing their use or stopping altogether. It provides individual, group and family work tailored to each individual's needs. It has outreach projects in local estates and hospitals, drink-drive and criminal justice education projects and a number of developing services, including a service for older people.

2. Action on Addiction

Action on Addiction offers residential care and structured day care for people with alcohol and drug problems. It operates mainly from a medical model perspective, using an abstinence-based programme that is linked to the 12 steps of the Alcoholics Anonymous and Narcotics Anonymous fellowships. It also works with families, offers training courses and actively supports research with academic partners in London and Bath.

3. Community drug and alcohol teams

Most regions in the UK have community alcohol and/or drug teams. In some areas these will be a combined team, in others they will be separate. While services can be contracted out to charitable organisations, the community teams can be statutory teams too. What services are offered will differ in structure and availability according to local need, but they will usually include assessment, individual counselling, group work and a substitute medication prescribing service. The models used usually include both abstinence and harm reduction approaches.

Introduction

Specialist alcohol and drug services take many forms. These range from the two-person outreach team contacting people in the community, to the office-based community service delivering counselling, family or prescribing services, or the residential service that combines medical detoxification and intensive rehabilitation. Some services work with both alcohol and drug issues, others address only one. Some services specialise in working with particular groups of people, for example, young people, people on court-ordered treatment programmes or those using a particular substance, for example, crack users; others work with whoever comes through the door. Some services adopt medical models of understanding and responding to people with alcohol and drug problems; others are underpinned by social models and theories of social learning and use the language of 'intervention', as opposed to treatment. Some services use a mix of both.

Having a beginning understanding of the range of services and approaches available is necessary in order to be able to support service users who need, and accept, specialist intervention for their substance use. You need to be able to refer the person to the right place, according to their needs and wishes. Without some knowledge of the local services and what they offer, there is a danger of making an inappropriate referral that results in the service user not attending the service and being put off trying again.

Working effectively with specialist substance use colleagues is a two-way process. The key to effective partnership working is good communication and an understanding of the other person's and other agency's practice. Understanding why a substance use specialist will not tell you the details of a person's therapeutic counselling session, even when you have concerns about their child, for example, is important to ensuring that the relationship doesn't fall at the first hurdle. It is equally important for specialist agency staff to understand your role, duties and priorities and why you are so concerned and requesting information. Obstacles often arise when a *basic* understanding of each other's perspective has not been reached, leading to unnecessary and unhelpful defensiveness on both sides. This understanding does not happen by osmosis and requires people from each agency to take the initiative to educate each other prior to joint work proceeding, and to be aware of any existing information-sharing protocols.

This chapter will outline some of the key models underpinning specialist substance use practice and the types of specialist help available and will highlight the main referral routes into specialist services.

Partnership working

At the core of improving practice with people affected by problematic substance use is the ability to work in partnership with specialists in the alcohol and drug field. This does not mean passing the buck or relinquishing any interest or intervention relating to your service user's substance use once a specialist has become involved. The service user's substance use is still highly likely to have a bearing on the reasons for your involvement and support. In a survey of social workers in England, practitioners who worked in partnership with specialist colleagues rated their advice and support highly, stating that it gave them added confidence in working with these issues. They also felt that involving substance use specialists as partners shared 'the burden' that a person's substance use added to often complex cases (Galvani et al 2011).

Historically, social care and substance use services have not worked well together, due to a number of reasons, including different priorities, such as the adult or child, the different power relationships between helper and client and different philosophies and theories underpinning practice.

In particular, child welfare work has historically been underpinned by theories that stem primarily from psychology and sociology. The emphasis of this work has been on attachment processes and family and environmental systems. The focus has been on the child more than the adult, and interventions are often mandated rather than voluntary; thus, relationships and trust take longer to build. In addition, both parties know that social workers have a great deal of power, for example, the ability to remove children from the family home if they believe that there is good reason to do so. In adult work there appears to be little acknowledgement and exploration of substance use unless it has become obvious and problematic.

The philosophies and theories that underpin substance use services have historically worked within medical theoretical frameworks and been led by health professionals. Recent years have seen moves towards more social models of substance use, and community-based services are commonplace. The nature of the relationship between service user and professionals is one of support and motivation rather than of monitoring and challenging. Unlike some areas of social work practice, the helper–client relationship has rarely been one that has powerful or punitive sanctions at its disposal – apart from specific criminal justice programmes – and the confidential, therapeutic nature of the relationship has been sacrosanct.

Anecdotal evidence suggests that the medical and social models clash most frequently when parental substance use is having a negative impact on child welfare. The key tension is the different time-scales to which child protection and substance professionals work in terms of their assessments and interventions. People will often need several attempts to change their substance use, as relapse or dropping out of formal treatment services is not uncommon. For example, in 2009–10 only 38% of people leaving formal drug treatment services in England during the year were 'discharged successfully', that is, left specialist services 'free of their drug dependency' (Roxburgh et al 2010). Others were referred on to services in the community or criminal justice institutions, but clearly, a significant number will have returned to substance use. In the same year the NTA published its first longitudinal study of outcomes following treatment (NTA 2010a), which found that more than half of those exiting treatment in 2005–06 were subsequently involved in the criminal justice or drug treatment systems up to four years later.

However, time is a luxury that some service users, who are being negatively affected by a loved one's substance use, cannot afford. Where there are immediate concerns about adult or child abuse, it is clear that social workers cannot allow time to pass, given that people's safety is at risk. Consider, for example, child welfare procedures. These are designed to safeguard children and have strict time limits within which to assess, discuss and take action. Herein lies one of the biggest challenges between the two worlds of substance use and child and family welfare. Young et al (1998 cited in McAlpine et al 2001: 135–6) present 'four hourglass clocks' to illustrate the conflicting time frames:

1. *Child welfare mandates for decisions regarding permanency*: clear deadlines are given for assessments and decision making.
2. *The slower pace of change for substance use behaviours*: people often need several attempts over a long period of time before they successfully change their substance use and associated behaviour.
3. *The relatively speedy maturation of children*: children mature quickly, and developmentally they cannot be 'put on hold during a parent's addiction and recovery' without developmental consequences.
4. *Time limits for welfare recipients*: this is not, as yet, applicable in the UK, although current changes in the benefit system are proposed and could well result in increasing demands being placed on people receiving substance use treatment to work in exchange for their benefits or, alternately, risk losing their benefits.

There can also be tensions around where the expertise lies – for example, if social workers insist on abstinence-oriented treatment, or if they believe that hair testing for drug use provides a reliable measure of subsequent parenting behaviour.

In spite of these tensions and seemingly opposing perspectives on practice, there are also a number of similarities. Social learning models and cognitive behavioural interventions that are used within social work practice have become increasingly prevalent in alcohol and drug services. Indeed evidence has shown that cognitive behavioural interventions are among the most effective treatments for alcohol and other drug problems (Gossop 2006; Raistrick et al 2006), and these are recommended by the National Institute for Health and Clinical Excellence (NICE 2011a).

As with social work teams, alcohol and drug teams, particularly those within the voluntary sector, are often located in the community, and this provides opportunities for joint working with local social care providers. Similarities also exist in terms of some key challenges that substance professionals and social work professionals face. Both work to minimise harm or the risk of harm to self or others – for substance professionals this is about supporting people to reduce or stop their substance use and for social workers it is about offering a range of support, depending on the needs of the service user.

In the substance use sector, there is increasing recognition of the potential harm to children, families and communities from individuals' substance problems and acknowledgement that services need to provide appropriate services and support (HM Government 2010a). National substance use policy is increasingly focusing on longer-term recovery (Box 3.1) from substance problems and recognises the need for support by and within families and communities (HM Government 2010a). The policy suggests that a far more holistic approach to support is going to be expected from specialist services, alongside a partnership approach with other health and social care agencies (HM Government 2010a).

Box 3.1: The new 'recovery' agenda

An emerging agenda in substance use policy and practice is renewed emphasis on the notion of 'recovery'. A range of definitions and uses of 'recovery' exist. In the substance use field, it originated in the Alcoholics Anonymous movement. People belonging to these fellowships will often talk about 'being in recovery' from their substance problem, meaning that they are abstinent from substance use.

Current policy definitions adopt a broader focus emphasising an improved quality of life, and do not require people to be abstinent from substances. For example, the UKDPC (2008: 6) defines recovery as: 'The process of recovery from problematic substance use is characterised by voluntarily-sustained control over substance use which maximises health and wellbeing and participation in the rights, roles and responsibilities of society.' The UKDPC is explicit that its definition includes people who choose to be abstinent or maintain a particular level of reduced substance use.

The English government has avoided being explicit about abstinence as part of its concept of 'recovery' in its strategy documents (HM Government 2010a), although treatment initiatives such as 'payment by results' and related targets may judge success as abstinence only. The government has adopted the language of longer-term 'recovery' to support its redesign and reorientation of treatment services. However, this use of the recovery concept falls far short of the original recovery-oriented movements, which have at their core a commitment to peer-, user- and carer-led involvement.

A further similarity between the professions is the absolute importance of the quality of relationships between professionals and service users; it appears key to the on-going engagement of parents with social services and between substance professionals and service users. Both professions work with uncertainty, and with people who may need to, or are required to, change their behaviours. This is not a quick and easy process, particularly when people's living environments and any social networks may be more supportive of risk behaviours. Both professions also work with people who have multiple problems and who often have histories of abuse and neglect, as well as with people who have often sought to deny or minimise their problems or support needs and may well have been in touch with legal or social or other statutory services in the past. However, importantly, both professions are also committed to the work and understand people's ambivalence over making changes. Both sets of professionals work with people in crisis and understand that the outcomes may be uncertain. The remuneration of their work is not generous, and work environments and resources are often limited. Evidence suggests that shared values and working environments are among the key elements of effective collaboration across child welfare and substance use services (Drabble 2007).

Thus, in spite of historically different theories and models for working, there is an increasing merging of roles, values and goals, particularly in light of the introduction of care pathways, case management and mandatory attention to children and family issues within the substance use field, and the increasing pressure on social services to identify substance use and actively work in partnership with specialists. This offers opportunities for improved collaborative working relationships and paves the way for increased attention to effective methods of working that can be shared.

Models underpinning substance use interventions

There is no single model, theory or method that underpins specialist substance use interventions. Broadly, however, services are based upon either a medical or social model of substance use. Understanding the difference between the models is important, given the implications they have for service delivery and, subsequently, their suitability for different service users. For example, a medical-model approach views substance problems as a medical problem, a disease, and includes a discourse that people are sick and that the 'cure' to their illness can be found in lifelong abstinence from their drug of choice and any other mood-/mind-altering substance. There is no middle ground of reducing their drug or alcohol use to non-problematic levels. This is the model used by Alcoholics Anonymous, Narcotics Anonymous and other similar groups. It is also the model used by organisations adopting the Minnesota Model and the '12-step' approaches to substance use, which emphasise powerlessness over the substance use.

A social-model perspective approaches substance problems as learned behaviour; the individual continues using because of benefits and rewards that result from their substance use, even if those benefits or rewards are to 'feel normal' or 'avoid withdrawal symptoms', rather than more overtly positive effects. Interventions based on the social model focus more on exploring the function that substance use has in a person's life and on helping someone to decide how to reduce the negative impact it may be causing to themselves or others. This approach works with people's beliefs about their substance use and their subsequent behaviour. Motivational and cognitive behavioural interventions, therefore, often underpin such approaches in order to help people 'un-learn' what they've learned about substance use and feel empowered to make their desired changes. The emphasis is on people learning about how their beliefs about their substance use relate to their use of the substance and what functions substance use serves in their lives. From this they can start to look at alternatives to substance use and at what additional support they may need to help them overcome the related or underlying problems. The goal of intervention or treatment is usually set by the client and may still be abstinence oriented, but it may also include a goal of reducing their substance use to less harmful or more manageable levels.

Box 3.2: Terminology

Every profession has a range of specialist terms or jargon that it uses, whether consciously or not. In social work practice, examples are 'empowerment', 'person-centred practice' and 'the assessment framework'. Often this language is based in the origins of the profession and the perspective or tools that it adopts. Substance use practice is no different. Services that are underpinned by medical models and perspectives often use terms such as 'treatment', 'alcoholic' and 'addict' and talk of being 'in recovery', while services that work from social models of substance use tend to use terms such as 'intervention', 'problematic substance use' and 'drink/drug problem'. Reflecting on the meaning in language and what it conveys to others is an important part of sensitive and skilled communication.

Ultimately, the type of model that services adopt and the theories underpinning it will be largely unimportant to most service users (and also to many services!). What we know from research into the effectiveness of alcohol and drug interventions is that the quality of the 'therapist' or 'worker' is among the key factors influencing outcomes (Project MATCH Research Group 1998; Okiishi et al 2003; Gossop 2006). Commonly known as the 'therapist variable', the relationship and trust that are built between worker and service user appear to be far more important than the particular model underpinning service delivery. That said, some service users will object to accusations that someone is 'in denial' if they feel that they can reduce their substance use to manageable levels rather than stop. Similarly, someone wanting to achieve abstinence may not be receptive to suggestions of targets that simply reduce their substance use. They may also reject self-labelling concepts such as 'alcoholic' or 'addict', so careful use of terminology is important. As is common with social work practice, using the service user's language is important – unless that language is negative or labelling.

Structure of substance use services

There is a vast range of services that are delivered to meet the needs of people with, or at risk of developing, alcohol or other drug problems. Attempts have been made to construct a framework within which these services sit, depending on the level of service they provide and the intensity of the intervention or treatment programme. In 2002 the NTA in England[1] introduced a four-tiered framework[2] designed to ensure that interventions for substance use could be delivered at all levels of need and by a range of health and social care providers, not solely substance specialists. Social workers and other non-substance specialist professionals in health and social care came under Tier 1 services (Table 3.1).

Table 3.1: Tiers of service

Tier	Interventions
Tier 1 Non-substance specific service providers	This tier consists of a range of interventions that can be provided by non-substance specialist providers in health and social care, including social workers. Local partnership arrangements with specialised drug services are expected to be in place or developed
Tier 2 Open access drug services	Interventions that are geared to engaging people in treatment, supporting people through to more structured treatment, providing aftercare services and working with people to keep drug free – for example, advice and information services, drop-in services, needle exchange, outreach, brief interventions
Tier 3 Structured drug services	Interventions that require a greater degree of structure and care planning than tier 2, for example, structured counselling, day programmes, detoxification, prescribing, offenders on drug treatment and testing orders, regular key working and case management, related aftercare
Tier 4 Residential services	Interventions including in-patient detoxification and rehabilitation services, residential crisis services

There are two main reasons why social workers need to understand this structure. First, social workers need to be clear about what the expectations are for their practice with substance use issues. As outlined in Chapter Two, the requirement for social workers, other non-substance specialists front-line health and social care staff is to be able to identify problematic substance use, screen and assess it, provide advice and information and, where needed, refer on to specialist services working in partnership with them (DH/NTA 2006; NTA 2006[3]). Research suggests that there are very few social workers who feel confident or competent to meet these criteria but that social work qualifying or post-qualifying training is equipping them to do so (Galvani and Hughes 2010; Galvani and Forrester 2011a; Galvani et al 2011). Historical evidence shows that social work educators have not routinely incorporated alcohol and drug training into the curricula, in spite of decades of calls for them to do so (see Galvani 2007 for a review). However, at the time of writing, reviews of social work education and practice are under way and have identified substance use as both an area of work for which social workers need to be prepared and a key concern in the environment in which many social workers practise, specifically within children's social care (Social Work Taskforce 2009; Munro 2011). There have also been calls from within the profession for social work educators, employers and individual social workers to take responsibility for becoming more informed about substance use (BASW Special Interest Group in Alcohol and Other Drugs 2010).

Second, social workers need to ensure that referrals made with, or on behalf of, service users are appropriate. They should be based on knowledge of the range of services available and made with informed consent. Someone who wants to speak to a substance use specialist for the first time, perhaps to explore whether or not they have a problem or what help is available, is more likely to need an open access service, in the first instance, than a residential service or a highly structured day programme. Referring people to the right type of service initially and giving them information on what to expect is key to maximising the chances that the person will attend and engage with the service. Taking that first step to speak to a specialist agency takes courage and determination. Getting the referral wrong may lead to the person not wanting to go through it again and provide them with a reason for not attending more appointments. Importantly, social workers need to make personal contact during the referral, not just signpost someone to it. This ensures a feedback loop and allows for follow-up, particularly if the appointment or referral is not a successful one. It also allows supportive professional relationships to develop between the social worker and substance use specialists.

Further, there is much overlap between the different levels of service and many organisations offer services that fall into several of the NTA's tiers. The most reliable way to understand what services offer and to find out crucial practical information is to contact your local services directly – for example, is there a waiting list, is the service on a bus route, or is there a crèche? Asking people for advice and help prior to the referral is likely to result in far better partnership working and appropriate support for service users than making a referral 'cold'.

Accessing substance use services

There are various ways to access an alcohol or drug service. The broad structure of services identified earlier gives some indication of how people might access services.

- Tier 1 services are not specialist substance use services; they include social services, housing, GPs and so on. In theory, this first tier of service should be accessible to everyone and there should be a basic level of knowledge of substance use and brief advice and intervention available at this level. Unfortunately, this is not always the case and the response people get from Tier 1 services in relation to alcohol and drugs can be very variable.
- Tier 2 services, by definition, should be 'open access'. They should be accessible for people to walk in off the street and ask to see someone or ask to make an appointment. They are also a resource for information

about services they provide and other related services in the local area. They will also accept telephone referrals from professionals, although some agencies may prefer the person attending the appointment to call in person. Some agencies may want to conduct a telephone screening consisting of some brief questions, just to ensure that the person is reaching the right service and to save any wasted journeys if a different service would be more suitable.

■ Tier 3 services may also have direct access, but many will often only take referrals from professionals or self-referrals. Again, there may be an initial screening process at the referral stage. Thus, it is important to know ahead of time the type of information that the agency will require, so as to save having to call a second time with the information. It is more likely, with this more structured service, that an appointment will be made for a full assessment of the person's needs. This can sometimes mean a waiting period of up to several weeks, so it is advisable to have a strategy in place in terms of how you can support the person during that time. You may even want to ask for advice from the substance use specialist about how best to do that. It might be that the person could access a Tier 2 service while waiting.

■ Tier 4 services cannot be accessed directly. These are usually accessed via referral from a Tier 2 or 3 service or from another medical or social care professional. One of the key reasons for this is that residential and in-patient beds are limited, so there is a screening process to ensure that they are being accessed by those most in need. With residential care, there also has to be a financial assessment, carried out by social workers, and funding needs to be sought and agreed prior to the person's entry into residential care. All this takes time, and often people's motivation to access support will have waned in the intervening period. It is therefore important that some support is put in place while the administrative wheels are turning – preferably a partnership arrangement between the social worker and substance specialist.

A number of routes into treatment are available through the criminal justice system. This is often the quickest way for some people to access substance use interventions. There are drug and alcohol programmes in prisons, with aftercare arrangements on the person's release. In the community there is a growing use of court-enforced community orders that include drug or alcohol rehabilitation requirements. The individual has to agree to take part, otherwise no order will be made and alternative criminal justice sanctions will be enforced. The treatment and interventions stemming from community orders relating to drugs and alcohol are delivered and monitored by the Drug Intervention Programme, which sits within the local drug and alcohol action team.

It is possible that social workers (who are, of course, in Tier I) will be involved in referring people to all the other levels or 'tiers' of substance use services. Referring the person to the right place and with the right amount of support is essential to maximising the chances of their engagement with the service and, subsequently, a reduction in the harm they risk causing to themselves and others.

Referring to specialists

There are two key questions that you should ask yourself before referring somebody to an alcohol or drug agency:

1. **What information will the agency need?**
    If you don't know this, call the agency and ask.
2. **What information will the service user need?**
    If you are going to suggest that a person seeks support for an alcohol or drug problem, you need to know what services are available and how they differ. Facing drug and alcohol problems is a huge step for people to take, particularly if the service user is considering getting specialist help for the first time. It is likely that they will have a lot of stereotypical ideas about what treatment is and will be fearful of taking that first step. You need to be able to answer their questions about the services available; for example, will they have to do groups, or is it individual work? Does the service insist on abstinence or will it work with the individual to agree their own goals around their substance use?

An inappropriate referral is likely to fail and will not encourage the service user (a) to have confidence in you or (b) to seek further help with their substance problem.

There are five key steps to good referral practice.

1. **Has the person agreed to a referral?** No matter how badly you think they need help, it is pointless making a referral if they're not going to attend.
2. **Do you have all the information you need to make a successful referral first time?** If you don't know, call the agency while you're with the person, and ask them what information they need.
3. **Does the person know what to expect?** If not, you need to tell them, or find out and then tell them. For example, do they know where the agency is and how they can get there? Have you explained the agency's expectations of the person attending (some people don't want to be in

groups for example)? Is there a waiting list and, if so, where could the person find support in the meantime?

4. **Does the person want some support to get there?** Can you take them to the appointment? If not, is there someone else the person can ask? This may need some exploration?

5. **Have you followed up after the referral?** This is important. You need to check how it went, what it was like and what the next steps are. If it didn't go well, why not? Do you need to make another referral elsewhere? It is important to act as the human safety net at this stage, wherever possible. Don't make the mistake of making the referral and thinking that your job is done, especially when the person, or someone around them, is at risk of harm. You need to follow up and provide encouragement. Do not give up on the person after the first attempt if it hasn't worked.

Confidentiality

The issue of confidentiality has been cited as a concern, and sometimes a stumbling block, for good partnership work between social services and alcohol/drug agencies.

The best way to overcome this is to:

1. Establish what the other service's confidentiality policy is.
2. Tell it what your confidentiality policy is.
3. Discuss what information you think you might need from it and why.
4. Be open to hearing its view and negotiating boundaries.
5. Establish an agreement between yourself, the service user and the alcohol/drug agency – in writing if necessary. This may state that the agency will discuss certain matters with you – for example, attendance at counselling or group sessions. If you have the agreement of the service user about what can and cannot be discussed, then confidentiality will not be an issue. Both substance use and social care services are rightly concerned about upholding confidentiality, but service users may be happy to share information rather than repeat it to different services.

Anecdotal reports from alcohol/drug agencies suggest that social workers often expect them to provide information that they cannot provide – for example, details of the content of their counselling sessions. These details need to be confidential between the counsellor and client in order for the therapeutic relationship to be established. If the client knows/thinks that the details of their sessions will be revealed they are unlikely to fully engage with treatment, thus ultimately increasing potential risks to themselves and others. However, the exception to this is when information is disclosed that suggests that the person may harm themselves or others, and you may want to put your own mind at ease by checking about this with the agency and talking with the person's allocated worker.

The other information that some social workers have requested is for the allocated specialist to make judgements about whether the person's substance use has reduced to the extent that they are no longer a risk to their children. This type of question is often based on the erroneous assumption that stopping or reducing substance use will mean that the person's behaviour will instantly improve, or that any identified risks will disappear. *Stopping or reducing substance use does not necessarily make someone a better person or behave differently.* Indeed, given the uncomfortable withdrawal symptoms and the emotional, physical and mental struggles that someone might be dealing with during this time, they may well need *more support*, when they are cutting down or stopping, to ensure that they are coping with responsibilities such as parenting. Such assumptions are often grounded in a genuine lack of knowledge about substance use, its effects and what it does and does not 'cause'.

What an alcohol or drug agency will usually be able to tell you is whether the person has attended their agreed sessions and how the person *appears* to be progressing towards their goals. However, it will remain your responsibility to assess whether or not the person's behaviour has changed to the extent that any social work concerns are diminished. Do not assume that change in drug or alcohol use means change in other behaviour, particularly when other people are at risk.

Methods of intervention

Drug and alcohol services use a range of methods as part of their interventions. Some will adopt one particular approach, others will mix and match a range of interventions. As in social work training and practice, the range of methods used in substance use interventions is diverse. As previously stated, some of the interventions that are most effective overlap with key methods used in social work practice – for example, cognitive behavioural interventions. Motivational Interviewing (MI) also has a strong evidence base in alcohol and drug interventions and is expanding into other areas of practice, including children and families work.

In 2006 two comprehensive reviews of the effectiveness of drug and alcohol treatment approaches were undertaken, by Gossop (2006) and Raistrick et al (2006) respectively. Their conclusions were remarkably similar, in spite of the fact that the studies drew on two different bodies of research literature. They both found good evidence of effectiveness for Brief

Interventions, Motivational Interviewing and 12-step facilitation therapy. In addition, for drugs, Contingency Management and Relapse Prevention were effective; for alcohol, additional evidence was found for the effectiveness of the Community Reinforcement Approach (CRA) and Coping and Social Skills Training.

The following is a summary of these methods, with the exception of Relapse Prevention, which has been summarised in Chapter Two.

Brief Interventions (BI)

BI comes in many forms. As the name suggests, it is an intervention that is time limited, ranging from one to several sessions. Miller and Sanchez (1994 in Rollnick and Miller 1995) identified six key aspects of Brief Interventions, using the acronym FRAMES:

- **F**eedback of personal risk or impairment
- **R**esponsibility for change
- **A**dvice to change
- **M**enu of alternative change options
- **E**mpathy on behalf of the practitioner
- **S**elf-efficacy or optimism in client facilitated by the practitioner.

Unlike counselling, BI is a more direct intervention providing advice, and is often used in the context of professional authority. A different type of BI is known as Motivational Enhancement Therapy, or MET. Based on MI, it is designed to be delivered over a maximum of four sessions and focuses on strengthening internal motivations for change. The first two sessions focus on building motivation, including structured feedback, plans for change and enhancing motivation, while the second two sessions focus on strengthening the person's commitment to change, reinforcing progress made and reflecting on the process of change (Miller et al 1995).

Motivational Interviewing (MI)

MI is 'a person-centered counseling style for addressing the common problem of ambivalence about change' (Miller and Rollnick, in press). Fundamentally, it is 'a method of communication for strengthening a person's own motivation for and commitment to change' (Miller and Rollnick, *in press*). It is underpinned by four phases of relationship building: engaging with the person, focusing on the issues of concern, evoking 'change talk' and planning next steps (Miller, personal communication, 2011).

There is no set time frame to MI – it can be used as a brief intervention or can underpin a much longer period of support. MI assumes that people are ambivalent about change because, if they were not ambivalent, they would have already made the change. Its initial stages focus on exploring and resolving ambivalence through acceptance, empathy and reflective listening. A key element of MI is what Miller and Rollnick (2002) refer to as the 'spirit' of MI: the accepting, compassionate, partnership-oriented, non-judgemental style in which it is done. It is the worker's understanding, skill and ability that support the client to realise their own motivation, and consequently time and resources need to be put in to training for MI and on-going supervision.

Miller and Rollnick stress the collaborative nature of MI and the importance of respecting the client's expertise on themselves and of understanding that the responsibility for change rests with the client. They state: 'Implicit is the belief that such motivation and resourcefulness do lie within each individual and need to be evoked rather than imposed' (Miller and Rollnick 2002: 41).

MI has been rigorously evaluated, resulting in clear evidence of its effectiveness in a range of practice settings.

12-step facilitation (TSF) therapy

The following description of 12-step facilitation (TSF) therapy is taken from the preface to a manual for TSF written by Mattson (1995). While it refers to alcohol, TSF can be applied to drug use too, with NA/CA (Narcotics/Cocaine Anonymous) being two of the illicit drug equivalents of AA.

> This therapy is grounded in the concept of alcoholism as a spiritual and medical disease. The content of this intervention is consistent with the 12 Steps of Alcoholics Anonymous (AA), with primary emphasis given to Steps 1 through 5. In addition to abstinence from alcohol, a major goal of the treatment is to foster the patient's commitment to participation in AA. During the course of the program's 12 sessions, patients are actively encouraged to attend AA meetings and to maintain journals of their AA attendance and participation. Therapy sessions are highly structured, following a similar format each week that includes symptoms inquiry, review and reinforcement for AA participation, introduction and explication of the week's theme, and setting goals for AA participation for the next week. Material introduced during treatment sessions is complemented by reading assignments from AA literature.

Contingency Management (CM)

This approach has been a controversial one, in so far as it rewards people, often with vouchers or payment, for achieving particular goals in the course of their substance use treatment. It relies on people being regularly monitored for adherence to their treatment regime, which primarily means being tested for the absence of the substance, usually opioids or stimulants, via urine tests. The vouchers or incentives increase, the longer the person stays abstinent (NICE 2007). The guidelines for use of CM state that staff must ensure that:

- the target is agreed in collaboration with the service user
- the incentives are provided in a timely and consistent manner
- the service user fully understands the relationship between the treatment goal and the incentive schedule
- the incentive is perceived to be reinforcing and supports a healthy/drug-free lifestyle.

(NICE 2007: 14)

Community Reinforcement Approach (CRA)

The CRA focuses on engaging the individual's social environment in responding to the person's alcohol or drug use. It works with family, friends and work colleagues, for example, in helping them to reward the individual's reduced substance use and to leave intoxicated behaviour unrewarded. The following list shows the types of training that can be included in the CRA:

- communication skills training
- problem-solving training
- drink-refusal training
- job finding
- social and recreational counselling
- behavioural marital therapy
- muscle relaxation training
- relapse prevention
- motivational counselling.

In addition, some CRA implementations will offer substitute drugs and monitored compliance with the medication regime as part of the intervention.

Methadone and other substitute medications

There are various medications that can be used to help people reduce or stay off alcohol and drugs. All need to be prescribed by a doctor, although people do buy them illegally on the street. Prescribed medication needs to be suitable for the individual, taking into account any other health problems they may have so people, will need to see a GP or medical specialist via an alcohol or drug service.

The following is a select list of medications that you may come across most often:

- *Methadone:* a synthetic opioid prescribed as a replacement drug for heroin users. It usually comes in the form of a sticky green liquid. Some drug users report worse withdrawal symptoms from methadone than from heroin. People are usually prescribed slowly reducing amounts of methadone to help ease them off the substitute. The main complaint from some users is that GPs never prescribe enough to realistically substitute for the heroin, and then wonder why they 'top up' with heroin.
- *Subutex/Buphrenorphine:* a synthetic opioid in tablet form, used in the medical treatment of heroin use.
- *Antabuse/disulfiram:* a tablet prescribed to some people with alcohol problems who have difficulty being abstinent through other means. It is taken regularly and has a *very* unpleasant reaction if used with alcohol.
- *Naltrexone:* blocks the effects of alcohol and heroin, thus the user doesn't get the effects they would normally get from using the substance.
- *Benzodiazepines:* for example, diazepam. 'Benzo's' are prescribed to help people cope with/lessen the effects of withdrawal.
- *Vitamins:* many people who have used substances to problematic levels will need 'industrial' doses of vitamins to help boost their body's immunity and functioning. These can be administered in tablet or liquid forms, the latter by injection.

Box 3.3: Detoxification

Detoxification is the process by which a person is physically detoxified of a particular substance(s). Where someone has been using substances regularly over a significant period of time they will often experience physical withdrawal symptoms as their body gets rid of the substance. These symptoms are likely to increase, the more of the substance a person has been using, particularly if they are using these amounts on a daily basis. However, everyone's body is different and will respond differently, so there are no set responses to the detoxification process.

It is advisable that detoxification is carried out by medical experts, who will be able to monitor the person's physical health. Drug and alcohol use has an impact on most organs of the body and these organs will react to the withdrawal of the substance in ways that can be dangerous to health. However, psychological interventions should accompany medical detoxification, given that people will respond to detoxification both mentally and physically and will need support with both.

Detoxification and rehabilitation are commonly discussed together, but it is important to recognise the difference. Rehabilitation follows the detoxification process and refers to the on-going intervention, treatment or aftercare that supports people to maintain any changes they have made.

You must never suggest to someone that they just stop using or drinking without first ensuring that they have had a medical consultation.

Coping and social skills training

This is a set of skills training that have been found to be effective for people with alcohol and drug problems. It can be delivered in both group and individual settings. Different versions of this training have been tested and evaluated, but the key components comprise:

- communication skills, including building interpersonal relationships and assertiveness training
- coping with emotional stress and fluctuating moods
- improving daily living skills and responding to stressful events
- coping with cues that have previously led to drug or alcohol use.

What all these methods have in common, to a greater or lesser degree, is cognitive behavioural components. Cognitive Behavioural Therapy (CBT) works with how people think and how this relates to the way they behave. Ouimette et al (1997) describe interventions as targeting two areas in relation to substance use, '(a) changing distorted thinking about the abused substances, and (b) increasing adaptive coping responses'. A range of individual and group sessions comprise CBT, depending on the length of the programme and goal of interventions, but they can include relapse prevention groups, cognitive skills training, behavioural skills training, abstinence skills training and therapy groups.

Most social workers will have been introduced to CBT during their qualifying training and will therefore be able to understand the techniques and theory underpinning the above processes and methods.

Alternative therapies

Some agencies will also offer alternative or complementary therapies as part of their programme, including ear (auricular) acupuncture, aromatherapy, relaxation and so on. Evidence shows that service users respond well to these therapies and value them for helping them to relax and deal with their anxieties, although there is no rigorous evidence that they have any impact on substance-using outcomes.

What the alcohol and drug treatment effectiveness reviews concluded is that no one type of intervention is going to suit everyone. Indeed Gossop (2006) concluded that it is likely that a combination of interventions plus additional support is needed to avoid people falling through gaps in single-approach services. The treatment effectiveness studies also clearly point to some key factors that are important in delivering successful outcomes for service users, including the quality of the staff, the importance of engaging and retaining people in treatment and some indications that more intensive work may have benefits in helping people to stay motivated and supported. Social workers therefore play an important role in ensuring that a referral is appropriate because this, in turn, will maximise the chances that the person will stay in treatment. Similarly, social workers' on-going support to help the person stay motivated once any intervention has started is equally important. The research evidence also found better outcomes when supplementary and additional services were in place, and here the social worker has a pivotal role in linking the person with other necessary services, which may include parenting support, financial advice, housing, health care and so on. Complementary therapies are often provided in alcohol and other drug treatment services, with ear (auricular) acupuncture and other interventions being commonly available. While they are not effective as 'stand-alone' treatments, there are some anecdotal reports that these interventions may improve the likelihood that service users will attend treatment.

Summary

There are obvious benefits for social workers and substance use professionals in joint working. The mutual understanding and support that it facilitates can make professional challenges far more manageable. More importantly, there are obvious benefits for service users in professionals' joint working, in terms of the quality of the service they receive. The key challenge for social workers and substance use professionals is operating within environments that have developed mythologies about what the 'other' cares about and is able to understand. Stereotypically, the substance use professional will not disclose any information about their client, regardless of who else is at risk in their household. On the other hand, the social work professional is often seen either as being too focused on the children or as having high expectations of substance use interventions as a 'cure all' for the service user. In some contexts these mythologies still exist, but increasingly substance use services are moving towards more family-oriented approaches and services for the families of the person with the alcohol or drug problem. Social workers, particularly in children and family roles, or those in mental health or older people settings, are increasingly being faced with service users with alcohol and drug problems. They need the knowledge to know what to ask and how to intervene, and good working relationships with substance use partner agencies can provide just that.

At the heart of partnership working is good communication. Asking for information and advice, or developing joint working or training arrangements, comes down to individual managers and professionals seeking help from their specialist colleagues. Armed with information about local services, referral processes and some information about the approaches used by substance use services, social workers can be more confident about what to do when working with someone with alcohol or other drug issues.

Notes
[1] The NTA will no longer exist as an independent health authority in 2013. It is to be merged into a new body Public Health England.
[2] Under review at the time of writing. The tiers of service are expected to go; however, it is a useful framework for understanding the range of services available as these will remain regardless of the framework they sit within.
[3] Both policy documents under review at the time of writing.

Discussion questions/exercises

1   What are the similarities in working practices between substance use and social work professionals?
2   Find out the three nearest alcohol or drug services to your workplace and what their referral requirements are.
3   Consider the pros and cons for using two of the approaches listed for working with substance problems.
4   What must you never tell someone with a chronic alcohol problem to do?

Further learning resources

- www.patient.co.uk will provide information on any prescribed drug.

- To find a local drug service or for more detailed information on illicit drugs or medications in the medical treatment of alcohol and drug problems, go to the website of drug charity Drugscope – www.drugscope.org.uk. The 'Helpfinder' facility will help you to find services; the 'Drug Search' facility will help with information on any drug, prescribed or illicit.

- Stirling University library has an excellent online resource, including a link to the Methadone Handbook and other pieces of legislation and key policy documents: www.drugslibrary.stir.ac.uk/index.php

4

Substance use among black and minority ethnic people

Practice example

Dilshad (aged 19) has been using cannabis daily for two years. He lives at home with his mother, elder sister and grandparents and does not like to leave the house. His father is not at home and is only ever mentioned in passing by his mother, and in a negative way. Dilshad is unemployed and has been experiencing some mental health problems. He refuses to take prescribed medication. He reports hearing voices at times and the family are concerned that these are bad spirits. Dilshad refuses to go to any drug or alcohol agency and believes that Allah will help him. Mum is trying to support him and has been taking him to see the imam in another city, who prays with him. Dilshad and his family live within a tightly knit Asian community, members of which are starting to comment to his family that he should be working and that he needs to get himself sorted out.

Introduction

> Those interested in drug use within the black community are continually torn between unveiling the nature of black problem drug use and avoiding the promotion of racial stereotyping. (Kalunta-Crumpton 2004)

In social work training and practice, emphasis is placed on understanding the needs and differences of individuals within their families and communities. Learning to think about values, cultures and life-styles that are different from our own and how that difference impacts on our practice is part and parcel of basic training (Department of Education 2011). The same learning and reflection is necessary for considering how to work with people from black or other minority ethnic groups whose use of substances is problematic. Much evidence has highlighted how substance use among minority communities is ignored or overlooked at all levels of planning and service commissioning (Bashford et al 2004a, b), as well as in the research that sets out to provide an evidence base (Bhopal et al 2004). Exploring how to respond in social work practice so as to ensure that these issues are recognised and addressed sensitively is the focus of this chapter.

This chapter cannot cover the hundreds of minority groups in the UK. The Office for National Statistics' (ONS) population estimates list only the top 60 nationalities resident in the UK (ONS 2010). Excluding the European Union nationalities and residents from North America and Australasia, the main nationalities resident in the UK include people from the Asian and African subcontinents, such as people from India, Pakistan, Bangladesh and China, and Nigeria, South Africa, Zimbabwe and Somalia. This chapter therefore focuses primarily on key black and minority ethnic groups, with a brief consideration of Traveller communities, who are often overlooked as a minority group.

Prevalence

There are very mixed messages about the prevalence of alcohol and other drug use among people from minority ethnic groups. While some of these will be due to the different methods used within research studies, some of it is also because there is diversity within diversity! For example, factors that will make a difference within particular ethnic groups include gender; different generations and their degree of acculturation; age and income. Thus, in terms of social work practice, an understanding of the overall picture has to be supplemented with an understanding of the nuances that each of these elements may bring. It is also important to remember that people are individuals who simply make different choices about their substance use, regardless of their nationality or ethnic origin.

The British Crime Survey of England and Wales includes questions about illicit drug use that, to date, are published annually. In an analysis of three years' survey data and a nationally representative sample, drug use among Asian and Black ethnic groups was far lower than that among White groups and Mixed ethnicity groups (Hoare and Moon 2010). Asian and Asian British groups had the lowest levels of drug use, followed by Black and Black British groups, with Mixed ethnicity and White groups reporting highest levels of use. Class A drug use was highest among these latter two groups. Importantly, however, the authors report that the age of users was important when looking at drug use, with the high use of cannabis among younger people accounting for much of the difference between groups in terms of overall rates of drug use. Gender was also a significant factor in illicit drug use; across all ethnicities, men's use was higher than women's.

There is a similar picture in relation to prevalence figures for alcohol consumption among a range of minority ethnic groups. In a review of the literature, Hurcombe et al (2010) found evidence for higher rates of abstinence among non-White groups as compared to White ethnicity groups, particularly among those from Muslim backgrounds and for people from Pakistan and Bangladesh. Those from Mixed ethnicity backgrounds drank more heavily than other non-White ethnic groups. However, again, some differences were apparent according to generation, gender and income.

Hurcombe et al's (2010) review found that, in spite of generally lower levels of alcohol use and higher levels of abstinence, when men from Muslim or Pakistani backgrounds did drink, they drank more heavily than other non-White or religious groups. They also found that income was an influencing factor. Among people from Indian, Chinese, Irish and Pakistani backgrounds, higher income was associated with people from these ethnic groups drinking above recommended limits.

When people start drinking and using also appears to differ by ethnicity. Wu et al (2010), in their study of initiation into substance use among women aged 18–31 years from different ethnicities in the US, found that the African-American and Hispanic women started using substances at a later age, but ultimately were as likely to use illicit drugs as were the White women in their sample. In the UK, Hurcombe et al (2010) found that while women in all ethnic groups drank far less than men did, there was evidence that heavy and frequent drinking among Indian women and second-generation Sikh girls had increased, as had frequent and heavy drinking among Chinese men.

Prevalence rates of alcohol and other drug use among adolescents are also a focus of research that explores ethnic differences. However, in the overall picture there are few differences from the adult findings. Generally, lower levels of alcohol and other drug use are found among youth and college students from minority ethnic groups (McCabe et al 2007), and where the young people or their families follow Islam, use is even lower (Van Tubergen and Poortman 2010). Van Tubergen and Poortman also found that students from Mixed ethnicity families had higher levels of alcohol use than students from single-minority ethnicity families.

The influence of religious beliefs on substance use appears to be strong. Denscombe and Drucquer's smoking and drinking survey (2000) of 15- to 16-year-olds in the East Midlands found different levels of use among the different religious affiliations of young people, although overall their level of use was far lower than that of their White counterparts. Between the two time periods covered by their survey (1990 and 1997) there was a significant overall increase in smoking and drinking among young people, but particular patterns emerged when religious affiliation was considered. For example, Hindu boys drank rather than smoked, and vice versa for Muslim boys. Also, over the two time periods there was little change among Muslim boys in relation to alcohol consumption. Thus, the important point that Denscombe and Drucquer's study makes is to avoid assumptions or analysis based on broad ethnic groupings, to explore further within groupings for differences and to ensure that responses are tailored accordingly.

Given the lower level of use by non-White or Mixed ethnic groups, it is easy to see how Dilshad's use in the practice example above is relatively unusual. Combined with religious disapproval of substance use, it is easy to see how his family could be at a loss to know how to respond and why they are keen to address the issue outside the local community in which they live.

However, in spite of lower levels of use among ethnically diverse youth, some research has also found that this is not sustained as they mature, and that use among Black ethnic groups equals or increases as they age (Vogt Yuan 2011). Vogt Yuan suggests that this is primarily due to the higher levels of disadvantage among Black groups as compared to Whites.

In terms of alcohol use, Rao (2006) reports on higher levels of alcohol-related health problems in the UK among migrant Irish men and migrant Sikh men as compared to rates in their countries of origin, and higher rates for both of related morbidity and mortality than among the general population. Sikh men are reportedly overrepresented among cases of liver cirrhosis (Hurcombe et al 2010). Hurcombe et al also report that, despite their drinking less, dependence rates among ethnic minority groups are similar to those among the general population. North American data concur. Godette et al (2009) found that among Black young drinkers there was less risky or heavy drinking than among all groups except Asians,[1] but that the prevalence of alcohol-related problems, while lower than among Whites and native Americans, was still a cause for concern. This was reiterated by a study of adolescents in one area of London, where researchers found that alcohol-related problems still occurred among 'substantial' numbers of Black African and Black Caribbean teenagers aged 14–16 years, despite their drinking less overall (Stillwell et al 2004: 185).

Given some of the barriers to accessing treatment and specialist support that minority groups often face, this raises concerns about how these people are seeking help or coping with their drinking problems.

Acculturation

For many people migrating to the UK, the use of alcohol and drugs and the general attitudes towards them will be very different from those of their native culture and religious beliefs. Acculturation to the new culture's norms is often one of the reasons given for the increase or changes in substance use among migrant communities. It is defined as follows:

> acculturation refers to the assimilation by one group of the culture
> of another which modifies the existing culture and so changes

group identity. There may be a tension between old and new cultures which leads to the adapting of the new as well as the old. (Sociology Guide 2011)

What the definition does well is identify the potential tensions in the cultural transition, and evidence suggests that this is likely to be the case in relation to substance use.

Both Rao (2006) and Hoare and Moon (2010) found that migrant groups in the UK used more substances than did their 'home' populations. One explanation for this is what MacAndrew and Edgerton (1969), in their classic anthropological text *Drunken comportment: A social explanation*, view as the influence of the society and culture in which these migrant groups now live:

> persons learn about drunkenness what their societies impart to them, and comporting themselves in consonance with these understandings they become living confirmations of their societies' teachings. (MacAndrew and Edgerton 1969: 172)

Of course it may not all be learned behaviour. It could be that those who migrate just happen to be heavier alcohol or other drug users, or are more open to the influences of Western societies, given their choice to migrate, but this is unlikely, given the consistency of lesser use across such diverse ethnic groups. It is far more likely that acculturation is a significant influencing factor.

In a Canadian qualitative study of seven ethnic groups, Agic et al (2011) explored cultural differences and the subsequent implications for addressing alcohol problems within those communities. They found differences in sizes and types of drinks between countries of origin, different cultural views on what was thought to be excessive drinking, and that norms and beliefs about alcohol problems differed from the dominant culture in which the people now lived. The authors point out that health messages (in this case about alcohol) that are located within the context of the dominant culture are unlikely to have immediate relevance to those from other cultures. They also suggest that their findings call into question the relevance of substance use assessment tools and similar resources that have been designed and developed for people within the dominant culture.

Specific drugs

Particular drugs have often been associated with particular ethnic groups. The stereotype is of the White professional using powder cocaine, the use of crack-cocaine by Black men in particular (Kalunta-Crumpton 2004) or the use of Khat by Somalis. No generalisations can be made, as patterns of substance use change as a result of a number of factors, including availability, cost, fashion, legal status and individual choice. However, research suggests that some ethnic groups use particular drugs more than others. What it is important to consider for practice is that stereotypes can influence both the attitudes and values of professionals and can also detract from a thorough assessment of a person's use of licit and illicit substances.

The Crime Survey for England and Wales suggests that White and Mixed ethnic groups are more likely to use Class A drugs such as heroin, powder cocaine and ecstasy. Mixed ethnic groups have the highest levels of cannabis use, although within the Black and Black British groups, Black Caribbeans have the highest levels of cannabis use (Hoare and Moon 2010). Cannabis is also the drug of choice for young people, and Hoare and Moon point out that this needs to be considered when looking at the ethnicity figures, as the Mixed ethnicity sample has a far higher number of young people, proportionally, than the other ethnic groups.

Research exploring drug use among young people challenges this further. Cannabis remains the most commonly used drug for girls and boys (15- to 16-year-olds) (Rodham et al 2005), but there is also evidence that youths from different ethnicities are more likely to use different substances. For example, Asian females reported more use of opiates than did their White counterparts, but significantly less use of cannabis (Rodham et al 2005).

To summarise, the research data from the UK, Europe and the US suggest that when the issue of substance use is explored by broad ethnic categories, White ethnic groups consistently have higher levels of use of alcohol and other drugs than do non-White groups. As Kalunta-Crumpton (2004) points out, 'the conception that many blacks misuse drugs is a myth derived from racial stereotypes rather than evidence'. However ethnicity is only part of the picture. Age and generation appear to make a significant difference to the use of substances. The types of substances used appear to vary between different ethnic groups. Further, the literature suggests a range of risk and protective factors, with particular protection being found among individuals maintaining close family and religious links.

Risk and protective factors

Despite clear evidence that substance use among Black or Asian minority ethnic groups is generally lower than among White or Mixed ethnicity groups, there are particular risks that heighten the chances of substance use and problematic substance use. The following is a summary of some of the available research evidence:

- being male (Hoare and Moon 2010)
- being a younger black or Bangladeshi male, aged 18–30 (White 2001; Godette et al 2009)
- poor proficiency in English (Reid et al 2001)
- poor access to education and lower educational attainment (Reid et al 2001)
- unemployment or low income (Reid et al 2001; White 2001; McCambridge and Strang 2005; Fountain 2009b; Godette et al 2009)
- mental distress resulting from the trauma that preceded, and led to, migration; also trauma as a result of the migration process (Fountain 2009b)
- separation from family (Fountain 2009b)
- intergenerational conflict (Reid et al 2001)
- acculturation issues and peer pressure (Reid et al 2001)
- poor knowledge of drug treatment services (Reid et al 2001)
- peer influence among young Caucasian people (Corbin et al 2008)
- positive alcohol expectancies (for White and Hispanic youth) (Chartier et al 2009)
- childhood conduct problems (for Black youth) (Chartier et al 2009)
- social disadvantage (Vogt Yuan 2011).

Reid et al (2001) summarised the risk factors as a 'general underlying problem' of social and economic disadvantage among many minority ethnic communities.

However, there is some evidence of a small set of protective factors. Four factors are consistently found in the research and offer some element of protection against the initiation of substance use or development of substance use problems:

1. strong religious beliefs (particularly in the case of Islam) (White 2001; Harrell and Broman 2009; Hurcombe et al 2010; Van Tubergen and Poortman 2010)
2. close contact with family/strong family ties (White 2001; Corbin et al 2008; Hurcombe et al 2010; Van Tubergen and Poortman 2010)
3. strong ethnic identity (Holley et al 2006; Hurcombe et al 2010)
4. strong local community ties (Hurcombe et al 2010).

For Dilshad, in the practice example at the start of the chapter, there are clearly a number of risk and protective factors present. Any social work intervention with Dilshad needs to be underpinned by an understanding of these factors. In any discussion with him and his family, this knowledge can be used to promote the strengths of Dilshad's family and cultural context and determine whether there are ways that they can support him further, particularly if he accepts a referral to specialist services.

> ### Box 4.1: Mental health and substance use among minority ethnic groups
>
> Coexisting mental health and substance use problems are explored in Chapter Nine. However, it is worth noting that compulsory detention in hospital is far higher among Black than White ethnic groups (Care Quality Commission and National Mental Health Development Unit 2011). Institutional racism and stereotyping by psychiatric professionals are often seen as the reasons for this. Combined with substance use, evidence has shown that Black British men (as opposed to Black Caribbeans, for example) were far more likely to be hospitalised under the Mental Health Act 1983 than are other minority groups (Afuwape et al 2006). In social work practice it is important to be conscious of this and to ensure that all practice is sensitive to potential racist assumptions and bias.

Policy initiatives

Two main bodies of policy can be drawn on to inform practice responses to people from black and minority ethnic (BME) communities who are living with substance problems: first is the wider policy on equalities and fair access to services, and second is the more national/local level policy focusing on substance use and the degree to which it recognises differences for those from BME communities.

As Johnson et al (2006: 15) highlighted, the 'Race Relations (Amendment) Act 2000 placed a general duty on public authorities, and lays down the government's expectations for public authorities to pursue race equality within all their processes and outcomes'. As they state, if people are refused a service on the grounds of ethnicity or receive 'less favourable' treatment, both the individual and the services will be breaking the law. For social workers negotiating access to specialist substance use services or supporting BME people who are seeking to attend those services, this is helpful information. Subsequently, the Equality Act 2010 (HM Government 2010b) has reinforced the requirement for equal access to services, imposing an 'equality duty' on all services. However, it is also worth noting that the equality duty, as it relates to class differences, has been scrapped by the current English Coalition government. Given the overlap between lower class status and ethnicity, this begs the question as to whether or not other elements of the Act will be politically supported in practice (Gentleman 2010).

Many substance use services also sit within the mental health service provision and commissioning arrangements, and therefore are also subject to scrutiny under mental health strategy and legislation. The government's strategy at the time of writing is *No health without mental health: A cross-government mental health outcomes strategy for people of all ages* (HM Government 2011c). The strategy recognises, as do its many predecessors, that people from some BME communities are overrepresented in the mental health system (for example, African Caribbean people are more likely to be compulsorily detained), while other communities are seriously underrepresented in the system (for example, South-East Asian women). Further, it calls for better involvement with communities at a local level to inform service development needs. Importantly, however, according to the Mental Health Acts 1983 and 2007, it is noteworthy that 'alcohol and drug dependence' are not, on their own, considered mental health problems for which mental health services need to be provided.

At a level of exploring policy relating to substance use service provision the NTA published a good practice guide for substance use services, *Diversity: learning from good practice in the field* (NTA 2009). The key tenets of good practice are to:

- fulfil statutory duties
- assess equality needs and conduct impact assessments of responses
- ensure equality data collection including consultation with local groups
- demonstrate a commitment to embedding diversity into the system
- help different communities to become aware of local treatment services
- ensure that staff are competent in relation to all aspects of diversity.

The document also calls for senior leaders of substance use services to become diversity 'champions', ensuring their response to diversity is embedded at all levels of the organisation. The NTA has since developed an online 'Equality analysis: audit tool' (NTA 2010b) that allows services to audit the extent to which they are complying with the requirements of the Equality Act 2010. However, no other data have been published that clarify how well commissioned substance use services are doing in relation to equality of access.

Substance use treatment: barriers and access

The majority of people in treatment for alcohol and other drug problems are white. According to NTA's monitoring data (DH/NTA 2011) 88% of people in *alcohol* treatment are White British, while White Irish and Other White groups each accounted for 2% of people in treatment and other ethnic groups accounted for no more than 1% maximum. There are very few Bangladeshi, African, Chinese or Pakistani people in treatment, or people from mixed ethnicity Black and White or White and Asian dual heritage. This suggests significant barriers to people accessing treatment, even accounting for the lower overall levels of substance use among these ethnic groups (DH/NTA 2011). Some regional differences are evident, with the London area seeing a larger number of people from non–White ethnic groups in treatment (18%).

There is a similar picture in relation to *drug* treatment. White British account for 83% of people attending drug treatment, followed by Other White (3%) and Caribbean (2%). Again, there are very few Chinese people, mixed ethnicity White and Asian or White and Black African people in treatment (Roxburgh et al 2010).

Appropriateness of existing services

The reasons for lower levels of minority ethnic people in drug and alcohol services are many. Among them is the fact that the prevalence of alcohol and other drug use appears to be lower among minority ethnic groups, and this will be reflected in lower numbers attending specialist services. However, this is not considered to be the primary reason for lower numbers. The primary concern is the appropriateness of existing drug treatment services for people from minority ethnic groups and the extent to which they offer a service that meets their needs, particularly in terms of cultural and religious understanding and in terms of language. In general, existing services, particularly those set up for supporting people with illicit drug use, are seen as catering for the white injecting heroin user, using methods of intervention that focus on individual interventions. This creates a barrier when, for example, African-Caribbean people are more likely to need stimulant or cannabis services (Sangster et al 2002; Kalunta-Crumpton 2007).

Asian and Black Caribbean communities in particular highlighted the need for services to provide women's services where, culturally or for other reasons, men's presence was not appropriate, and to provide support for families and carers (Luger and Sookhoo 2005; Fountain 2009b, c; Hurcombe et al 2010).

Kalunta-Crumpton (2004) states that mainstream services are 'reluctant' to recognise and address cultural differences in service provision and this reluctance is reflected in a lack of national and local policy addressing the needs of minority ethnic people with substance problems. Fountain concurs (2009a, b, c, d, e). In a series of reports exploring the particular needs and issues for five broad minority ethnic groups, she calls on service commissioners to work more closely with minority communities to ensure that their needs are met and to understand their sensitivities and issues around drug use and services. She also states that communities must also become involved with commissioners and learn more about drugs and drug services. This would be one way to overcome the inherent mistrust of existing drug services, as well as the perception that they are primarily there for White heroin users (Wanigaratne et al 2003; Fountain 2009a, b, c, d, e). Kalunta-Crumpton (2007) points out that the stereotypes such as 'black people don't inject' do little to help those in minority communities who do inject (or who use drugs in ways not commonly recognised among the community) to seek help. Such stereotypes can also keep their true needs hidden. The national plan *Tackling crack* (Home Office 2002b: 4) noted that the needs of ethnic minority people needed to be 'met more effectively'. Kalunta-Crumpton (2007) states that this signalled 'overt recognition' that there had been gaps in services for crack users, many of whom are African-Caribbean.

However, Bashford (2003) reported that resources about minority ethnic substance use on which services can draw to improve their cultural competence are seriously lacking, as are educational and prevention opportunities.

Importance of family and friends

Fountain's research found that family, friends and GPs were among those whom people were most likely to turn to for support when they had alcohol or other drug problems. However, she also found a lack of awareness of drugs and drug services among the five communities that she studied (2009a, b, c, d, e), which raises questions about how family and friends are responding when substance problems are disclosed to them. In the case of Dilshad in the practice example, his mother and the imam were the two people in his support network who were trying to help him with his substance use and possible mental health problems. While praying may help his spiritual strength before, during and after any attempts to change his cannabis use, it is unlikely to be enough to help him reduce or abstain. Kalunta-Crompton (2004) highlighted the importance of the family in supporting and directing people to specialist drug services in order to help individuals overcome racial and ethnic barriers to substance treatment. Any substance use service that Dilshad received in future would do well to ensure the involvement of his mother and imam, if Dilshad agreed.

Stigma and taboo

A particular barrier to minority ethnic people's accessing substance use services is the stigma and taboo surrounding use and problematic use.

Consistently, research evidence shows that it is the key barrier for people from various minority ethnic communities. Fears about contravening moral codes such as 'izzat' within Islam, which means maintaining honour and respect for oneself and family, keeps people away from seeking specialist support and help (Wanigaratne et al 2003). However, even outside particular concepts or community codes, many minority ethnic groups have strong taboos about alcohol or other drug use, often underpinned by religious doctrine. As a result, problematic use and the use of specialist services outside the community will be seen as bringing shame on those associated with the individual, and may risk the community and others finding out. In her reports on substance use issues among minority ethnic groups, Fountain (2009a, b, c, d, e) emphasises how the taboo and stigma cannot be underestimated as a barrier. She states that the barrier extends to serious concerns about the confidentiality of services, as well as the relationship between specialist services and other authorities, including the police or social care. Many of the groups Fountain spoke to felt that there was a lack of staff from ethnic backgrounds within services. This, in turn, may result in a lack of sensitivity to the needs of minority ethnic groups and serve to reinforce their isolation and exclusion in substance use services. However, anecdotal evidence from practice suggests that some people from minority groups prefer workers of a different culture because of concerns over potential breaches of confidentiality if they are working with someone from their own culture and community.

Institutionalised racism is also a fear (Wanigaratne et al 2003) and moves a step beyond Fountain's emphasis on the need for culturally competent services.

Sangster et al (2002: 3) provide two examples in their study of how particular types of treatment may not be appropriate for people from particular cultures, and so this needs to be explored prior to referrals being made:

> there is a widespread fear among the African Caribbean community of being kept in a medical institution for a mental illness they do not have. This has led to deep distrust of residential rehabilitation services. Vietnamese clients reacted badly to group counselling, which reminded them of the humiliation faced by drug users who were forced to confess under communist policies in Vietnam.

Lack of information

Another key barrier is the lack of information on drugs and drug services within the community and in language that people can understand (Luger and Sookhoo 2005). The lack of knowledge and awareness was highlighted both for the individual and for family and community members who needed or wanted to support a loved one (Fountain 2009a, b, c, d, e). In a small study of specialist substance use professionals and service users, Vandevelde et al (2003) found that communication difficulties were paramount, and particularly in terms of understanding how some cultural differences, including perceptions of honour and respect, prevented some people from speaking openly or about their emotions.

UK researchers have called for better community engagement (Luger and Sookhoo 2005; Fountain 2009a, b, c, d, e; Hurcombe et al 2010) as the best way to reach people who are 'hiding' their substance use because of fear of dishonour or exclusion within their families and communities. Such engagement would also support communities to learn more about substance use.

Specialist minority services?

A possible solution might be the setting up of specialist alcohol and drug services focusing on people from BME groups. However, the research evidence shows little support for this suggestion. As Raistrick et al (2006: 50) state:

> people's lives are too complex to align them with a single special population service; perverse inclusion and exclusion criteria can quickly appear and then detract from the usefulness of a service which was set up with good intentions. Most people seeking help for a drinking [or drug] problem will have certain general or common identities as well as one or more special identities. The potential for special identities is vast and may focus on any or all of demographic, social, political and other factors.

Raistrick et al state that religion is one of the key dividing factors and that there is a better case for thinking about ways in which existing mainstream services can make themselves more responsive and accessible to those from different faiths, rather than for setting up specialist services.

Wanigaratne et al (2003) point out that political will is needed to break down the barriers to effective service provision. Table 4.1 summarises the key barriers identified by Fountain in her studies on drug issues among different ethnic groups in the UK.

Table 4.1: Summary of the needs of minority ethnic groups, based on five Fountain (2009a, b, c, d, e) studies

Ethnic group	Lack of knowledge and informtion on drugs and drug services	Drug services unaware of needs/ lack of cultural/ religious compe- tence	Com- munity members want advice/ support	Perceived lack of confi- dentiality/ trust	Language or commu- nication barriers	Fear of contact with police or other sevices/ authori- ties
South Asian (n=10,485)	✓	✓	✓	✓	✓	
Black African (n=4,657)	✓	✓	✓	✓	✓	✓
Black Caribbean (n=1,863)	✓	✓	✓	✓		✓
Kurdish, Cypriot, Turkish- Cypriot (n=1,395)	✓	✓	✓	✓	✓	✓
Chinese- Vietnamese (n=315)	✓	✓	✓	✓	✓	✓

Treatment outcomes

The evidence on whether the outcomes of substance use interventions or treatment are any worse for people from minority ethnic communities, once they have accessed specialist services, is limited. Treatment effectiveness studies in the UK have found it difficult to follow up people from minority ethnic groups over a period of time (Jones et al 2009), while others have highlighted the lack of inclusion of ethnicity as a variable in effectiveness studies (Simeons et al 2004). Several large UK outcomes or effectiveness studies fail to consider or report on the impact of ethnicity (UKATT Research Team 2005; NTA 2010a).

Overall, the evidence, primarily North American, is equivocal. In a North American study by Field et al (2010), both a Brief Motivational Intervention (BMI) for drinkers in a trauma care setting and a 'treatment as usual' comparison group were found to reduce drinking among White, Black and Hispanic participants at 6 and 12 months follow-up points. However, there were significant reductions among Hispanics in the BMI group. In a study of treatment attrition among young people from minority ethnic groups in the US (US-born Hispanics, foreign-born Hispanics and African-American youth), Austin and Wagner (2010) found a lack of cultural or ethnic factors affecting attrition. Attrition increased if people had to be placed on waiting lists and if their parents used crack-cocaine or had never used alcohol. In the UK's *Drug Treatment Outcomes Study*, Jones et al (2009) found that 'non-white' participants were significantly more likely to continue crack-cocaine post intervention than were white participants, but no other significant ethnic differences emerged.

However, concerns have been raised about the extent to which the evidence base is reliable. In a review of ethnicity measures in outcome studies involving adolescent substance users, Strada et al (2006) found that a minority of studies incorporated ethnicity into their design and very few studies conducted adequate analyses to reliably determine different responses to treatment according to ethnicity.

Clearly some improvement is needed in the research evidence base looking at outcomes of alcohol and other drug treatment for people from minority ethnic groups. Until this happens, few firm conclusions can be made.

Good practice: assessment and intervention

Once barriers have been identified, it is easier to see what needs to be done to overcome them and to develop good practice. While some barriers relate specifically to specialist substance use services, others are barriers that social workers need to address in their own practice.

Castro and Alarcon (2002) point out how cultural variables that are shown to reduce substance use need to be incorporated into interventions for substance problems. It is important to note that substance use intervention does not start at the substance use service: it begins with the social worker asking about substance use as part of initial assessment processes. Therefore, *awareness of the cultural variables* needs to be incorporated into social workers' practice from the start. As previously stated, there is evidence that people with strong ethnic identities and strong family ties are less likely to develop substance problems – these protective factors should form part of a *sensitive exploration of substance issues*. For example, discussions around identity and substance use can be used in motivating or maintaining change, or it may be appropriate to discuss with the family practical and emotional ways in which they think they can support their loved one. Of course, family work such as this must only take place where it is safe and appropriate to do so. Given the high levels of overlap between substance use and domestic abuse, care must be taken to screen for domestic abuse *before* family or partner work takes place (see Chapter Six).

Similarly, evidence suggests that observance of religious beliefs can be a protective factor against using substances or developing problems. However, where problems have developed, White (2001: 1823) asserts that *religious beliefs should also be incorporated into service delivery*. They may provide a spiritual support for changing substance-using behaviours. White states that overlooking the opportunity to discuss someone's beliefs in relation to their substance use may be a 'costly mistake'. Again, this needs a skilled approach in order to avoid sounding moralistic or proselytising in tone.

The evidence has very clearly highlighted the lack of knowledge and awareness of both substances and substance use services among minority communities. Social workers can easily *provide information* in a range of languages and formats to meet these needs, for example, through printed leaflets about local services or through providing a list of online resources or names of people to contact for advice and confidential discussion.

In the example of Dilshad at the beginning of the chapter, he, his mum and the supportive imam may need information about cannabis use and its impact on people's physical and mental health. They may need information about services that can support Dilshad, and particular reassurance about the confidentiality of services. First and foremost, a discussion of their concerns about Dilshad's receiving specialist help will identify what their main concerns are. Further discussing with Dilshad and, where appropriate, his mum and imam, how his faith helps him and how it can continue to help him if he receives specialist support, will also be important.

It is also an appropriate role for social workers to *facilitate joint working* with specialist substance use agency workers either to make educational visits within communities or, where individuals and their families need support, to arrange joint home visits or meetings outside the community with those concerned. In Dilshad's case, where the social worker has established a relationship already, their involvement in facilitating joint working and introductions could be vital for him to engage with services. A referral to the service alone will not do.

As well as looking to their own actions and responsibilities, social workers also need to be aware of substance use services' barriers and to be able to *ask substance use agencies about the cultural sensitivity* of their services prior to referral. Failure to do so can lead to inappropriate referrals and reinforce negative stereotypes of specialist services and their lack of responsiveness to the needs of people from minority groups. Where services are not culturally sensitive, social workers could work alongside an agency to develop appropriate materials or to discuss the particular needs of a family or individual. The substance use agency may not be aware of the negative perceptions that minority communities have about mainstream services. Discussing some of these in relation to confidentiality, in particular, can help the substance specialist to know how to structure an initial meeting or discussion with an individual and/or their family members. Also, *discussion of any potential language difficulties* and the need for interpreters and the sensitive use of interpreters could take place.

Assessing substance use is part of the social worker's role, to some degree. In particular, if someone is unwilling to engage with drug or alcohol services but has engaged well with the social worker it may be that the social worker needs to do that *assessment*. Johnson et al (2006) state that it is important to include questions about culture and spirituality in the assessment process and to include those factors, where applicable, in the subsequent care plan. They also state that the worker needs to learn about the person's family structure and gender roles. Current evidence suggests that alcohol assessment tools such as the AUDIT (Babor et al 1992) show no bias when used with people from minority ethnic groups (Volk et al 1997) even though they tend not to include more culturally sensitive questions. It is also important to note that assessment instruments cannot be easily translated into other languages, as often the concepts or meanings in one language are not recognised or retained in another, and research has been criticised for not adequately recognising this (Bhopal et al 2004).

Social workers also have a role to play in the minority communities in which they work in terms of *informing them about substance use and service provision*. This will help to overcome the lack of knowledge that people have in those communities about help that is available to them or their family members. Finding an appropriate and culturally sensitive way to do this will need careful consideration. Johnson et al (2006) point out that the building of trusting relationships takes time, and therefore patience and persistence will be required.

Consideration may also need to be given to gender sensitivities. Women with substance problems are likely to have experienced abuse or other forms of trauma (see Chapter Six). Research shows significant improvements in drug abstinence (Amaro et al 2007) where additional attention is given to addressing trauma within substance use interventions. Further, mixed gender services may not be appropriate for some minority ethnic groups, and therefore it is important to explore which services run women-only groups or other forms of service provision.

In sum:

- Ensure that discussions or questions about substance use with individuals and families take place in the context of understanding the sensitivities and stigma in particular communities.
- Be aware of how different religions perceive alcohol and other drug use and be sensitive that individuals and families who follow a particular religion may adhere to this and find any use, let alone problematic use, difficult to discuss.
- Be prepared to ask about what their religion has to say about substance use, as it may be possible to help motivate people to change with reference to their religious beliefs. This will need to be done carefully to ensure it does not sound judgemental or proselytising.
- Referrals that you make to substance use services need to be informed referrals; discussions with prospective substance use service providers need to check that appropriate service provision is available – for example, language barriers, women's groups, family work, BME counsellors.
- Where individuals accept the need for support, discussions need to take place about whether they would like family and friend support. With your service user's permission, you can have discussions with, and provide information to, family members about how to support and cope with their loved one's use.
- Some agencies will offer family support where families are already aware of a loved one's substance problem and want to attend services with them. Check what the local substance use services offer for families and ensure that they do so safely – for example, that they do not undertake family work where there is on-going domestic abuse or where domestic abuse is suspected.
- Discuss with substance specialists your service user's fears about confidentiality breaches and information sharing. Ask them to discuss this very carefully with your service user (and family where appropriate). One particular fear is of deportation, and this could be discussed explicitly, where relevant, to allay fears.
- Provide leaflets and information about alcohol and other drugs and local services. Ensure that they are in the appropriate language and that, by

providing them, you are not jeopardising the safety and confidentiality of your service user, that is, if others find the leaflets the person could be in serious trouble with their family and/or community.

■ Ensure that your communication and empathy skills are regularly updated through training and supervision.

In spite of calls for improvement from the five broad ethnic groups that Fountain (2009c: 8) researched, she also found that:

> The cultural competence of drug services was perceived by many study participants as being characterised by 'friendly staff' who were 'understanding', 'welcoming' and 'non-judgemental' (especially of drug-using mothers) in a 'relaxed' environment.

In other words, cultural competence is not necessarily about understanding the history of a particular culture and the intricacies of its norms and religious underpinnings; it can also be about good social work skills and warmth and understanding.

Traveller communities and substance use

Practice example

The Dowling family are from a Traveller community and have recently settled in a house adapted for the needs of their disabled children. Dad, Colin (42), has used heroin on and off for a number of years and has previously detoxed on his own, without medical or specialist support. He is using again, and after being caught in possession of drugs by the police, he was referred to the local alcohol and drugs service for support. Colin also has a history of heavy drinking but does not appear to be drinking currently. He has supportive parents who live locally. His partner, Julia (36), does not use substances. The four children are aged between 7 and 15 years and two of them have degenerative physical disabilities that require a great deal of personal care. Due to Colin's substance use, he spends a great deal of time out of the home and therefore does little to support Julia with the children. The police and school have raised concerns about the well-being and care of the children, in particular their physical care. The family has been in contact with social care for several years, on and off. Colin is reticent about accessing specialist drug support, but pressure from his family, combined with the referral from the police, has prompted him to go. His attendance is sporadic.

There is an overwhelming lack of research on the Gypsy and Traveller communities generally. While they are recognised in British law as a minority ethnic group, few data are collected about their needs (Van Cleemput 2010). As from 2011, Gypsies and Travellers are included in the UK census (Van Cleemput 2010) and this recognition may help provide evidence that the social and health needs of this group of people are worthy of attention.

Nature and extent of substance use

Due to the lack of research on Travellers, obtaining a representative picture of substance use across this population is not possible. The National Drug Treatment Monitoring System (NDTMS) does not record Travellers as a separate minority ethnic group. The following information is therefore taken from two key studies and is based primarily on qualitative data (Fountain 2006; Van Hout 2010a, b).

Fountain (2006) reported on the Irish Traveller community's drug use, following literature-based research and interviews with both Travellers (n=122) and workers from agencies (n=34) from different disciplines who worked with them. Van Hout (2010a, b) also studied a sample of Travellers (n=57) and agency workers (n=45) from the West of Ireland.2 Their findings are remarkably similar, although Van Hout (2010a) included alcohol as well as illicit drug use in her study.

Both studies highlight the importance of recognising the social exclusion that Travellers face and how this ties in to higher levels of poverty, unemployment and poor living conditions in deprived neighbourhoods that are often tied to alcohol and other drug problems.

Alcohol is the primary drug of choice for people from Traveller communities, followed by cannabis and sedatives, tranquillisers and antidepressants (Fountain 2006). The substances least used are heroin, crack-cocaine, LSD and solvents, and levels of injecting drug use appear to be low.

Alcohol levels are generally high for both men and women (Van Hout 2010a). Heavy drinking is seen as normal, with only serious problems being frowned upon and left for the family to deal with. These are often hidden or covered up by the family, due to the shame and stigma. The Traveller community are considered a very religious community, and heavy drinking takes place around religious ceremonies such as weddings and funerals. Van Hout (2010b) reports that drug use is perceived as a more recent problem within the Traveller community; only in the last 10 years has drug use emerged as a problem with the community.

Motivations for use of substances

There are no simple reasons for the apparent increase in the use of drugs and heavy use of alcohol among Traveller communities. The risk factors that apply to anyone's problematic use of alcohol or other drugs are often present in Traveller communities – for example, poor education, low levels of employment, insecure housing/homelessness, poorer health status, drug-using peers or social networks, living in a disadvantaged area/poorly resourced environment (Fountain 2006). The marginalisation and social exclusion experienced by Travellers not only place them in a position of increased risk for substance problems but are also a barrier for service access. In the practice example above, a full assessment of Colin's needs, and those of his family, would help you to determine how many of these risk factors could be applied, as well as providing direction in terms of support needs.

Suggestions from Travellers and agency workers suggest that the ease with which people can currently access alcohol, particularly young people, has not helped to combat heavy drinking. Young Travellers in particular are seen to be using substances to 'fit in' with their non-Traveller peers, and the women in the community are reported as being the people who are trying to deal with them within the community (Pavee Point 2007). Travellers report ready supplies of substances being available in both the school and home environments (Van Hout 2010b). Parents of young Travellers are particularly concerned about the fact that young people are leaving school early and are using drugs more (Pavee Point 2007).

Alcohol, for some, is considered a coping mechanism (Fountain 2006), due both to the perceived disintegration of the community and also the discrimination that Travellers face. Some Travellers also report that in people's choosing to 'settle' in a disadvantaged community – for example, accepting council housing – the Traveller culture has been diluted. This includes increased contact with others who are using drugs and alcohol. In the practice example earlier, Colin and his family have recently 'settled', due to the health problems of their children, and it is possible that among the motivations for Colin's use are difficulties in 'settling' and becoming part of a housed community.

As in other minority ethnic groups, young men in Traveller communities are those most likely to use substances; overall there are low levels of female use. Van Hout also reported that marital status was relevant to drug use, in that Travellers reported that more care was taken by those who were single, as being known as a drug user could damage their eligibility for marriage (Van Hout 2010b).

However, some agencies and Travellers report high use of alcohol by women, particularly in conjunction with prescription medication (Van Hout 2010a). The agency workers in Van Hout's studies also report high levels of domestic violence, assault and damage as a result of Traveller drinking. Women's drinking to cope with their experiences of domestic violence and abuse has been well documented (Barnett and Fagan 1993; Gutierres and Van Puymbroeck 2006) and may be one explanation for women Travellers' drinking and prescription drug use.

Barriers

The barriers to accessing services that are faced by people from Traveller communities are the same as those faced by other minority ethnic groups. However, for a group that is already stigmatised and marginalised, Travellers have expressed great concern about substance use becoming an extra reason for excluding them (Pavee Point 2007).

Fountain (2006: 19) lists some of the cultural competence issues specific to Travellers:

> the incompatibility of drug service procedures with Traveller culture: the lack of inclusion of the family in drug treatment; waiting lists; the appointment system; acceptance for treatment being dependent on catchment areas; the predetermined privileges that clients at a therapeutic community must earn; the necessity for medical cards before treatment can begin; questionnaires and form-filling on registration at a treatment service; and the inclusion of counselling sessions in drug treatment programmes.

In addition, Travellers have reported literacy difficulties within the community as preventing them from being able to access information and services that may be available to them (Pavee Point 2007).

Van Hout (2010a) also found that approaching services was seen to be stigmatising, embarrassing and ultimately unlikely for most Travellers. This emphasises the importance of outreach and for those supporting the Traveller community to facilitate contact. For Colin, the contact and referral was made by the police, even though his partner and family had been pressuring him to do something about his substance use. Van Hout also found that those who did attend specialist services were only men – women usually did not approach specialist substance use services.

Good practice responses

There are both similarities and differences in how to respond to Travellers with substance problems, as compared with other minority ethnic groups discussed earlier in the chapter. The main approaches are to:

■ *Provide information and outreach:* There is a need for social workers to help provide Traveller communities with appropriate information on drug use and, in particular, how to deal with drug problematic use. Effort will need to be made to engage the community where relationships do not already exist, possibly through Traveller organisations, GPs, schools or other professionals working with the community. Such effort will also need to consider that literacy may be an issue for some Travellers.

■ *Facilitate and mediate:* Travellers' needs are generally not considered by drugs services in the development of their services, therefore a social worker's role could be to link Travellers with services and to adopt a facilitative role in briefing both the specialist service and the person concerned about what to expect or what their concerns might be.

■ *Involve the family:* As with other minority ethnic groups, the immediate and extended family is important in Traveller communities. Fountain (2006) reports that family influence is considerable, and therefore consulting with all the family, where safe to do so, may be helpful in marshalling additional support for the individual and/or to rule out whether the family influence is a negative one. Families, particularly women, also appear to be given the responsibility to 'sort out' their loved one's substance problem, therefore discussion with them will help to determine what has been tried before and how effective it was.

■ *Encourage protective factors:* Protective factors, including association with non-drug-using peers within or beyond the Traveller community, or the support and closeness of non-using extended families, could be encouraged, particularly where someone is needing to fill the void left by previous associations with drinking or drug-using associates.

■ *Act as educator:* It has already been stated that Travellers reported knowing little about how to prevent or tackle substance use. A number of strategies that they used could, however, be built on with the advantage of supporting existing solutions identified within the community, in addition to offering new ones. One strategy the Travellers reported was talking to young people about drugs. Providing further information that specifically targets young people would be helpful and encourage on-going discussion within families and communities with young people.

■ *Develop peer educators:* Accessing Traveller communities and building trust with them may not always be easy, given their distrust of dominant cultures and the marginalisation and exclusion they experience. For this reason, and for the longevity of the message relating to alcohol and other drug education, peer educators could be trained. Given the transient life-style of many Travellers, this would also ensure that the learning and education travelled with them. Facilitating partnerships with local substance specialists and local Traveller communities or their representatives would be an effective role for social workers to play in helping Travellers and their children to learn more about the risks of substance use. (Adapted from Fountain 2006 and Van Hout 2010a, b)

Other approaches to changing substance use, such as attempting to detoxify ('detox') people at home, which was reported in the research studies, could be dangerous and potentially life threatening – particularly for alcohol. Therefore, information should be provided on what detox involves, the medical support needed to facilitate home detox processes, and information on specialist services.

As with a number of religions, the research shows that a number of Travellers with substance problems reported finding support through their faith, and abstinence pledges to priests were reported. Discussing with someone how their faith can help support them is therefore an important step.

The messages from the research were not all about what others need to do to support Travellers, however. Travellers also recognised the need for their community to take responsibility and to work actively with agencies so as to be able to support members of the community with substance problems (Van Hout 2010a).

In Colin's situation, the initial engagement process will be key. Working with him both within and outside the context of the family serves to acknowledge his important role and responsibility in the family, while giving him the privacy of discussion outside of it. It will be important to discuss with him whether his sporadic attendance at treatment is related to his substance use or to something about the service that he doesn't like. Ask him to talk about the negatives of the service he is attending and then the positives. Find out what support he wants to be able to give his children, both physically and emotionally, as this may be another motivating factor. Ask how his current use of substances may prevent him from supporting his children or his partner. Highlighting his strengths in attempting to work with specialist services and listening to his family's wishes for him to change his substance-using behaviour is important to building a sense of self-efficacy that may support his continuing attempts to change his substance use.

In sum, this brief section has drawn on two main studies of the Traveller community and their experiences of substance use. Travellers are a minority group who are not adequately recognised in policy and practice and, like other minority groups, struggle to seek help or to know where to start when problems arise. As for everyone who experiences problems with alcohol or other drugs, there is a huge amount of stigma and taboo around admitting to such problems. This means that outreach, education and information are vital to supporting this community.

Notes

[1] In North America, 'Asian' generally refers to different ethnic groups than in the UK. In the UK 'Asian' generally includes people from India, Pakistan, Bangladesh and sometimes China. In the US, it refers primarily to Chinese, Vietnamese, Filipino and Korean people.

[2] There are a number of Traveller communities, including 'English or Romany Gypsies, Welsh Gypsies, Irish Travellers, Scottish Gypsy Travellers and also Roma from various countries in mainland Europe … Other groups of Travellers include show-people and New Age Travellers (more often referred to now as New Travellers)' (Van Cleemput 2010). However, the Traveller communities stemming from Ireland appear to be the largest Traveller group and are the focus here.

Discussion questions/exercises

1   What are the key protective factors relating to substance use for people from minority ethnic groups?
2   Find out in which languages your local alcohol and drug services have information.
3   Consider the local community where you are based – which are the main ethnic groups locally, and how do they find out about alcohol or other drug services?
4   List three ways of getting information to local Traveller communities to support their attempts to deal with substance use within their communities.

Further learning resources

- Beddoes, D., Sheikh, S., Khanna M. and Pralat, R. (2010) *The impact of drugs on different minority groups: A review of the UK literature. Part 1: Ethnic groups.* Available online at: www.ukdpc.org.uk.

■ Hurcombe, R., Bayley, M. and Goodman, A. (2010) *Ethnicity and alcohol: A review of the UK literature. Summary report*. York: Joseph Rowntree Foundation. Available at www.jrf.org.uk.

■ Van Hout, M.C. (2010) 'Alcohol use and the Traveller community in the West of Ireland', *Drug and Alcohol Review*, 29, 59–63.

■ *Ladged no longer*. DVD on the impact of drugs on the Gypsy community. Available from Jake.Bowers@btinternet.com.

■ Travellers Aid Trust – www.travellersaidtrust.org/.

Practice examples

1. Mum – Jackie (19), Dad – Ian (21), Children – Ruby (2), Lily (9 months)

Jackie and Ian have been using heroin for some time. The referral to social services was made by Ian's parents, who are worried about their grandchildren and don't know what to do next. Both Ruby and Lily have disabilities that require them to have regular feeding and attentive care. The grandparents live in the tower block next to their grandchildren. Jackie and Ian have sold all the furniture in the flat except for the baby's cot, but they still feel very committed to their children and want to look after them. They are clearly not managing to do this and have a lot of their own problems that they need help to address. The grandparents are willing to look after Ruby and Lily.

2. Son – Billy (11), Dad – Eric (51)

Billy was referred to social services by his school, who reported that he was not attending and expressed concern for his welfare. Billy is a young carer for his father, who has been drinking heavily for many years and has brain damage as a result of his drinking, that is, Korsakoff's syndrome. Eric clearly loves Billy and spends lots of time with him, giving him a great deal of love and affection. However, he is unable to take care of Billy at all. Billy is skilled beyond his years in all adult tasks and has stated very articulately that he wants to look after his dad.

3. Grandmother – Pauline (53), Mum – Sarah (26), Children – Max (6), Eliza (2)

Sarah is a single mum and controlled heroin user. Because of Sarah's heroin use, Pauline has removed the children without Sarah's consent and contacted social services for help. The children have different fathers, both of whom are also heroin users and do not want any involvement with their children. Pauline is the paternal grandmother of one of the children and blames Sarah for her son's heroin use. Sarah's controlled heroin use allows her to care for the children well. Max always gets to school on time and both children are clean and cared for. Sarah wants to continue caring for her children. Max also wants to stay with his mum.

Introduction

Alcohol and other drug use by parents may have no negative effects on children and young people at all. Many adults use drugs or drink alcohol to levels that do not cause problems or have any impact on their parenting behaviour. However, alcohol and drug use that is problematic can have serious and occasionally extreme negative effects. These include tragedies such as child deaths or children who are physically, emotionally and psychologically scarred into adolescence and adulthood. Unfortunately, there are also children whose lives have been similarly affected but whose parents did not use alcohol and drugs. They simply had parents who were not good enough and whose abusive or neglectful parenting behaviours had nothing to do with alcohol or drugs.

When working with parental substance use, it is vital to make professional judgements on parenting behaviour and its impact on the children, and not jump to conclusions based on one factor alone – in this case, the parents' alcohol or drug use. There is evidence to suggest that even where there are maternal substance problems, other environmental factors are more likely to have a negative impact on parenting than the mother's substance use alone; for example, low socioeconomic status and the mother's perceptions of the child's 'maladaptive' behaviour (Suchman and Luther 2000).

Of course, parental substance use is one risk factor among many for potential harm to children, and should be explored where it is identified. Any parental substance use should sound alarm bells and prompt further questions. The responses may lead to more in-depth assessment by social workers and/or substance use professionals. This needs to be done skilfully, underpinned by knowledge of substance use and after reflecting on your values with regard to substances and the people who use them. Research evidence suggests that negative responses by social workers, who are often ignorant about substance use issues, have caused parents in need of support to distrust social work contact at best and, at worst, to be openly hostile to it (Cleaver et al 2007; Woolfall et al 2008). Another criticism of social workers is that drug use is often demonised, whereas alcohol use can be completely overlooked, in spite of research evidence showing that it poses as many risks, if not more, to children and young people (Harwin and Forrester 2006; Mariathasan and Hutchinson 2010).

What is clear is that working with parents who use substances requires a focus on *the behaviour resulting from* the substance use, not the substance use per se. Poor parenting behaviour is the determinant of harm to children, whatever the reasons for it. Where substance use is negatively affecting the parenting behaviour, then action must be taken, but it would be wholly inaccurate, and potentially dangerous, to assume that once the substance use is reduced, or has stopped, parenting behaviour will be 'good enough' and the risks will disappear. The parent may still not be a good enough parent, without the alcohol or drug use.

This chapter will summarise the policy and evidence base in relation to substance use by parents and its impact on children. It will highlight risk and resilience factors for the children of substance-using parents and outline good practice in the assessment and intervention process.

The policy context

There are no accurate figures on the number of children negatively affected by parental substance problems. Surveys and other attempts to establish the extent of the problem are always likely to be best-guess estimates, particularly given the likelihood that people will deny illegal drug use or underestimate their alcohol or other drug use. In a study attempting to pull together estimates from three UK national household surveys, Manning et al (2009) suggest that previous estimates may have significantly underestimated the actual problem, particularly if 'binge' drinking and any use of illicit drugs are taken into account. In terms of alcohol, the authors report that nearly 30% of children under 16 years of age could be living with a binge-drinking parent, although this is reduced to 22% if 'hazardous drinking'[1] only is considered. Figures for illicit drug use are lower; however, they indicate that approximately 8% of children live in a household where a parent has used illicit drugs in the past year, and that 2.8% of children live with a 'dependent drug user'.

Clearly, use and problematic use differ, and either one does not automatically indicate actual harm, but these figures suggest that increased risk of harm for a substantial number of children is likely. In addition, Copello et al (2000b) estimated that for every person with a substance problem, two other people are negatively affected. Taken together, such estimates suggest that all family members will, at best, be concerned about a loved one's substance problem and, at worst, be harmed by it.

Safeguarding children is the dominant concept governing current childcare policy and practice. What has been helpful about the safeguarding agenda is that is has focused on issues that affect children's safety and well-being and on parenting behaviour that may be unsafe. Substance use and domestic abuse are among these potentially harmful behaviours and are increasingly recognised in national policy as negatively affecting families and children.

A raft of guidance for local policy and practice development has emerged under the safeguarding agenda that addresses many other situations or personal contexts in which children live. These include children living with parents with learning disabilities, looked after children, disabled children and those who are sexually exploited and trafficked. Along with the more general policies, it has emerged under the umbrella of the Every Child Matters initiative.[2]

At the core of the safeguarding agenda are five key aims, as laid out in the original Every Child Matters Green Paper (DCSF 2003). These aims were subsequently enshrined in law by the Children Act 2004 and followed by the 10-year strategy, the Children's Plan (DCSF 2007), which set out key aims in child education, poverty and health.

These five key aims are for children to:

- be healthy
- stay safe
- enjoy and achieve
- make a positive contribution
- achieve economic well-being.

The impact of alcohol and drugs on children's health, safety, enjoyment and achievement will vary enormously, depending on the extent to which parental alcohol and drug use is affecting parenting behaviours. However, it is clear that where there is heavy alcohol or other drug use by parents, social work assessment and intervention will need to consider the extent to which these aims are being met.

It is only relatively recently that attention to parental alcohol and drug use has emerged within the policies and practice guidance for social work. Many social workers are still leaving social work education without training on substance use (Galvani et al 2011), making it even more imperative that post-qualifying training and practice guidance is provided. In England, guidance has emerged primarily from charities (Adfam 2008; NSPCC 2008; Delargy 2009) or at a local government level within local safeguarding children board guidance on child protection procedures (Camden Safeguarding Children Board 2009; Birmingham Safeguarding Children Board 2011). The Welsh and Scottish governments have been ahead of the game in producing policy and practice guidance for working with parents using substances (Scottish Education Department Social Work Services Group 1988; Scottish Executive 2001). Indeed the Welsh Assembly Government recently introduced legislation to mandate joint working between health and social care in setting up integrated family support services (Welsh Assembly Government 2010). The initial remit of the new integrated services is to focus on parental substance use, in particular.

The introduction of the Common Assessment Framework (CAF) and associated guidance (HM Government 2006a) – following the Children Act 2004 – highlighted how parental substance use and/or the young person's substance use are examples of when a CAF would be undertaken:

> common assessment may be appropriate when significant changes have been observed in children who are, have been or are at risk of (being): ...

> ■ presenting challenging or aggressive behaviours (e.g. bringing a knife into school), abusing/misusing substances or committing offences;
> ■ experiencing physical or mental ill health or disability (either their own or their parents');
> ■ exposed to substance abuse/misuse, violence or crime within the family.
> (HM Government 2006a: 4)

The CAF process is designed to be completed by any professional and to increase integrated working across disciplines. The assessment form contains two prompts on substance use under 'behavioural development' and 'family history and functioning'. The extent to which these prompts are used routinely rather than when substance use has reached a crisis point is not known.

National reports and inquiries, including the Laming report (2009), the Social Work Task Force (2009) and the Munro review (2011), have all identified substance use as a key issue that social workers need to be able to work with in order to support families and safeguard children. This may indicate a greater emphasis on substance use in preparing people for social work practice. Only time will tell.

National substance use policy has been even slower in recognising the role of social work and social care in working with people with substance problems. Traditionally, drug and alcohol services have been focused primarily on the individual with the substance use problem with, at best, advice and very limited services to adult partners or family members. Where parental substance use is mentioned, it tends to be in the context of a strategic focus on young people's use of substances and the impact of parental substance use on the young person's family environment. However, the last two drug strategies for England have given slightly greater recognition to the impact of substance use on families (HM Government 2008b, 2010a). Indeed, the latest strategy also recognises the need for support for family members in their own right:

> We will encourage local areas to promote a whole family approach to the delivery of recovery services, and to consider the provision of support services for families and carers in their own right. (HM Government 2010a: 21)

Further, the NTA (2011), which currently oversees the commissioning and monitoring of drug services,[3] has produced guidance on the development of joint protocols between substance use and social care services for working with parents using substances. There has also been a growth of specialist services across the UK for parents and children living with substance problems, but provision is patchy and resources for such services are limited.

In sum, there is increasing attention to parental substance use and its impact on parenting and on children's welfare. Social workers working with families will continue to need training and support so as to work effectively with these issues (Galvani 2007; BASW Special Interest Group in Alcohol and Other Drugs 2010), particularly given the overlap with other problems, including domestic violence and parental mental ill-health (Laming 2009).

The following section will focus on the possible impact on parenting of parental alcohol or drug use. It will be your remit to assess the extent to which these types of behaviours occur and whether children are at risk of harm or potential harm as a result.

Impact on parenting

There is a great deal of research looking at the impact of alcohol and other drug problems on families, in particular parents and their children. Some of the negative impact on parenting relates directly to the impact of the substance use on the parenting ability of the parent(s) using the substance. However, the impact can also be on the parenting of a non-using partner as they seek to cope with the different moods, behaviours and needs of their using partner, as well as their absence, physically or practically, when they are under the influence of substances.

The types of problems that are commonly reported as resulting from parental alcohol and drug problems include:

- *Disorganisation within the family:* The effects of the substance (and the often time-consuming process of getting hold of it) can often disrupt family routines or lead to their being neglected in favour of the substance-related activities. In addition, there are practical difficulties relating to the effects of substance use; for example, a parent not getting up in the morning in time to get the child to school, or a clean school uniform not being ready (see Practice Example 2 at the start of the chapter).

■ *Broken promises:* When someone has a drug and alcohol problem it can often take over their plans for the day, and that promised trip to the park or the promise of time spent playing or watching a video together may be broken. Ultimately, broken promises give clear messages to children that parents will say one thing and do another.

■ *Emotional inconsistency:* Because of the impact of alcohol and drugs on a person's mind and body, mood swings are common. Consider what you know about the effects of alcohol and other drugs (see Chapter Two). The artificially induced highs and lows that accompany substance use will change when a person is sobering up or coming down from a high, or vice versa. The withdrawal process can be physically and psychologically uncomfortable. People can experience a range of emotions and be tearful, volatile, edgy and withdrawn to name a few. The children may experience a parent with volatile mood changes. This lack of emotional stability can be damaging to children, who need a consistent level of love and affection and clear boundaries about what is and isn't acceptable behaviour or a proportional response. In addition, the attention given to the substance-using process and its after-effects can result in a lack of attention to the child. The importance of recognising emotional neglect was a clear message that emerged from research with children who had lived with parental substance use (Templeton et al 2006).

■ *Neglectful or authoritarian parenting:* Related to the emotional inconsistency is evidence that parenting styles can be either neglectful or authoritarian. The time and patience required for parenting are not available to parents who have substance problems. The heavier the substance use, the poorer the parenting.

■ *Coexisting mental health problems:* The overlap between alcohol and drug problems and mental ill-health is very clear (see Chapter Nine). The relationship between the two is bi-directional. Alcohol is a common, legal and available 'solution' for people who, for instance, suffer trauma, depression or anxiety. Similarly, we know that alcohol and other drug use is associated with temporary or permanent mental health problems. In addition, people with serious mental health problems will often self-medicate their mental health symptoms or the side-effects of their psychotropic medication with substances. Given the unpleasant side-effects of such medications, it is arguable that using substances is a reasonable response rather than a deviant behaviour, as it is often viewed. The relationship is certainly a complex one, but nevertheless it is a strong one and support may be needed for people to address their mental health issues at the same time as they are seeking support for their substance use. Coping with both substance problems and mental health problems is difficult and the impact on the parenting capacity will need to be monitored carefully. In addition, the stress and pressure placed on a partner or other carers will increase and may well have a negative impact on their mental health.

- *Financial problems:* Drinking and drug use costs money, and problematic use will strain the finances of many a household. In particular, those whose income is lower or who are reliant on benefits will be more noticeably affected. Consider the living environment of Jackie and Ian's family (in the Practice Example 1 at the beginning of the chapter), compared to that of a family with a far higher income. Financial difficulties will be far more quickly apparent for those living in relative poverty than for the middle- or upper-income earners. In worst cases, the level of debts with loan sharks, family members, friends, local shopkeepers and so on may result in parents having difficulties affording the basics for their children.
- *Physical health problems:* One of the more obvious signs that someone has a problem with alcohol or drugs is when they start to feel physically unwell. Some of this may be a result of withdrawal from a substance they have used, but some of it may be a result of damage to the body's organs, as in the case of Eric in the practice example at the start of the chapter. While the ill-health may be either temporary or permanent, the results for the child are similar: a parent who is sick and unable to function fully as a parent and fulfil key parenting tasks. In addition, where there is a non-using partner, he/she may end up taking care of the health needs of their partner, thus leaving less time available for their children, in terms both of time spent with them and of monitoring or supervising their activities.
- *Domestic abuse:* Research clearly shows the high rates of overlap between substance use and domestic abuse. In general, research suggests that there are higher levels of conflict between parents where there is an alcohol or drug problem. This may not be of such a frequency, pattern and impact that it constitutes domestic abuse, but it may be. Where both issues are present, the impact on the children in the household is magnified (Templeton et al 2006).

In a review of three years of Serious Case Reviews (SCRs), Brandon et al (2010: iii) conclude:

> As in previous studies [of SCRs] domestic violence, substance misuse, mental health problems and neglect were frequent factors in the families' backgrounds, and it is the combination of these factors which is particularly 'toxic'. The incidence of these risk factors is, however, likely to be under-recorded in the notifications.

In a review of the literature conducted by the author and colleagues (Templeton et al 2006), it was apparent that many parents with alcohol or drug problems had often suffered child abuse and neglect in their own childhoods. While this is far from suggesting that the cycle of child abuse and adolescent and adult substance problems is inevitable, it does reveal a high risk of intergenerational suffering, with children at risk of suffering harm from one generation to the next. For practice, this means that early identification and intervention can not only protect the child, but also, potentially, can interrupt the cycle of high risk that their own children may face.

Parents' views

There is limited research evidence representing parents' views of the impact of substance use on their parenting. For obvious reasons, a parent may not want to discuss the negative impact that their alcohol or other drug use will have on their parenting, through fears of the children being removed into the care system.

Redelinghuys and Dar (2008: 42) found this to be the case in their interviews with 66 parents in a London-based detoxification unit, in which 41% of the parents stated that they were concerned about the impact of their substance problems on their children, either currently or in the future, and in particular with 'substance related difficulties'. However, the majority reported no concerns. Eleven parents said they would not contact any professional for help on behalf of their child, while the remainder said they would most likely contact their GP (n=33) or specialist substance services (n=30). Only nine said that they would contact social services and even fewer said they would contact paediatric services (n=3) or child or adolescent mental health services (n=5). As the authors suggest, this was most probably due to concerns about the children being removed from home or the stigma attached to those particular services.

However, establishing parents' views is essential for research and social work practice, especially for developing a more positive, trusting and strengths-based approach to services and interventions. Establishing the views of Jackie, Sarah and Eric in the examples at the start of the chapter has to be the starting-point. Too many times, social workers are accused of not listening to parents (Woolfall et al 2008) or not acknowledging how hard parents have been trying to change their use or how scared they are of losing their children. It is important for social workers not to miss these crisis moments, which may be a trigger for change.

The motivation of parents' possible separation from their children as a driver for change was reinforced in a study by Mahoney and MacKechnie (2001). In their consultation with parents and children attending drug and alcohol services in Liverpool, they found that, while parents knew they had an alcohol or drug problem and that it had a negative impact on their children, they often felt powerless to change and felt that social services lacked knowledge and understanding. Some parents, but not all, stated that, on reflection, the substance use was more important than their children's needs. The parents were aware that some children might blame themselves for their parents' use, but also identified their children as an important motivation for change. Further, they wanted workers and services that supported them with a range of needs over the long term, and home visits too. Part of what they wanted was support in getting their family structure right once they had reduced or stopped their substance use. They didn't want short interventions for the drugs and alcohol alone: they wanted services that were flexible, confidential and offered counselling to both parents and children. Finally, they wanted social services to be open about child protection concerns and not to threaten them with proceedings, because that increased secrecy. While this can be a difficult balance for social workers to achieve – that is, being open and transparent without it being seen as threatening – it is the communication skills that will make the difference. The tone that is used, the body language and the context in which it is used are key to achieving this balance.

In the practice examples earlier, Sarah's efforts need to be recognised and openly acknowledged, and it appears that she may need support to get her children back; Jackie and Ian's situation appears a lot more serious, but nevertheless their wishes need to be heard because their impending crisis with regard to their children's care may be the trigger that they need in order to seek help and to change. Even if their children are placed in someone else's care, they need support and help to work towards their return if that is what they wish and what is deemed best for the children.

One Australian study focused on the strategies that 22 heroin-using mothers used to reduce the harm to their children from the negative impact of their substance use. Richter and Bammer (2000) reported seven strategies that emerged from the mothers' reports and suggested that these strategies could be used by professionals as measures of the mothers' success in changing their substance use and reducing the harm to their children. The seven strategies were:

1. stop using completely;
2. go into treatment ...;
3. maintain a stable small habit;
4. shield children from drug-related activities;
5. keep the home environment stable, safe, and secure;
6. stay out of gaol [jail];
7. place them with a trusted caregiver and maintain as active a parental role as possible.

(Richter and Bammer 2000: 404–5)

The authors report that the women saw the various strategies as a ladder, with the least desirable option being number 7 and the most desirable being number 1. What is clear, however, is that the mothers were trying to balance good parenting with using. From a strengths-based perspective, this provides a number of strengths on which social workers can build self-efficacy and self-esteem, which contribute to motivation to change (Miller and Rollnick 2002). At the same time they will need to use skilled reflection and communication to encourage parents to talk about how their substance use conflicts with their desired goals of protecting their children. In the Richter and Bammer study, the mothers were aware of their limitations and self-critical of their parenting:

> "I remember when I first went to the rehab house, I remember I could never, now it might sound strange, but I just didn't know how to even like hold her or cuddle her. And you used to find a lot of parents that come in that didn't know how to give your child any affection because you had no love or respect or self esteem or anything for yourself. So it was really hard to give to someone else."
> (Leor in Richter and Bammer 2000: 405)

As with the relationship between Billy and his dad, Eric, in the practice example earlier, research has found that children provide both a practical and also a social support for their parents in helping them to overcome substance problems. Tracy and Martin (2007), in a review of the status and roles of children in relation to women in treatment, found that children often provided as much support for sobriety as did adult members in their mothers' networks. Further, children who either lived with their parent or lived in foster care were also perceived as providing social support to parents. Children are often aware of this role, and therefore any suggested change in the relationship, even with the best of intentions, can be met with resistance.

Consider Billy's relationship with Eric: while roles are reversed and our 'ideal' of childhood is unlikely to match the reality for Billy, he appears to feel loved and knows that he is the most important support for his dad. Whole-scale change is likely to meet with resistance from both of them, but it may be helpful for both if respite arrangements are made on a regular basis. However, first things first: what are the options available to them, including family substance services? Have you explained your concerns and the options clearly? Have you given them time to think about them? Have you then asked for their thoughts on what should happen? You will need to be skilled in your communication and sensitive to their relationship. You will need to understand that anything that suggests permanent separation may well be rejected outright, although it may be one of a number of choices you give them.

This section has focused on the impact that alcohol and drugs can have on parenting, drawing on research with parents and touching on the practice realities of working with parents and children in a relationship that we may not consider ideal but that is nevertheless an important one. The next section will explore the impact of parental drug and alcohol problems on children.

Impact on children

There can be a negative impact on all family members from living with, or being close to, a loved one with problematic substance use. The potential harm does not discriminate according to age, but children are clearly more at risk, due to their increased vulnerability and their inability (or reduced ability, depending on age) to make choices to leave the home or spend time elsewhere.

There is a lot of research on the negative impact of parental substance use on children, both *in utero* and after birth, through their youth and teenage years and into adulthood. A number of reviews have helpfully summarised this literature and drawn out the implications for practice and research (Cleaver et al 1999; Tunnard 2002; Kroll and Taylor 2003; Templeton et al 2006). They show the many ways in which parental substance problems can have a negative impact on children, including:

- physical health, for example delayed development and intellectual difficulties;
- emotional health, for example confused emotional attachments, premature maturation. Children will sense the shame and stigma of having a parent with alcohol and drug problems and may even be teased about it – they will learn not to talk about it and will keep secrets;
- mental health, for example low self-esteem, and other psychological or psychiatric problems;
- behavioural changes, for example appearing withdrawn or, conversely, aggressive'
- educational problems, for example poor school attendance and achievement;
- social development; for example children and young people can become socially isolated, either as an adverse effect of their parent's social isolation or because they are stigmatised, unwilling or unable to have friends to play and visit their home;
- disrupted leisure time;
- relationship difficulties; for example, evidence suggests that these children experience their own problems with relationships and the parenting of their own children, as well as being at increased risk of domestic abuse;

■ increased risks in childhood/adolescence, for example multiple forms of abuse, developing their own substance problems.

This wide range of potential negative impacts highlights the importance of a full assessment not only of the child's needs but also of the substance use of the parent and the impact it is having on their parenting ability.

Research looking at young people in the care system shows that a large number of them have histories of parental alcohol and drug use and other behaviours that often co-occur – for example, domestic abuse, mental health problems, poor parental supervision and so on (Cousins and Milner 2006; McAuley and Young 2006). However, given the high rates of overlap between substance use and mental ill-health and between substance use and domestic abuse, these issues are not solely significant to young people in the care system: they are also the realities for children and young people living with their parent/s.

FASD[4]/NAS

In utero there is a danger, albeit still a minimally understood one, of children's being physically and mentally damaged by heavy maternal substance use. Two main diagnoses have been developed to describe a list of symptoms and problems that children may suffer as a result. For alcohol, this is Foetal Alcohol Spectrum Disorder (FASD); for illicit drugs, it is Neonatal Abstinence Syndrome (NAS).

There is currently more research into FASD than into NAS, with the former having a body of work and resources available, including national charities and websites, whereas such resources are far more limited for NAS. What evidence there is suggests that FASD most likely stems from regular high-dose drinking during the first, and possibly third, trimesters of pregnancy. The child can subsequently suffer a number of health problems and social problems on a spectrum from mild to severe. These include:

■ pre- and post-natal growth deficiencies, for example shorter body length, small head, failure to thrive;
■ physical anomalies, for example small upturned nose, heart and kidney problems;
■ a damaged central nervous system, resulting in cognitive and learning difficulties.

These problems will require extra attention and will result in a baby that is more demanding than normal. This poses particular problems for a parent or parents who are less able to cope as a result of their substance use and may be particularly vulnerable themselves. An affected baby may well go through a process of withdrawal from the substance, often lasting up to several weeks, and may need medicating to help them through it safely. Alcohol and drug use is also a risk factor for the baby dying from SIDS (Sudden Infant Death Syndrome), particularly when co-sleeping with a parent in bed or on a sofa (Blair et al 2009).

Box 5.1: Information on FASD/NAS

National Organisation on Fetal Alcohol Syndrome (NOFAS-UK)
– www.nofas-uk.org
NOFAS-UK promotes public awareness about the risks of alcohol consumption during pregnancy, with the goal of reducing the number of babies being born with FASD. It also acts as a source of information for the general public, the press and medical professionals.

FAS Aware UK – www.fasaware.co.uk
This website has been designed to raise awareness, and provide informed choice, information and support for people affected by or interested in FAS.

Neonatal Abstinence Syndrome (NAS), Information for you
This is a three-page leaflet designed by a lead midwife in substance use based in London. It is a helpful resource for professionals and service users. www.bhrhospitals.nhs.uk/maternity/pdfs/nasleaflet.pdf.

Neonatal Abstinence Syndrome
This is an excellent six-page leaflet about NAS produced by Health Scotland. www.healthscotland.com/uploads/documents/10536-_Neonatal%20 Abstinence%20Syndrome.pdf.

Evidence suggests that, as affected children grow, they may often have no sense of time, no understanding of risk or danger, and will often require one-to-one attention (BMA Board of Science 2007). Social skills can be limited and sometimes inappropriate and short-term memory can be poor, although longer-term memory is better. Concentration can be difficult and they may need to have clear instructions repeated continually. Consider the difficulties of raising a child affected by FASD or NAS and the potential for the child to be labelled as naughty by parents, teachers and others who may be ignorant of the child's background and diagnosis.[5] For social work practice the key requirement will be to recognise the behaviour, support the parents – for example, arranging respite – and ensure clear communication to teachers and other carers or professionals so that children are not labelled as 'bad'.

As yet, the prevalence of FASD and of NAS is not known. Much more evidence is needed about these conditions, but there is increasing recognition that maternal heavy intoxication can result in health problems for the child, ranging from short term and mild, to lifelong and severe. Current medical advice is that, until more is known, parents should not drink alcohol or use drugs during pregnancy.

Box 5.2: Pregnancy, domestic violence and substance use

- Pregnancy is also a high-risk time for domestic abuse, with physical abuse often aimed at the woman's abdomen, and emotional and psychological abuse relating to her appearance – for example, increased weight. Given the high rates of overlap between alcohol and drug use and suffering domestic abuse, this is also an important point to be aware of in practice and to ask adults and children about in a safe and sensitive way, that is, not in front of other people.
- Research suggests that the combination of parental substance use and domestic violence increases the negative impact, in many areas, on children's growth and development, and this impact continues into their own relationships and experiences in adolescence and adulthood.

Children's views

Children's voices have not been well heard in the research on parental substance use and its impact on the family. What little research there is suggests that they are fearful of losing their parent and often feel responsible for their parent's use or for helping their parent to change. In the practice example of Billy and his dad, Eric, it is clear that he feels very responsible for caring for his dad, although, as he gets older, he may also become increasingly aware that he is losing out in comparison to the activities of his peers. As for Max, he too wants to stay with his mum, although his grandma, Pauline, wants Max and Eliza to stay with her.

In a review of the literature by Templeton et al (2006), the themes of isolation, secrecy and conflict dominated the literature. These themes have been reflected in the experiences of children who called Childline, a telephone helpline service for children in the UK. Evidence from a review of calls received from children powerfully illustrates how extremely distressing and upsetting these issues are for the children who call Childline (Mariathasan and Hutchinson 2010: 1):

> "I want to run away from home. Both my parents use drugs and alcohol and they fight. My mum brings men home all the time. I really hate their way of living and would like to get away. I did try to get away with my sister but my sister is partly disabled so she couldn't keep up and we came back home. I am really unhappy to be left alone in the house all night." (Sanjay, aged 14)

> "My mum and dad don't feed me. I have to steal money from people so I can get food. When I cry, Mum and Dad hit me. They are drinking all the time. I can't tell anyone because I am scared my mum and dad might do something and hit me." (Jonathan, aged 10)

Kroll and Taylor (2003) report that children learn from an early age what to keep secret, and the implications if they do not do so. They learn quickly whom to trust and the risks of telling anyone, particularly outsiders. Thus, encouraging children to speak out in way that feels safe and not disloyal to their parent/s will be a key task for social workers when working directly with children. Kroll and Taylor (2003) reported that social workers were seen by some children as a threat rather than supportive, and stated that children only disclosed a small amount of information if they did talk.

Childline also found that concerns about parental alcohol consumption far outnumbered those about parental drug use (Mariathasan and Hutchinson 2010). It also found that these children were three times more likely than other callers to Childline to talk about experiences of physical abuse. What the children's voices highlight is the presence of domestic abuse and physical abuse of children in households where parents have alcohol and other drug problems. Fear of physical and sexual violence or death is a major issue for children of substance-using parents. Kroll and Taylor (2003: 169) reported that it was the 'greatest problem' for children in the studies that they reviewed.

While these overlapping issues are vitally important in assessing risk to children (and adult victims), it is also important that the social worker does not consider the removal of the substance use as the answer to stopping the violence and abuse. In a study that asked the children of parents with substance problems for their views on healthy relationships, Galvani (2010b: 28) found that even when specialist substance use services were involved with parents, children found that this did not always improve relationships:

> "Not always, cos like, the person who's [using drugs] might get quite annoyed, saying that they're not doing it, or that they don't

need help. Cos if you admit you need help it's like saying there's something wrong with you."

"It does and it don't because if they get help then they'll build a stronger relationship, but still, they would still have time to bring back the past."

"Sometimes. Because it would be like well done, but in your mind you'd probably think they're still taking it ..."

"It does and it doesn't as well. Because they might be both taking drugs at the same time and they might be comfortable with that but it does make your life better as well cos at least you're not gonna hurt yourself by doing damage to your body."

Templeton et al (2006) found that the research exploring the childhood experiences of adults whose parents had alcohol or drug problems highlighted the emotional abuse and neglect they had suffered. Many such adults felt that these were far less recognised and addressed than sexual or physical abuse, yet they were just as damaging.

In spite of the incredible hardship of living with parents with substance problems, it is clear that children typically still love their parents and want things to be normal. They worry about their parents rather than themselves, and are looking for ways to help or to make things better (Mariathasan and Hutchinson 2010).

In social work practice, as in research, exploring children's views and self-identified needs is the first step in attempting to offer support and assure better outcomes for them. The parental substance use may not always be the main issue concerning the children, particularly considering the range of overlapping issues that the parents, and children, often face. It is clear that factors including parental conflict and domestic abuse and parental mental health significantly affect children too.

Risk and resilience

While many children will be at risk from parental alcohol and drug problems, other children cope with a parent's substance use without suffering significant harm. Some children and young people are more resilient than others to parental abuse and neglect, whatever its cause or origins.

Knowledge of risk and resilience factors, and how to enhance protective factors around a child, is part and parcel of social work education for those working with children and families. Studies specifically looking at resilience in children living with parental substance problems have confirmed the transferability of such protective factors to the particular needs of this group of children (Velleman and Orford 1999).

Newman and Blackburn (2002) highlight the difference between resilience and protective factors, stating that resilience builds within a child – it is an internal mechanism that is particular to that child. Resilience can be enhanced as a result of protective factors within the child's environment, or as part of the child's skills and cognitive abilities. Understanding the difference between the two factors, and the professional's ability to influence each one, will be hugely helpful in social work interventions with children and families affected by problematic alcohol use. The protective factors, in particular, can be used as a measure of child's support systems and can be discussed openly with parents and others involved in the young person's care. Table 5.1 provides a list of the protective and resilience factors, drawn from the research literature.

Table 5.1: Protective and resilience factors

Protective factors	Resilience factors
Basic needs met: food, clothing, hygiene	Feeling safe and secure
Good relationship with non-alcohol- or drug-using parent and supportive grandparents and siblings	High verbal and cognitive skills
Someone to talk to and share problems with	Experience of success and achievement
Peer support/talking to other children and young people in the same situation	Ability to use adults as resources
External support, for example, school	Strong self-esteem
Education about parent's alchohol or drug use	Ability to play
Reassurance that they are not to blame	Deliberate planning by child for a better future
Structure and routine to life	Understanding that parent is trying to stop/reduce their substance use
Community resources, for example, clubs, church	Feeling loved and cared for
Being able to get away from home and do something outside the house	
Good communication between parents, and between parents and children	

Working with other family members

It is not just the children who can be negatively affected by the alcohol or drug problems of a parent. The impact of substance problems can be felt by partners, other family/household members and extended family, all of whom may have some role in supporting the children in the household. Regardless of the rights or wrongs of her actions, Pauline, in the practice example at the start of the chapter, is clearly concerned about the well-being of her grandchildren. Similarly, Ruby and Lily's grandparents are worried enough about them to make a referral to social care and risk damaging their relationship with their daughter, Jackie.

Family and friend relationships will often be strained or damaged when a loved one has a substance problem, and people's way of coping may be to stop or reduce contact. There is increasing evidence that the mental and physical health and well-being of others living in the household of an individual with substance problems is negatively affected (Copello et al 2000b). However, increasingly there is research showing that support for family members in their own right, rather than as part of the intervention focusing on the person with the substance problem, can substantially improve their health and ability to cope with their loved one's substance use (Orford et al 2007).

For those not living in the household, there is also the frustration of how to help or whether to help at all. Extended family frequently become carers or surrogate parents, and recent evidence of the increasing recognition of kinship care has highlighted the number of grandparents who are parenting their grandchildren as a result of parental substance use (Goodman et al 2004; Barnard 2007). Support by a non-substance-using family member or carer is important, given that a history of parental substance use is also a risk factor for the child's development of adolescent substance use problems.

Nor is it just parental substance use that can negatively affect family members. Barnard (2005) explored the experiences of a sibling's problematic substance use on the family, noting feelings of anger, sadness and loss, as well as impotence at their inability to change the course of events. It also created problems between partners and between parents and other children, who lost both a sibling and parental attention as a result of their parents' focus on the sibling with the substance problem.

Thus, it is crucial to recognise the impact that substance use has on other family members and to ensure that you give time, attention and support to others in the family, not just to the parent with the problem and the child who is most vulnerable. Supporting the others around the parent and the child can have protective effects for the health of these others, and also encourage the parent to seek help for their substance use. In the practice examples, supporting the grandparents in their own right will not only help them and their grandchildren, but may also facilitate better relationships with Sarah and Jackie.

To summarise, it is clear that parental substance problems can have negative effects on parenting ability and child welfare, and these effects can range from minor to severe and life threatening. Parental substance problems can also affect other family and friendship networks, resulting in social isolation from the people who would normally be there for support. The physical and emotional isolation gives clear messages to adults and children about having to cope alone, as well as reinforcing messages about stigma and the need for secrecy. This provides a very clear indication of what skills social workers need in order to support families affected by substance problems, as well as the focus of their intervention.

Implications for practice: values, knowledge, skills

Understanding the potential impact on parenting and child welfare of problematic alcohol and drug use is important. However, equally important is an honest reflection on your skills and values relating to substance use. Service users will pick up in an instant on what you know and do not know, and what your attitude to them is; therefore you need to have got there first!

At the most basic level, you need to understand that (a) people don't start using alcohol or drugs intending to develop a problem and (b) there is a tremendous amount of shame and stigma attached to problematic alcohol and other drug use. Knowledge of alcohol and drugs, their broad effects and why people use substances is essential. You don't have to be an expert, but some knowledge is required, as is the acceptance that the service user is the expert in their own use. You need to ensure that you acknowledge that and ask them how it impacts on them and their behaviours and roles (see Chapter Two).

You also need to be able to understand and communicate, in a clear and empathic way, the potential risks of being a parent with substance problems and the potential impact on the children. As already shown, children are often a key driver for change and it can be both necessary and helpful to explain what your concerns are and how you can support the parent to ensure that the children are not affected. Don't assume that parents know the potential harm their use may cause, or how to avoid it. This is where an understanding of the risks and the resilience and protective factors can help, as these can be discussed openly with the parents and can provide some immediate and practical solutions that both meet the child's needs and assuage some of the professional's concerns.

Ultimately, what will make the difference between your engaging or not with the parents and children are your communication skills. You need excellent communication and interpersonal skills; for example, you need to have considered what type of questions you can ask, in what tone you will ask them, what you can offer, how you might overcome the difficulties presented earlier and so on. We cannot take good communication for granted, particularly in a pressured situation and a professional environment that is often dominated by procedures and administration. In a study by Forrester et al (2008b) the responses of 40 social workers to vignettes involving parents with alcohol problems were recorded and analysed. They found that, overall, social workers' responses were confrontational and aggressive and consequently were unlikely to facilitate change or allow for partnership working with the service users.

Assessment and intervention

Assessment will clearly precede any intervention, although the two are not as distinct and separate as they may at first appear. On-going assessment is an important part of any intervention and review process. Chapter Two provides insight into how assessment of substance use can be approached in a way that will maximise openness and relationship building without sacrificing the duties and concerns that need to be addressed. Again, the key is communication and attention to the words and tone used.

Interventions in families where there are substance problems will be with three groups of people:

- parents
- children
- other family members.

You may be responsible for working with one or all of these groups, or working in partnership with other professionals. It may also be possible to work with the whole family as a unit, but this needs to be done with care, particularly considering the high rates of overlap with domestic abuse among people with drug and alcohol problems. Working with whole families where there is on-going domestic abuse is unsafe at best, and dangerous at worst.

If your remit is to work with only one of these groups, then it is your responsibility to ensure that the appropriate referral is made, or support is found, for the others. All need environments where it is safe to talk. This means not just physical safety from issues such as domestic abuse; people also need to feel emotionally safe – particularly children. Children are unlikely to talk openly in front of their parents for fear of being disloyal or getting into trouble. Providing that safe environment, both physically and emotionally, is a crucial task.

Whichever member of the family you work with directly, they will be likely to have some features in common:

- They will not know to what extent they can trust you.
- They will probably feel ashamed and therefore minimise and deny their use or how they are affected by it.
- They will find it hard to speak openly to you.

Ultimately, it is your empathy, communications skills, warmth and honesty, that will maximise your chances of developing a trusting relationship with people living with alcohol and other drug problems. Asking people what the positives of their substance use are and listening to the responses, then asking what the disadvantages of their substance use are, will immediately suggest that you are willing to listen and to hear their view, and that you are not automatically assuming that all substance use is bad.

During your training you will have been taught a range of methods for social work intervention, most of which will be underpinned by a clear theoretical base, including methods such as task-centred practice, cognitive behavioural interventions, crisis intervention, group work and possibly solution-focused or motivational methods. A number of these are also used in substance use settings and there is evidence of their effectiveness – for example, motivational and cognitive behavioural interventions.

Whichever group you are working with, the key is to be clear about the purpose of your assessment, visit or meeting that day. It is important to be open about this, while providing support and choices and focusing on people's strengths alongside their support needs.

Consider the examples at the beginning of the chapter. In addition to a core assessment, interventions with Jackie and Ian clearly need to begin with an assessment of their substance use (as individuals and as a couple) and how they feel that impacts, positively and negatively, on their parenting. Highlighting their strengths and what they think these are needs to happen up front. Strengths may include their ability to parent Ruby and Lily up to this point, particularly considering the children's additional physical needs, their love and commitment to their children, their willingness to work with you and the fact that they have family support close by. Seeking their views about their needs and their concerns about their parenting and the children comes next, prior to expressing your own views and concerns. Having a number of options that can be discussed with them in relation to services for their substance use will enable them to feel that they have choices. Clearly, a joint visit or assessment with a substance professional is required. An assessment of the grandparents and their capacity to provide care may also be needed – including any indications that they are also using alcohol or other drugs problematically – if they are to be involved in the children's care.

In Sarah's case, her efforts at stabilising her substance use and caring for her children appear to have been successful. It must therefore be extremely distressing for her that these are neither recognised nor respected by Pauline and that her children have been removed by Pauline against her wishes. She will fear social services' involvement, in spite of her achievements. The focus of intervention is therefore on supporting her to get her children back (unless there are indications that this would not be a suitable move), alongside discussions with Pauline about her action in terms of removing the children. Where both are agreeable, work with the grandmother and Sarah together to see what arrangements can be made for visitation and contact. Importantly, Max's views must also be heard and his views taken into account.

Specialist services that work with families, and individually with children and parents, are available, although service provision is patchy and future funding is uncertain. Your local drug and alcohol action team (DAAT) will have a directory of services in your area, or you can use freephone or online resources such as FRANK, the 'Helpfinder' database from national charity Drugscope, or the NHS alcohol services directory via Alcohol Concern:

■ FRANK helpline – 0800 77 66 00; has a list of services by area
■ Drugscope Helpfinder – www.drugscope.org.uk/resources/databases/helpfinder.htm
■ Alcohol Concern – link to alcohol service directory www.alcoholconcern.org.uk/concerned-about-alcohol/alcohol-services

Working with family members in their own right will not only improve their own well-being but will also help them to support their loved one in the best way possible. As the child's welfare is paramount, it is essential to secure positive and on-going support for the parents, through family and friendship groups, to enable them to be the best parents they can be.

Copello et al (2000b) have developed a five-step model for working with family members in their own right. It is designed to educate and support family members to support their friend or relative. The five steps are:

1. Giving the family member the opportunity to talk about the problem;
2. Providing relevant information;
3. Exploring how the family member copes with/responds to their relative's substance misuse;
4. Exploring and enhancing social support; and

5. Exploring the need for and the possibilities of onward referral for further help and support.

(Templeton et al 2007: 138)

Evaluations have shown the five-step model to be effective in terms of reducing both the physical and psychological symptoms that family members suffer, as well as helping them to cope with their relative's substance use (Orford et al 2007). In some cases the approach has also led to a change in the alcohol or drug use by the relative with the problem, as well as improving family relationships. This model facilitates self-help, focusing on the family member, and it could be adapted for working with children.

There are also a number of bright, colourful and easy-to-use resources available for working with children who have a parent with alcohol or drug problems – these are accessible online, through local services and through links from the national charities Adfam, Drugscope and Alcohol Concern.

Summary

A wealth of information and advice is available to support social work practice with adults and children living with parental substance problems. While there is limited formal training on substance use in social work education, social workers have to take responsibility for seeking this out as part of their continuing professional development. Parental substance use may have no negative impact on children or other family members, but it may also have serious consequences. Understanding the impact of parents' substance problems on parenting and on the children is part of being prepared to respond appropriately. Understanding the risks and resilience factors and discussing these with parents provides them with information and choices about their parenting of which they are otherwise unlikely to be aware. In some situations where children are at immediate risk of harm, the parent may not have the luxury of choices. However, it is important to ensure that, wherever possible, you have made skilled attempts to engage with the family, build relationships and provide the care and control in appropriate measures. Only honest reflection on your values, knowledge of substance use and communication skills is likely to ensure that this happens.

Notes
[1] '[D]rinking between 22 and 50 units per week for men and between 15 and 35 units per week for women' (Drummond et al 2004: 9).
[2] What can be confusing is that Every Child Matters was originally the name of a Government Green Paper (DCSF 2003) that marked a significant change

in the focus on children's well-being. The name is now also used to headline all the government policies and practice guidance relating to safeguarding.
[3] The NTA is due to be disbanded and its functions transferred to a new government body, Public Health England, in 2013.
[4] FASD information has been taken from the British Medical Association Board of Science review of the evidence published in 2007.
[5] Powerful case studies through the voices of parents and one man who lives with FASD can be found in the BMA's Board of Science report (2007).

Discussion questions/exercises

Consider the three practice examples at the start of the chapter.

1   From the little information that you have, what are the risks to the children and what are their resilience or protective factors?
2   What words would you use (a) to introduce yourself to Eric, to Jackie and Ian and to Pauline, and (b) to elicit their views about the impact of substance use on their children/grandchildren?
3   If you encountered domestic abuse in a family with substance problems, how would this affect the way you talked to and worked with members of the family?

Further learning resources

■   Adfam – www.adfam.org.uk. National charity working to support family members and friends of people with alcohol and drug problems. Website includes a range of resources and publications for professionals and family members/ friends and a list of support groups for families in the UK.

■   *Children talking to ChildLine about parental alcohol and drug misuse.* Childline Casenotes series. Produced by NSPCC (2010). Available online at: www.nspcc.org.uk/inform/publications/casenotes/clcasenoteparentalalcoholdrugabuse_wdf78112.pdf [accessed 16 August 2011].

- Whittaker, A. (2011) *The essential guide to problem substance use during pregnancy. A resource book for professionals*. London: Drugscope. Contains lots of good, accessible information as well as useful appendices that include information for parents and professionals and examples of forms and tools used in the assessment and care planning process for families affected by parental substance problems.

- *You are not on your own*. Colourful, child-friendly online booklet to help adults and children talk about a parent's drinking. Targets young people aged 8–12. Produced by the Children's Commissioner (2011). Available online at: www.childrenscommissioner.gov.uk/content/publications/content_498.

Domestic abuse and substance use

Practice examples

1. Brigid (56)

Brigid suffers from depression. She is divorced and has a long history of suffering domestic abuse, of living in hostels and of street homelessness. She has been drinking heavily for many years and also gambles what little money she has. She is in contact with a number of services, including mental health and housing services. She has periodically attended alcohol services and Alcoholics Anonymous self-help groups. She is in danger of being evicted from her housing association accommodation.

2. Kayleigh (9) and Solomon (5)

Kayleigh and Solomon have been referred to social services by the police, who have made several visits to their home address as a result of incidents of domestic violence during which the children were present. Mum, Sonia, disclosed that she is worried about her partner, Wayne's drinking and the effect it is having on the family. Wayne was made redundant a year ago and has recently been drinking very heavily. Sonia has made unsuccessful attempts to stop him drinking by taking away his bank cards and controlling the money. They have huge arguments that have involved Wayne being physically violent to Sonia. Solomon has become scared of Wayne and doesn't like to go near him. Kayleigh often takes care of Soloman and does chores around the house when her Mum is too tired. Sonia has an elder daughter, Toni (15), who has taken to staying out overnight at friends' houses. Sonia is very worried and doesn't know what to do.

3. Tracey (27)

Tracey uses crack-cocaine and heroin and occasionally exchanges sex for drugs. Her 'boyfriend' (James) has recently come out of prison and has moved into her flat. Although Tracey was getting help for her substance use and attending a day programme she has recently missed many appointments and has been involved in prostitution on a regular basis. James often has friends around to Tracey's flat to 'party'. If she refuses to go out to prostitute or refuses his sexual advances in front of his friends, James becomes violent towards her. Tracey is afraid of him, but because he is also kind to her at times she doesn't want him to leave. She has threatened to throw him out before, and he has said that he will get help for his 'temper'. At other times he has said that if she does throw him out, he will kill her.

Introduction

The relationship between domestic abuse and substance use is a complex one. There are no easy explanations for the link between the two, but they often go hand in hand. Both substance use and domestic abuse are issues that cut across social work specialisms – they affect both adults and children, whatever their ages, abilities, mental or physical health problems. They cut across socioeconomic and ethnic groups, and affect people in different kinds of relationships.

The two issues are most commonly linked in intimate adult partner relationships, both heterosexual and same-sex relationships. However, evidence also shows that they coexist among young people who use substances and are violent and abusive to their parents, as well as within intimate adolescent relationships.

This chapter will provide an overview of the nature and extent of the links between substance use and domestic violence before looking at their impact and their implications for practice.

Definitions and terminology

Domestic violence encompasses a range of violent and abusive behaviours. The term 'violence', however, is often interpreted as physical violence only. For this reason some organisations have taken to using the term domestic *abuse*, as this more clearly suggests a range of abusive behaviours within the home environment or within 'domestic' relationships. As with many terms used in everyday language, the term you use will depend on the context in which you are using it. There are parallels in the drug and alcohol field. 'Substance use' is often interpreted as use of illicit drugs only, rather than its more accurate meaning, which also includes alcohol and licit drugs.

Whichever term you use, the important point is to have a clear understanding of what constitutes domestic violence and abuse. One of the most commonly cited definitions is that used by leading domestic violence charity Women's Aid:

> Domestic violence is physical, sexual, psychological or financial violence that takes place within an intimate or family-type relationship and that forms a pattern of coercive and controlling behaviour. This can include forced marriage and so-called 'honour crimes'. Domestic violence may include a range of abusive behaviours, not all of which are in themselves inherently 'violent'. (Women's Aid 2007)

One of the changes in definitions in recent years is the inclusion of forms of violence and abuse specific to particular minority ethnic communities – for example, 'honour crimes' – as well as clarity over a range of abusive behaviours, as contrasted to physically violent behaviour. Another change is the British government's acknowledgement of the gender bias in domestic and sexual abuse and a willingness to define it as such. Current government policy uses the definition drawn up by the United Nations Declaration (1993) on the Elimination of Violence Against Women:

> Any act of gender-based violence that results in, or is likely to result in, physical, sexual or psychological harm or suffering to women, including threats of such acts, coercion or arbitrary deprivation of liberty, whether occurring in public or in private life....Violence against women and girls can include, but is not restricted to, domestic abuse, sexual assault, stalking, forced marriage, so-called 'honour' based violence, and female genital mutilation. (HM Government 2011a)

In the UK, recognition of domestic abuse and its implications for the safety of (primarily but not exclusively) women and children has occurred only recently at government and policy levels. For example, it took until 2005 for childcare policy to recognise the impact of witnessing or hearing adult violence on children and to include it in the legal definition of harm under section120 of the Adoption and Children Act 2005. Arguably, the impact of this tardy political recognition has been to keep domestic violence and abuse at the political and policy margins and to result in limited service provision for people who experience it.

Domestic abuse is not a new phenomenon and is one that victims have had to learn to cope with, live with, or attempt to escape from. Acts of domestic violence and abuse breach our very basic assumptions about love, intimacy and trust. It is therefore unsurprising that, in a context of limited services, people find their own ways to cope, numb the pain, escape or forget. The use of alcohol and drugs is one way to do this. Consider Brigid and Tracey in the examples earlier and think empathically about what it must be like to live with fear, trauma and abuse. In such circumstances the use of alcohol and other drugs may feel like a reasonable response.

The impact of domestic violence and abuse

While physical and sexual violence and abuse are often viewed as the most shocking and serious forms of domestic abuse, victims[1] report that it is the psychological and emotional impact of domestic abuse that has the most long-lasting negative effects. In the example above Brigid is clearly living with the long-term effects of her abuse and, like most victims of domestic abuse, suffers varying degrees of emotional, psychological and mental ill-health. This can range from nervousness, anxiety and low self-esteem to post-traumatic stress disorder, severe depression and suicide attempts.

Most often, domestic violence and abuse is not a one-off event. Repeat victimisation is common and figures show that domestic violence currently has the highest rate of re-victimisation, as compared with any other crime. Nearly three-quarters (73%) of victims recorded in the Crime Survey of England and Wales 2010-11 were repeat victims. Of those who were interviewed, 24% had experienced three or more incidents of violence and abuse (Parfrement-Hopkins 2011). Such violent and abusive behaviour can be lethal. Statistics show that each week nearly two women are killed by a partner or former partner, and that the majority of murdered children under the age of 16 were killed by a parent (Coleman et al 2011). Lesser physical abuse can result in bruises, burns, broken limbs or permanent scarring and disfigurement.

In children and young people the emotional and psychological abuse is seen in a range of behaviours, including withdrawal, aggression, anxiety and bed wetting, to name a few. In Practice Example 2 earlier, Toni is coping by getting out of the house as much as possible and Solomon is scared of Wayne and doesn't like being near him, while Kayleigh appears to be acting at times as a young carer for both her sibling and her mother.

The extent of overlap between substance use and domestic abuse

Evidence of the overlap between alcohol and drugs and domestic abuse comes from a range of sources and needs to be interpreted within those contexts. For example, we have research on domestic abuse suffered by women receiving formal help for alcohol or drug problems, and on the perpetration of domestic abuse by men receiving help for substance problems. There are data based on samples of women and men receiving domestic abuse services, as victims or perpetrators, and on their use of substances. There is also evidence in the British Crime Surveys, which collect data based on victim reports only. However, the BCS surveys victims who are aged 16–59 only and asks for their *opinion* on whether the perpetrator was under the influence of alcohol or drugs. Thus, as with all statistics, the data are limited in various ways and must be interpreted with those limitations in mind.

A summary of key prevalence data follows.

General population samples

- In the 2007–08 Crime Survey in England and Wales, reports by victims of domestic abuse suggest that 37% of offenders were under the influence of alcohol, while 12% were under the influence of drugs at the time of the assault (Kershaw et al 2008).[2]
- For 'serious sexual assault' since the age of 16 36% of victims thought the offender had been drinking; 9% of victims thought the offender had been under the influence of drugs (Hall 2011).
- 25% of victims of serious sexual assault reported that they were under the influence of alcohol in the most recent incident; 2% were under the influence of drugs that they had chosen to take (Hall 2011).
- 6% of victims felt they had been drugged by the offender prior to the sexual assault (Hall 2011).

Substance use 'treatment' samples

- Schumacher et al (2003) found that 44% of men (n=658) had used one or more acts of physical violence in the year preceding treatment.
- Brown et al (1998) found that almost 58% (n= 59) of men in alcohol or drug treatment had perpetrated physical violence or abuse towards a partner or child in the previous six months. With the inclusion of verbal threats, this figure was 100%.
- A number of North American studies report between 60% and 80% of women in drug and alcohol services having suffered domestic abuse at some point in their lives (Downs et al 1993; Bury et al 1999; Swan et al 2001; Becker and Duffy 2002).
- In a Scottish study, McKeganey et al (2005) found that 62% women and 22% men were physically abused; and 36% women and 7% men were sexually abused.

■ In a study of 489 people in substance use treatment, Chermack et al (2008) found high levels of physical abuse, psychological abuse and injury. As with other research in this field, women were more likely to be injured.

Domestic violence services samples

There are far fewer data from domestic violence services samples for either victims or perpetrators. This is largely because, until recently, people with alcohol and drug problems have been excluded from these services. Indeed anecdotal evidence suggests that this practice still continues in some services. Evidence shows that:

■ 30%–40% of women in US shelters have problematic substance use, mainly alcohol (Downs et al 1998; Downs 1999).
■ One UK study surveyed six domestic violence services providing victim services. It found that more than half (51%) of those surveyed (n=75) had problems with substances (Humphreys et al 2005).
■ Easton et al (2000) studied 41 domestic violence offenders mandated to attend anger management classes. On average, 41% were diagnosed as substance dependent and 67% as abusing substances.
■ Other studies of domestic violence perpetrator programmes have found 60%–70% of men reporting substance use and problems (Gorney 1989; Brown et al 1999; Humphreys et al 2004).

In addition to these sources, there are data that demonstrate the presence of both substance use and domestic abuse in research focused on other issues. For example, research looking at young people's substance use or young people in the care system has repeatedly found evidence of both parental substance use and domestic violence at home (Chalder et al 2006; Kuntsche and Kuendig 2006; McAuley and Young 2006; Burkhart et al 2008). Similarly, independent scrutiny of Serious Case Reviews (SCRs), conducted as a result of child deaths or serious injury, shows that substance use and domestic abuse were often present in the homes of the children who were harmed. A third, and related factor, was parental mental health problems. Depressingly, these factors were reported as often being 'overlooked' by all of the agencies involved with the children and families, including social services (Ofsted 2008; Brandon et al 2010).

What these various forms of data show are high rates of overlap between substance use and domestic abuse among particular populations. Given the shame and secrecy attached to both substance problems and domestic abuse, it is beyond doubt that these figures are underestimates. As with all the data we collect in research or practice, we rely on people being willing to disclose their experiences, and also being able to recognise them as 'domestic abuse' or 'problematic substance use' in the first place. Sometimes what appears obvious to the social worker operating outside the person's environment is not at all obvious to the person who is living within it.

The association between domestic abuse and substance use can lead to some common myths and misconceptions about the nature of the relationship between them. These are often reinforced by media headlines and are not helpful in supporting victims, perpetrators and professionals to be clear about the impact of substance use on any type of violent and abusive behaviour. The next section explores some of these myths in greater depth.

Nature of the relationship

The nature of the relationship between alcohol or drug use and domestic abuse is complex. There is neither a simple explanation for it nor a simple solution to the difficulties it presents. However, this has not stopped people from trying! The danger is that overly simplistic explanations or solutions can lead to risky beliefs and risky responses. Below are some examples:

Risky belief 1: Alcohol and drugs *cause* people to be violent and abusive.

Risky response 1: Stopping/reducing people's use of alcohol and drugs will stop/reduce the violence and abuse.

Risky belief 2: Men who abuse women after using drugs or alcohol are not wholly responsible for their actions.

Risky response 2: Get him help for his alcohol or drug problem and/or speak to him when he's sober/not high and he'll not do it again.

In the practice example at the start of the chapter it would be easy to think that if Wayne stopped drinking and got himself a job the violence and abuse would stop. This is risky thinking. The reality is that there is no evidence of a direct causal link between alcohol and drugs and domestic abuse. In other words, the consumption of the substance does not automatically lead to a person becoming violent and abusive. Other factors need to be present. Evidence shows that perpetrators are violent to victims both with and without the substance and that they carefully select to whom they are abusive. Some studies have demonstrated a *reduced* level of violence and abuse perpetration among people who have attended substance use treatment (see Stuart et al 2009 for a review), but 'reduced' does not mean 'stopped'.

What can leave victims at risk of harm is the hope that substance use treatment will stop their partner's violence and abusive behaviour. It could result in the victim's staying in a risky situation for longer than they otherwise would, in the hope that their partner will change. Professionals must take care not to overlook the risks and safety issues to victims while someone is receiving substance use treatment. Thus, the implications for practice are to ensure that there is close monitoring of harm and abuse before, during and after a perpetrator receives substance use interventions. Research also shows that there is no difference between people who do not change their substance use and those who go back to substance use after a period of abstinence (O'Farrell et al 2004).

Substance use by the perpetrator has been found to increase the frequency of domestic abuse (Leonard and Senchak 1996; Brookoff et al 1997; Leonard and Quigley 1999; Fals-Stewart 2003), increase the severity of injuries inflicted (Leonard and Senchak 1996; Brecklin 2002; Graham et al 2004) and increase the mental and physical health problems of the abused partner (Dawson et al 2007).

Risky belief 3:   Women who use alcohol or drugs deserve, or could provoke, violence from their partner.

Risky response 3:   She needs to change. Provide the woman with substance use treatment/mandate her to attend.

This is dangerous thinking on a number of levels. First, people who are abusive and violent have to take responsibility for their own choices and actions. Even if the other person was behaving badly, the perpetrator had the choice of leaving, walking away or handling things differently. Excuses about 'provocation' in the context of domestic violence and abuse tend to be victim blaming and to minimise the responsibility of the perpetrator. This, in turn, colludes with the violent and abusive partner and reinforces the dynamic of power and control that underpins the perpetration of domestic violence.

Second, women who use alcohol or drugs often do so to cope with the violence from their partner or to numb or escape from the physical and psychological pain of the abuse (Clark and Foy 2000; Miller et al 2000; Corbin et al 2001; Galvani 2006). Women who are victims of abuse may have pre-existing substance use problems, and there is some evidence to suggest that these are worsened by domestic abuse (Downs and Miller 1994). Rivaux et al (2008), in an in-depth study of women in the early stages of residential treatment for substance problems, found women describing themselves as damaged goods and using drugs to protect themselves from getting hurt, as the intoxication helped them not to feel. A number of women had suffered sexual abuse in childhood or were ashamed of their relationships. For some of the women, using substances gave them the courage to stand up to their abusive partners, but for others their experiences demonstrated how some women appear to 'trade' their safety in order to stay in a relationship and avoid feeling lonely. Rivaux et al (2008) highlight how drugs and relationships served similar purposes for these women in terms of their being able to handle sadness, insecurity and past hurts. This complex and interlinking dynamic highlights how important it is that social work interventions recognise and address social support issues as well as the substance use.

Third, victim intoxication can increase a person's vulnerability to suffering violence and abuse, be it domestic, sexual (Mirrlees-Black 1999; Hall 2011) or other forms of violence (Room et al 1995; Rossow 1996). However, increased vulnerability *does not mean blaming the victim for not avoiding or minimising the abuse* they were subject to. An increase in anyone's vulnerability, be they adult or child, should engender a greater sense of responsibility in those who love, support or care for them, not less. People who choose to take advantage of that vulnerability in the form of violence and abuse need to be held to account.

James's abusive and violent behaviour towards Tracey is an example of this. Her crack-cocaine and heroin use places her in a vulnerable position that James appears to exploit and 'punish' if she does not behave as he wishes. It is likely that he knows that if she were to call the police or seek help from others she would not be believed because of her drug use. She is also ambivalent about having James around and is, as Rivaux et al (2008) suggest, possibly trading her safety for his company.

Risky belief 4:	Adults and parents think children can be protected from the domestic violence and abuse in the home (and the messages about its relationship with substance use).
Risky response 4:	Try to make sure that they're not around during the abuse, or remove them from the abusive situation.

Children are very sensitive to moods and tensions in the home. They will know that something is wrong, whichever room of the house they're in, even though they may think that angry and violent behaviour is normal and happens in all homes. However, children report that they are often scared for themselves and their parents. On the one hand, they want to protect their mother, who is usually the victim, and on the other hand, they may be afraid that their father will be in trouble and perhaps even be arrested and taken away if they do or say anything. Children often feel confused about what to do for the best, and may feel guilty, thinking that they are to blame for the anger and ensuing abuse. Research shows that they often end up trying to protect siblings and the parent who is being victimised, and want to make it all better (Stanley et al 2010). This places a tremendous pressure on children.

Children have reported witnessing, and often experiencing, extreme violence in the home (Cawson 2002; Mullender et al 2002; Gorin 2004; Wales and Gillan 2009; Stanley et al 2010). Where this comes to the attention of social work professionals the outcome may be the removal of the children into the care system. Research that focuses on young people in the care system has repeatedly found high levels of children's witnessing and suffering domestic abuse as well as parental substance use (McAuley and Young 2006). However, other research has shown that referrals to social care by police, following domestic violence incidents, rarely result in a social care assessment or intervention (Stanley et al 2010).

Erroneously, child abuse and adult domestic abuse have traditionally been separated in professional consciousness. This has overlooked the risks to children that could have been avoided. Research shows clear links between the perpetration of adult domestic abuse and of child abuse (Morley and Mullender 1994; Hester et al 2000; Cawson 2002; Wales and Gillan 2009). In addition, there are clear links between suffering abuse of various types in childhood and suffering abuse and trauma as an adult (see Barter 2009; Messman-Moore et al 2009). Often this later abuse and trauma leads to mental health problems, including greater use of substances (Bear et al 2000; Clark and Foy 2000; Corbin et al 2001; Galvani 2006). There is also a link between suffering child sexual abuse (CSA) and adult substance use. Engstrom et al (2008) found very high rates of CSA and domestic abuse among a random sample of 416 women in methadone treatment: 57.9% reported a history of CSA, 89.7% reported a lifetime's history of interpersonal violence, and 78.4% reported violence in the last six months.

The impact of such abuse is long lasting. As Bennett and O'Brien (2007: 407) point out, the 'effects of [domestic violence] last longer than the index aggression'. The psychological and emotional impact on children and young people can damage their physical and psychological development, as well as their ability to understand and maintain healthy relationships.

The following list summarises the many parallel negative effects of parental substance use and domestic abuse on children and young people:

- social isolation, stigma and keeping secrets
- emotional neglect and abuse
- behavioural changes or problems
- developmental delay
- damage to foetus/miscarriage
- psychological and/or psychiatric problems
- poor supervision
- inconsistent and poor-quality care

- overly punitive discipline
- feeling fearful and responsible
- disrupted play and leisure time
- disrupted routines, for example, school attendance
- low self-esteem and self-confidence
- physical and sexual abuse
- conflicting loyalties towards parents
- difficulties in their adult relationships.

One study highlighted how children quickly learn messages about the association between alcohol and domestic abuse. The following is an extract from an interview with a woman who had suffered domestic abuse and had separated from her partner, although the abuse continued:

> "You see at one point ... because they'd been through so much I started protecting them and not letting them see what was going on and then it just got worse and they know. Especially when they turn round and say 'oh but me dad had a drink he didn't mean it, it'll be alright won't it tomorrow'." (Kris in Galvani 2010c)

Kris's experience highlights not only her wish to protect her children, but also the realisation that she couldn't hide things from them. It also highlights the defensiveness of Kris's daughter towards her father and her use of his alcohol consumption as an excuse or reason for his behaviour.

It is not surprising that early messages about the relationship between substance use and domestic violence continue into adolescence. There is growing evidence of a tolerance of domestic abuse within adolescent relationships (Schütt 2006; Barter 2009), but there is also evidence that substance use coexists in the life of adolescent as well as adult victims (Silverman et al 2001; Howard and Wang 2003). As with adult victims, there is also a high level of victimisation among young people who drink more frequently (Hamburger et al 2008).

In a review of research, Templeton et al (2006) found evidence of increased negative impact on children where both domestic abuse and substance use were present. The impact was apparent in the children's development, their experiences in adolescence, their own intimate relationships and their parenting abilities as adults. The research also predicted adolescent psychopathology, with these children being at high risk for perpetrating child abuse and perpetrating or suffering domestic violence in adulthood, as well as being at higher risk for developing substance problems.

To summarise, the nature of the link is not as simple as one issue leading to the other. The relationship between the two is, however, firmly rooted in evidence and demonstrates the damage that abuse can have at any age and the potential for substance use to be a coping mechanism. However, a third issue that overlaps with these two is mental health. As discussed earlier in the chapter, domestic violence and abuse leads to a range of psychological and emotional difficulties. Similarly, substance use can stem from and lead to mental distress (see Chapter Nine). It is not hard to imagine how Brigid, Sonia and her children, and Tracey may struggle to deal with the challenges they face every day, and how living with the fear or memories of abuse will quickly lead to mental distress. Even if the substance use and domestic abuse are removed, the psychological problems are likely to remain.

The result of all these bi-directional and overlapping issues is that people who may present for help with one issue, for example, substance use, are likely to have multiple and complex needs. Where one issue is present the social worker needs to be aware that the others are highly likely to be present too. The skill is in assessing and supporting the person or people effectively without overwhelming them or trying to address all the issues at once. These are complex issues for service providers to respond to and are likely to require good partnership working, joined-up service provision and excellent and informed supervisors and managers.

The policy context

There is no law or national policy that directly addresses the overlapping issues of substance use and domestic abuse. However, various national- and local-level policies within each of the two areas offer some guidance.

Domestic violence and abuse

Legislation against the mistreatment of women and children dates back centuries. As with all legislation, it is only effective if it is enacted and enforced. In the 21st century the policy understanding of domestic violence (and violence to women and children more broadly) appears to have shifted. Domestic violence has clearly moved higher up the national policy agenda, with national and local government initiatives ensuring its inclusion in a range of policies and strategies affecting prevention, service provision and criminal justice protection.

The key pieces of legislation are currently the Domestic Violence, Crime and Victims Act 2004, the Crime and Disorder Act 2007 and the Protection from Harassment Act 1997. None of them includes a criminal offence of 'domestic violence'; rather, domestically violent behaviours are subsumed under other offences, such as common assault, false imprisonment, rape, attempted murder and actual bodily harm.

In 2011, the government published its action plan, *Call to end violence against women and girls* (HM Government 2011a). This signalled a significant move in terms of recognising the predominance of women and children as victims of domestic violence and abuse. However, it was clear that violence against men and boys would not be ignored. The action plan contains four main strands: preventing violence, provision of services, partnership working, justice outcomes and risk reduction, and it involves both financial commitment and a target time frame for each aspect of the plan.

Other relevant policies include those specifically relating to alcohol, drugs, children and adult social care.

Child welfare policy

A raft of policy in the childcare arena has emerged since the publication of *Every Child Matters: Change for children* (ECM) (DCSF 2004). Following publication of the Children Act 2004, the ECM agenda identified five key outcomes for all children. These are to: *be healthy, stay safe, enjoy and achieve, make a positive contribution, and achieve economic well-being*. Clearly, parental alcohol problems and/or domestic abuse can have a negative impact on all these outcomes. *The Common Assessment Framework for Children and Young People* (HM Government 2006a) was introduced in 2006 to enable all professionals to conduct an assessment where appropriate and includes domestic violence and parental alcohol and drug misuse among the factors that could prevent children from reaching the five ECM outcomes. The requirement for interagency working to safeguard children, including specific mention of alcohol and drug services, was set out in the *Working Together to Safeguard Children* policy in 2006 (HM Government 2006b). Further, the Think Family agenda (Cabinet Office 2008) is a cross-departmental government agenda to ensure that services for adults and young people and children are working together to ensure that individual problems that affect the whole family are considered.

Vulnerable adults

Important elements of adult social care policy focus on protecting or safeguarding vulnerable adults. Two key documents, *No secrets* (DH 2000) and *Safeguarding adults* (ADSS 2005), provide the principles and standards on which adult protection and safeguarding are currently based. *No secrets* is currently under review, and part of this review is the definition of vulnerable adults, although the government has stated that *No secrets* 'will remain as statutory guidance until at least 2013' (DH 2011). 'Vulnerable adults' often refs to older people or people with learning disabilities or mental ill-health, who can be vulnerable to abuse by family members, neighbours and health and social care staff, to name a few. The current definition of a vulnerable adult also includes a person who is 'unable to protect him or herself against significant harm or exploitation' (DH 2000: 9). While this could easily apply to people who have been made vulnerable as a result of domestic abuse, or those made vulnerable through their drug or alcohol problems, there appears to be relatively little recognition of these groups to date.

Substance use

The current national alcohol and drugs strategy for England makes no mention of domestic violence, in spite of its commitment to supporting individuals to 'long term recovery' and to better supporting families and communities (HM Government 2010a). This is disappointing, as previous national alcohol and drug policy had begun to recognise the links and incorporate them into policy documents. The first national alcohol strategy (Cabinet Office 2004) mentioned the link between alcohol and domestic violence, briefly acknowledging the need for perpetrators and victims to be offered appropriate help by alcohol and domestic violence services. The updated alcohol strategy (DH et al 2007) and policy governing the commissioning of alcohol and drug services (DH/NTA 2006, NTA 2006[3]) also highlighted domestic abuse as an issue related to substance use and relevant to be considered in alcohol interventions, particularly in relation to the assessment of risk of harm and referrals to domestic violence specialists.

What is apparent from this brief overview is that, while a separate policy is lacking, increasingly attention given has been to the overlapping issues within each policy area. The test is to ensure that policy is translated into practice.

Implications for practice

The challenge for social workers is where to begin. While these are complex and interlinked issues, there is no reason to be overwhelmed by them. However, research has highlighted how unprepared social services and social workers can be. In a study of social work responses to substance use and domestic abuse, Cleaver et al (2006) found that links were rarely made between domestic violence and substance misuse, despite the fact that both issues were presenting together more often than they did separately. They also found that working relationships between adult and children's services were generally poor and that few initial assessments resulted in a referral to services for domestic violence or parental substance misuse.

Social workers, particularly those working in children and family settings, repeatedly raise both issues as being at the core of their practice. In a study by Galvani and Forrester (2008) that explored newly qualified social workers' experiences of social work training and practice in substance use, one social worker stated:

> "I work within the assessment team, Children and Families. The bulk of our work is domestic violence, this is more often than not either drug or alcohol related, we face challenges every day that we have minimal knowledge of and are ill equipped due to the lack of training in this field."

In the same survey of 248 newly qualified social workers, the majority of respondents reported feeling inadequately prepared for social work practice with people with alcohol (53%) and drug (54%) problems, and 44% felt inadequately prepared for working with domestic abuse (Galvani and Forrester 2011a).

In social work education and practice the concepts of resilience and protective factors are well known and are most often considered in relation to children's experiences of abusive or inadequate parenting (see Chapter Five). However, such resilience and protective factors apply equally to vulnerable adults and those living in potentially harmful situations. The negative effects of domestic abuse, whatever the victim's age, are likely to be influenced by the victim's resilience and the number of protective factors that are available to them.

The following are prerequisites for responding well, and confidently, to the overlapping issues of substance use and domestic abuse.

Basic knowledge and understanding about (a) substance use and (b) domestic abuse

Without knowledge and understanding, social workers risk making assumptions that could lead them to intervene in an unsafe way or to suggest explanations and interventions that are wrong. For example, consider the Wayne and Sonia vignette at the beginning of the chapter. An incorrect belief that alcohol causes violent behaviour could lead to a social worker focusing on Wayne's drinking and recommending that he seek help for his alcohol problem. This may be a helpful thing to suggest if Wayne accepts that he has a problem and needs help. However, it would be wrong to think that this would solve the problem of domestic abuse. It would also be wrong and potentially dangerous for Sonia and the children to think that things would be better once Wayne had cut down or stopped drinking. This could encourage them to remain in a dangerous situation in the hope that things would change, but in fact it would be exposing them to protracted risks. It would also be wrong to focus on Wayne at the expense of offering support and interventions to Sonia and the children, who are clearly suffering as a result of his abusive behaviour. As discussed earlier, there are both immediate and long-term negative effects of suffering domestic abuse, for both adults and children, and support and counselling needs to be provided to help them come to terms with the abuse they have suffered and the fear it engenders. They may also need some guidance on what to do in future and to be encouraged to contact the police, Women's Aid, domestic violence helplines and specialist services for children. Remember that victims are usually ashamed of their experiences of abuse and therefore need support and encouragement to seek help and take action and to understand that it is not their fault.

Good communication skills

A requirement for 'good communication skills' is too often rolled out in prerequisites for jobs or 'good practice' interventions, without a clear idea of what this means. It covers a gamut of skills, including listening, challenging, questioning and discussion, negotiating, group facilitation, being a good professional partner and so on. The development of good skills takes time, and limited input during a qualifying social work programme is not in itself adequate; many of the required skills need to be honed and developed over years of practice. Some people will start with better skills than others and better knowledge than others, but with post-qualifying training, practice experience and on-going critical self-reflection, a person's skills will develop. Take the example of Tracey and James at the beginning of the chapter. Unless you have an established relationship with Tracey, getting her to open up about her drug use, prostitution and domestic abuse is going to take time and patience. It would be unsafe to talk to her about her relationship with James, in his presence. Considering how you might talk to her, when and where, and anticipating what her concerns might be about you and of James and how to minimise these for your meeting, are likely to be key in maximising the chances of engaging with her.

The essential communication skills for working with people where there is domestic abuse and substance use are as follows:

Engagement

Gaining someone's trust and establishing a good relationship with them is vital (see Chapter Two). Consider the shame people will feel about having an alcohol or drug problem and how this is likely to be doubled by the added experience of suffering domestic abuse. Consider the need to cover up that shame and to present to the outside world, in particular to social workers, as if everything is just fine. The social worker needs to work hard to gain the person's trust, and this is unlikely to happen in one single session. Brigid has had many years in and around the social care system and will have seen many professionals during her life. Ensuring that she takes the lead in identifying her needs is likely to maximise the chances of engagement with her.

Listening

This is an underrated and undervalued skill and something that social workers are criticised for not doing terribly well. Many people enter social work with the best intentions, that is, to try to support people in the difficulties they can face or to improve the service someone receives. The danger, however, can be to rush in too quickly to 'fix' things, to offer solutions before sitting and listening fully to people's experience. Listening can be an intervention in itself, allowing people the time to talk and giving them our attention when they do so, without imposing 'our' agendas. When dealing with people who are suffering domestic abuse and/or substance use, listening is key, for a number of reasons. First, people with substance problems are often seen as undeserving, liars and lacking in morals, will-power or concern for others. Their views will not have been sought often, even by those services that attempt to support them. Social workers must offer a different view and position for the sake of the individual and their family. Second, listening carefully where there is domestic abuse or it is suspected is vital. People do not usually suddenly disclose their suffering or perpetration of domestic abuse as part of a conversation; indeed, people often do not realise that is what they are suffering, if it has become so normal to them. Listen for clues – for example, 'what a temper/short fuse he has', 'I'll be in trouble/got into trouble for that' – which can be ways of disclosing and should be explored sensitively and safely. Third, when it is disclosed by adults or children, domestic abuse must always be believed. Sometimes, in our discomfort at what we hear, professionals can collude with excuses or offer them – for example, the perpetrator had been using drugs, had a bad day or was abused themselves. Worst is the suggestion that the victim/s may have done something to provoke the abuse. For example, Sonia might be criticised for trying to control Wayne's money in order to curb his drinking.

This would be poor practice, because not only does it begin to blame her for the violence and abuse but it also focuses on what she needs to do in order to avoid further violence and abuse, rather than on what Wayne needs to do so as to keep his family safe. Further, in this practice example the focus has to be on supporting Sonia and the children to be safe, not on criticising her attempts to improve the situation, however desperate and risky they may have been. That is a conversation that it might be worth having at a later stage – while being careful not to blame the victim.

Sensitive assessment that prioritises safety for victims

A key social work role is assessment: it is the basis on which social workers make judgements and discuss options for interventions. However, assessments are often paperwork led. While this is helpful as an aide-memoire or to meet agency targets, it should be used as a back-up tool only. Social work assessment forms usually do not tell you what questions to ask, and nor should they; assessment skills should respond to the context and to the individual needs of the person being assessed. In a situation where there is both substance use and domestic abuse, assessment forms can be particularly lacking. However, having a toolkit of good practice questions that could be asked about substance use and domestic violence and the links between the two will be helpful.

Box 6.1: The Stella Project toolkit

The Stella Project toolkit (Stella Project 2007) contains examples of questions on substance use, domestic abuse and the relationship between the two. It also provides information on safety planning, questions about children's safety and guidance for working safely with perpetrators of abuse. It can be downloaded from the website www.avaproject.org.uk/our-resources/good-practice-guidance--toolkits/stella-project-toolkit-%282007%29.aspx.

Thus, social workers need the knowledge and skills to ensure that they are highly sensitive to recognising potential abuse and are able to talk to victims safely about what support they have or may be able to access. Gently exploring how the person sees the relationship between their use of alcohol or drugs and their experiences of (or perpetration of) abuse is also an avenue to follow, but care must be taken not to suggest that substance use is to blame for suffering or perpetrating abuse.

Social workers must be confident enough, and have the skills, to know *what to say and what not to say* if they have concerns about possible abuse; for example, to know not to discuss any suspicions of abuse in a family setting that includes the perpetrator (however charming he appears), as family members are unlikely to speak freely, through fear of reprisals. Therefore where a visit or meeting involves the family or couple, one of whom is the perpetrator, these issues must not be explored. Good practice would be to see each person separately next time, minimising any suspicions by stating that it is agency practice to talk to people separately as well as together (which often it is). Also, understanding that women will often use substances to cope with abuse can help social workers to understand that focusing on the substance use alone may not be a helpful approach.

Be prepared with resources and information

Social workers also need to be able to *offer practical advice*; for example, they need to know how to help people suffering domestic abuse to remain safe and how to plan for their future safety and that of their children, including making referrals to specialist agencies. A number of agencies now have 'safety planning checklists' that can help both social workers and service users to plan ahead and think about strategies for maximising safety. Many even provide a checklist on what to take with you when planning to leave an abusive partner. These resources are easily accessible on the internet. Similarly, there are helplines for men who perpetrate or suffer domestic abuse that are easily available (clearly, information must only be given to a perpetrator of abuse where they actively acknowledge their behaviour, rather than as a result of anything the victim/s have disclosed). In the practice examples Wayne and James may benefit from leaflets and information about perpetrator helplines – but ONLY if they have disclosed and acknowledged their behaviour to you. Offering such information when only Sonia or Tracey had mentioned it would put them in danger of further harm for having spoken out of turn.

Mothers are often particularly concerned about the impact of abuse on their children, and therefore information leaflets targeting children of different ages, as well as information about support agencies, should be part of a social worker's resource pack. Where children are living with both parental substance problems and domestic abuse, research suggests that the negative effect on children is compounded. While social work interventions with children will depend on the nature of the professional role and the amount of time available for direct contact with the child, some key messages for practice emerge from the research. Mullender et al (2002) reported two clear messages for practice with children:

1. help them to feel safe (physically and emotionally)
2. give them space to talk about it.

Such discussion needs to be done at the children's pace and in response to sensitive questioning and encouragement from professionals. Children also need respite and support in regaining, for example, their play and leisure time. Work can also be done with the mother/adult victim and child to help them discuss what has happened and to help them both to cope with the effects. A number of resources for parents to help them discuss domestic violence with their children and for children wanting to talk to someone about their experiences are available (see Galvani 2006 for a list).

Care must be taken with supplying such information; for example, it must not be sent to a household where the perpetrator lives because he may open the mail and be angered by it. Information should also not be left during a home visit (unless agreed) because the victim/s then have to think about how to get rid of it before the perpetrator returns. This sensitivity to the potential harm of good intentions is crucial.

Knowing about the local drug and alcohol services or where to obtain information is also important if you have someone who is willing to get help or is asking for help with the impact of a partner's substance use on themselves or other family members. However, you will need to check the extent to which the agencies work with the 'other' issue. For example, some refuges will not accept women using alcohol or drugs, and many alcohol and drug services do not address domestic abuse and its relationship with substance use, nor work in partnership with local domestic abuse services. Knowing this ahead of time will ensure that any referrals you make are appropriate and informed.

Partnership work with specialists

Particularly important is the social worker's ability to seek advice and support from specialists working with people suffering domestic abuse and/or drug and alcohol problems. Discussing concerns with specialists can help with next steps or intervention options, or to identify different questions to ask. Importantly, it can help social workers to learn more about the specialist services available and encourage collaborative working. Any additional support or joint working can support both confidence and competence in working with both issues. For example, it might be very helpful to have a conversation about the effects of crack-cocaine before meeting Tracey, if you're not clear about this already. Similarly, knowing the psychological and medical impact of heavy drinking over many years might help you in responding to some of Brigid's needs.

Working with perpetrators

There are a number of do's and don'ts when working with perpetrators of domestic violence who may also be using alcohol or drugs:

(1) Don't think that you need to work with the perpetrator on their abusive behaviour and/or substance use in any depth

Both of these are specialist areas of work. You need to be knowledgeable enough and skilled enough to be aware of the issues and safety concerns and how to respond in your particular role. Of course this doesn't mean you will not talk to James or Wayne when you meet them. To do so is important in getting to know them and their views on the situation and forming some sense of the risk they pose. It does, however, mean taking care to not counsel them about their violence (particularly in the presence of the victims) or their substance use without knowledge and training in how to do that.

> **Box 6.2: Respect**
>
> Respect is a national charity that leads the work with perpetrators of abuse throughout the UK. It publishes principles and *minimal* standards for the conduct of work with perpetrators of domestic abuse, in particular for those working regularly with perpetrators of abuse or delivering perpetrator programmes. Governmental and non-governmental agencies have signed up to support the standards, including the Home Office, Children and Family Court Advisory and Support Service (CAFCASS), the Ministry of Justice, Women's Aid, the Association of Directors of Children's Services and Relate. For further information go to www.respect.uk.net.

(2) Do be clear that the perpetrator is fully responsible for their behaviour

Regardless of relationship dynamics and personalities, understand that violent and abusive behaviour remains a choice and that it is selective and intentional and serves a function for the perpetrator.

(3) Don't recommend anger management groups

Domestic violence and abuse cannot be resolved with anger management groups. Domestic violence is not about anger it is about controlling and power and is often a repeated abusive behaviour. Rather than the perpetrator being out of control it is usually a person who has demonstrated very clear control in selecting their victim and choosing when to abuse and how to do it.

(4) Don't blame, or allow the perpetrator to blame, their substance use

Alcohol and drugs can be used as an excuse for bad behaviour. Evidence of drugs' and alcohol's effects demonstrates that people retain control even when cognition and inhibitions are affected. Acknowledge that there is a relationship between the two problems, but provide accurate information about it. Do not ignore someone's suggestion that substances are to blame – it provides an opportunity to educate.

(5) Don't work with families or couples where there is on-going or recent domestic abuse, regardless of their current use of, or abstinence from, alcohol or drugs

Respect and Relate (2008) highlights the dangers of working with couples where there is current or recent domestic abuse. For example, the presence of the professional may provide a false feeling of safety to the victim/s, who may disclose the perpetrator's abusive behaviours and be punished for this later. Similarly, the victim may censor themselves during the sessions for their own safety, making work with couples less effective and reinforcing the perpetrator's control.

(6) Do place women's and children's safety at the centre of any intervention

Remember, when working with families and assessing risk, as well as when sharing information with others, that safety is paramount – not keeping the family together or trying to be all things to all family members.

(7) Do identify your own learning and training needs and be proactive in getting them met

Many social work courses cover domestic abuse and substance use only minimally during qualifying training, if at all. Ensure that you contact local specialists and ask what training they provide and how you can access it.

Summary

The combination of substance use and domestic abuse is a potent cocktail. The mix adds complexity to social work with men, women and children who live with it and heightens the safety risks for those involved. However, there are some simple messages that need to be understood by both professionals and service users alike. Alcohol and drug use does not cause domestic violence and responses by professionals need to ensure that this information is heard. Seeking help for alcohol and drug problems will not remove the violent and abusive behaviour, although it may, on occasion, reduce it. Good practice for working with adults and children who are substance affected and live with domestic abuse has to focus on safety and support. This must be underpinned by enough knowledge about alcohol, drugs and domestic violence to know how to respond without judgement or collusion and how to access the specialist support that is available.

Notes
[1] There is an on-going debate about the use of the term 'victim' as opposed to 'survivor' within the domestic abuse field. The latter is viewed as a more positive term, implying a transition from victim to survivor, while the former is viewed as suggesting a degree of 'helplessness'. The term 'victim' is used here, as it more clearly highlights where responsibility for abuse does and does not lie.
[2] Current data for the influence of drugs and alcohol on partner abuse alone have not been published. This figure includes all forms of domestic abuse, including family abuse. The data was collected in the main face-to-face surveys, which are thought to be a less reliable form of collecting data on domestic abuse than the self-completion surveys used in the past few years.
[3] Both models of care documents are under review at the time of writing.

Discussion questions/exercises

1   What are (a) the protective and (b) the resilience factors for each of the women and the children in the practice examples at the start of the chapter? How might you build on these in practice?

2   Name three key pieces of policy that underpin your work with issues of domestic abuse and substance use.

3   When working with someone who uses alcohol or other drugs as an excuse for domestic violence and abuse, how would you respond? What would you say and how would you say it?

4   Why might work with couples and families be unsafe where there is domestic abuse, or suspected domestic abuse, and substance use?

Further learning resources

■   Home Office: www.homeoffice.gov.uk/crime/violence-against-women-girls/. This website provides information about the government's strategy to end violence against women and girls and links to other sites, including sites relating to forced marriage and female genital mutilation, and to the National Domestic Violence Helpline: 0808 2000 247.

■   Respect: www.respect.uk.net/. Respect is the leading organisation offering advice and guidance to individuals and organisations working with perpetrators of domestic abuse. It also accredits organisations running perpetrator programmes and runs an advice line for men both suffering (Men's Advice Line) and perpetrating domestic abuse (Respect Phoneline).

■   Women's Aid Federation for England: www.womensaid.org.uk. The website is full of useful information and practical advice for professionals and for people suffering abuse or concerned about a child or someone else. It also includes links to research, resources and policy summaries.

Practice examples

1. Barrie (71)

Barrie was admitted to hospital following seizures. He was referred to the hospital social work team by the ward staff, due to his evident self-neglect and in the hope of finding him support to improve his health and hygiene. A social work assessment found that Barrie lives at home with his wife but has started to live and sleep only in the living room. His personal hygiene and health are poor. He has very limited mobility and is often unable to get on and off the sofa. Barrie's wife, Anne, is his main carer. He has two sons, one of whom has no contact with him. Anne has also suffered serious health problems and is unable to cope, particularly when Barrie is abusive to her. He also keeps her awake at night by shouting. Barrie has refused services in the past. His seizures and other health problems are thought to be related to his heavy drinking and smoking. Barrie says that he has always drunk and is not going to stop, although he promised to cut down when he left hospital. There is a suspicion that he suffers from depression alongside his heavy drinking.

2. Michael (66)

Michael is single and has no children. He has been accessing services for a long time for his heroin use. He has a history of polydrug use, including benzodiazepines. He is currently using cannabis as well as heroin. He is struggling to support his drug use financially and has presented to services asking for methadone. His brother, who is also a drug user, has been taken back into prison. Michael also has a criminal history, primarily of crimes to fund his drug use. He has a sporadic relationship with woman in her late 20s that has been going on for many years. Michael has shown some interest in building better social networks and at one point was interested in attending a day service, but didn't follow through. He has recently reported having memory problems.

Introduction

The population of the UK is ageing. National statistics show that while the population of under–16s is declining, there is a significant increase in the number of people aged 65 and over. Projected figures suggest that by 2033, 33% of the population will be 65 years and over, as compared to 19% aged 16 years and younger. The fastest rate of increase will be among those aged 85 years and over (Office for National Statistics (ONS) 2009a).

With the advantages of living longer come a number of related challenges. People are expected to work longer, and rises in the age of retirement have recently been introduced (DirectGov 2010). People will be living for longer in poorer health (ONS 2009b) and are likely to rely more heavily on family carers for support. In addition, older age often brings an increase in social isolation and people need to adapt and find ways to cope. Alcohol and other drug use (hereafter 'substance' use) is likely to be among those coping mechanisms.

There is some evidence to support the 'maturation' hypothesis, that is, that the process of ageing often leads to a decline in substance use (Hoare 2009; ONS 2009a). However, some researchers have questioned this, suggesting older drug users, in particular, are a hidden population, and point to equivocal evidence on the maturation hypotheses (Levy and Anderson 2005). What is agreed is that we will see an increase in the number of older people at risk of harm through their substance use. It is likely that more people will carry forward into older age the harmful or problematic use of substances developed when younger.

This chapter seeks to clarify some of the particular issues and challenges facing both older people with alcohol and other drug problems and those who work with them.

Box 7.1: When do you reach 'older' age?

Traditionally, in the UK older age is defined by social systems and structures. Retirement from the paid labour market is the key indicator that a person is approaching older age – retirement signifies an age where people can now relax and enjoy their later years without the physical and mental demands of paid work. This is accompanied by concessions for many public services in recognition of reduced income and advancing years. Services for older people, however, differ greatly in their age criteria. For some services retirement age marks the point at which people qualify to receive services, but for others a lower age of 50 years is used. In alcohol and other drug services there is no age requirement, but older people with alcohol and other drug problems are

▶

perceived to be comparatively few in number. The research literature is equally unsure of when older age begins. Cummings et al (2006) found that research relating to older people's alcohol services included people aged between 45 and 91 years. They point out that a number of generations are represented within this age range and that their needs will be quite different.

Prevalence and patterns of substance use

National statistics on the prevalence of substance use among older people are limited. The annual survey by the ONS of adults' knowledge of and behaviour with alcohol provides some information on alcohol consumption, but information on illicit drug use is far more difficult to find. As a result, prevalence figures, particularly for illicit drug use, come from smaller-scale studies within particular populations. It is important to note that there is a difference between use of substances without experiencing problems of any kind and the problematic use of substances.

Alcohol

The ONS research reveals an interesting picture of alcohol consumption by older adults (Robinson and Harris 2011). On average, older people (65 years or more) consume less alcohol than do other age groups. They are the age group least likely to have drunk alcohol in the previous seven days; however, they are also the age group most likely to have consumed alcohol daily:

> The age group with the highest proportion of people who didn't drink in the last week was the 65 and over group (47 per cent). This was also the group with the highest proportion of people who drank every day (14 per cent). The proportion of people who drink every day rises as age group rises. For example, 2 per cent of men and 1 per cent of women aged 16 to 24 had drunk every day during the previous week, compared with 19 per cent of men and 10 per cent of women aged 65 and over. (Robinson and Harris 2011: 54)

There are other clear gender differences in older people's average weekly alcohol consumption. Older men consume nearly three times the amount of alcohol consumed by older women, at 12.7 units and 4.6 units respectively (Robinson and Harris 2011).

> **Box 7.2: Units of alcohol and older people**
>
> Currently the unit benchmarks for alcohol differentiate between genders only. Men are advised not to regularly consume more than 3–4 units of alcohol per day, and women 2–3 units. Above these limits there are increasing risks to health. There are, however, growing calls for a revised number of units to be recommended for older people (RCP 2011). Physical changes in older age result in the body's not being able to process the alcohol as effectively, resulting in higher concentrations of alcohol in the body. The RCP advises that recommendations for older people's alcohol intake should be no more than 11 units weekly and 1.5 units daily (RCP 2011).

Further, 20% of men and 11% of women said that they had drunk more than the recommended number of units on at least one day in the previous week (Robinson and Harris 2011), while 5% of older men and 2% of older women had drunk heavily (over 8 or 6 units respectively) on at least one day in the previous week. While these statistics are considerably lower than the proportions for younger people's heavy drinking, they are still a cause for concern, particularly given the implications for older people's physical health at a time of life when it is likely to be less robust. Further, Wilkinson et al (2011) found evidence that 23% of older men and 16% of women underestimated the size of a 'standard drink' that they poured themselves. Thus, it is likely that a minority of older people are drinking far above the advised drinking limits.

The type of alcohol consumed also varies according to age. Older men are less likely to drink strong beers, lagers or ciders than are their younger counterparts, favouring wine or 'normal strength' beer, lager or cider in equal measure. The majority of older women drink wine more than any other type of alcohol, followed by spirits and normal strength beer, lager and cider in equal measure (Lader and Steel 2010).

Smaller studies in the US among older people in residential homes and 'frail and functionally impaired' older people living in the community have also identified alcohol problems in the population, particularly among older men (Emlet et al 2001; Klein and Jess 2002). Cummings et al (2006) highlight that more research is needed on alcohol use among older women, although the data on older people echo the patterns among younger people in that there are far higher rates of alcohol consumption among older men than older women.

In terms of the drinking environment, the annual UK survey showed that older people reported that their heaviest drinking occasion took place at home (Lader and Steel 2010). Older people were also the age group that was most likely to drink heavily on their own. This has been confirmed by qualitative research in Brighton, England. Ward (2008) explored the circumstances and contexts of older people's drinking. She identifies four different types of drinking context:

1. *Social – regular*: Older people perceived drinking as pleasurable and part of positive social contact.
2. *Social – occasional*: As above but often linked to eating or meals out and less frequent.
3. *Heavy lone drinking*: Often alone at home, and higher levels of consumption.
4. *Heavy drinking in a drinking network*: Higher levels of alcohol consumption, but set within a social context with friends who drink together.

Thus, the types of drinking context for older people demonstrate that heavier, more hazardous drinking is happening both alone and in the context of a drinking network.

The Institute of Alcohol Studies (IAS) (2010) suggests that greater levels of disposable income into retirement and the availability and acceptability of heavier drinking in their youth are among the reasons why our ageing population are more likely to drink more heavily than did previous generations. In its summary of research about older people and alcohol the IAS suggests three typologies of older problem drinkers:

1. *Early onset drinkers or 'survivors'*: people who have experienced alcohol problems in their younger age and who continue to drink problematically into older age;
2. *Late onset drinkers or 'reactors'*: people who have started drinking problematically in later life as a response to negative life events;
3. *Intermittent or binge drinkers*: people who drink heavily on occasions – but this may still cause them problems.

The extent of alcohol use, the range of drinking contexts, the patterns of alcohol consumption and the development of problems across the life course have clear implications for how professionals respond to older people's alcohol use. There is no 'one-size-fits-all' and consideration needs to be given to the different approaches required for older people whose motivations for drinking to excess may vary widely.

Of course, not everyone will fit these drinking contexts or typologies. Barrie, in the practice example, has been drinking heavily for some time. His drinking takes place at home, although there is no suggestion from the information we have that his wife drinks with him. From the information we do have and the apparent impact on his physical health, it appears that he may be an early onset drinker, but further assessment would be needed to determine this, as well as how much and what he was drinking.

Illicit drugs

The Home Office annually produces reports drawn from the British Crime Survey on the extent of illicit drug use in England and Wales. Unfortunately, the survey is limited to people aged between 16 and 59 years. The report states that 'the decision to exclude those aged 60 and over was an economy measure, reflecting their very low prevalence rates for the use of prohibited drugs' (Hoare 2009: 1). While this is true when comparing older people's use to younger people's use of drugs, Beynon (2009) points out that the decision reflects both a particular perception of the prevalence of drug use among older people and an attitude that older people do not use drugs. She states that many older people in the past did not use drugs in their youth and thus will not take drug-using habits into their older age. As our population ages, however, Beynon suggests, there will be a cohort of older people advancing into older age who did use drugs in their youth, a number of whom will continue to use illicit drugs and/or misuse prescribed drugs.

Gossop (2008) concurs, stating that drug programmes are now more effective at retaining people in treatment and reducing deaths from drug overdoses and that therefore the number of older patients will increase. He reports European statistics showing that the number of people over the age of 40 in treatment for opiate problems doubled in the three-year period 2002–05.

Gossop suggests that this is a trend that will be replicated across Europe. Current European estimates suggest that the population of older drug users will double between 2001 and 2020 (Gossop 2008). Han et al's (2009) research estimates that the number of people over the age of 50 in the US with substance use problems will more than double by the year 2020. They believe this figure is likely to be conservative at best.

Current data on illicit substance use among older people in England is drawn from the 2007 household survey of adult psychiatric morbidity (McManus et al 2009). The survey found that illicit drug use is lowest in the older age groups and that there was no consistent change in these levels when compared with two sets of previous data, from 1990 and 2000 (Fuller et al 2009). In the two age groups for over 65 years (65–74 years, 75+ years) the survey reported men to be using tranquilisers the most (0.5% and 0.2% respectively), followed by cannabis (0.4% and 0.3%), and that magic mushrooms (0.3%) were used by men over 75 only. For women, tranquilisers (0.7%) were the most-used substance in the 65–74 age group, followed by cannabis (0.2%). However, for women aged 75+ years magic mushrooms

(0.9%) were the most-used, followed by cannabis (0.7%). No explanation is offered for the somewhat surprising finding that magic mushrooms are the drug of choice for over-75s (Fuller et al 2009).

In the UK, Beynon looked at changing patterns of use within drug treatment services in the counties of Cheshire and Merseyside over a seven-year period. She found that the proportion of older men and women in treatment had significantly increased, as had the average age of injecting drug users (Beynon et al 2007). In 1998, the percentage of people aged 50–74 years in drug treatment in the two counties was 1.5% for men and 1.9% for women. In the financial year ending 2005, this had increased to 3.6% for men and 3.2% for women. In the 40–49 years age range the percentage of people receiving treatment more than doubled during this period, with 19.6% in treatment in 2005, as compared to 8.1% in 1998. There was also a significant increase in the number of people aged 50–74 years attending a syringe exchange programme (0.2% in 1992; 3.8% in 2004). Beynon's research finds support for the view that people who have problems with drug use are taking them into older age in a way that has not been seen previously.

Levy and Anderson (2005) conducted qualitative research in Chicago, US with 40 older injecting drug users, aged 50–68 years, to explore how their drug use had changed over time. Most of the sample were black, parents, single and male and and had begun injecting drugs in their teens, with some starting in their 20s. Most had been injecting heroin and cocaine for over 25 years, with one person injecting for 50 years. For some, their use had been sporadic, but for others their use was continuous. In addition, almost half reported smoking crack-cocaine, with a few people injecting it. They stated that alcohol and barbiturates became the substitute for heroin or other street drugs when they were unable to get hold of their drug of choice or when the effects of the street drugs were 'too harsh for an aging body to tolerate' (Levy and Anderson 2005: 250).

Gurnack and Johnson (2002) reviewed North American prevalence data on alcohol and other drug use among older people from minority ethnic groups. They found that limited data were available and only some of them explored older populations. What they did find was that the prevalence of alcohol and drug use (including tobacco) varied across ethnicities, depending on the substance used, highlighting the need for further research to take account of different drugs and patterns of use. They also recommended consideration of the cultural influences on substance use and the impact of a range of socioeconomic variables.

In Practice Example 2, Michael is clearly one of those people who is taking his longer-term substance use into older age, although there are indications that he is once again considering making some changes. What Michael's experience also shows is the non-medical use of prescription drugs as part of a cocktail of substances that people will use. As with the experiences of participants in Levy and Anderson's study (2005), it may also be that Michael is finding the acquisition and use of illicit drugs more difficult as he gets older.

Prescription drug use

According to the European Monitoring Centre for Drugs and Drug Addiction (EMCDDA), people over the age of 65 years use one-third of all prescribed drugs, often including benzodiazepines and opioid analgesics (Gossop 2008). The EMCDDA states that older women are more likely to be prescribed, and to abuse, psychoactive drugs. While some people may deliberately misuse medication – for example, by using more than prescribed, using it with alcohol or 'hoarding' it – Gossop suggests that for some people the misuse may be unintentional. He suggests that this could be a result of inadequate monitoring by health professionals, leading to (a) the prescription of drugs that contain properties that can lead to dependence and (b) the prescription of multiple drugs that do not interact well with other medications the person may be taking.

What difference does age make?

The reasons why older people use substances may be the same as those of their younger counterparts. Beynon's (2009) work exploring older people and illicit drug use concludes that little is known about the reasons why older people use illicit drugs and that this needs to be explored further. More is known about alcohol use, with a number of reasons identified that are more clearly likely to occur in later life.

Stress, loss and poor physical health can all contribute to the reasons why people use alcohol or other drugs, including prescription drugs. Ward (2008) found that feelings of loss were a key theme in people's reasons for drinking. Some of this was about loss of employment, physical health and mobility, or changes in relationships or housing, while some people described loss in relation to bereavement or the loss of daily routine and structure. Important for interventions to consider was the connection that some people made between their current and previous life-styles and accompanying drinking behaviour. Some people reported wanting to keep the connection with activities they had done in their younger days, in order to not feel so excluded as they moved into older age. Conversely, Ward (2008) found that a number of factors prohibited or reduced people's alcohol consumption in older age, including the cost and availability of alcohol, advice from their

GP not to drink, and taking prescribed medication with which they had to limit or avoid alcohol.

Brennan et al (2005) found an association between reported pain and the use of alcohol among older people. In a sample of 401 older people including current problem drinkers and non-problem drinkers with an average age of approximately 68 years, more reported pain was associated with higher levels of alcohol use to manage the pain, particularly among men assessed as having problematic drinking levels at baseline. However, at baseline this group of men also reported higher levels of pain and thus the directionality of the relationship between the two is unclear. Among people who were not assessed at baseline as having pre-existing alcohol problems, just over one-fifth (21%) reported using alcohol to manage pain, as compared to over half of those who were assessed as having alcohol problems (57% of men and 58% of women). Clearly, the relationship between pain and alcohol use or, indeed, the potential misuse of prescription drugs, has implications for practice and assessment processes.

Conversely, Harding (2009: 8), in her practice as part of a pilot alcohol project with older people in the London Borough of Kensington and Chelsea, said that she had found little evidence of people self-medicating with alcohol to reduce pain. The main reasons for alcohol use were 'unresolved emotional difficulties from the past' and 'loneliness and isolation due to being housebound'. A smaller number of people also drank as a result of the loss of a partner or of status in the community, or as a result of feeling unprepared for retirement.

Barrie (in Practice Example 1) has a number of these losses in his life, from the information that we have. Given his angry and abusive behaviour, these could be overlooked in any assessment or intervention but they are important to acknowledge and address. Given his longevity of drinking and smoking, it is unlikely that any intervention that focuses solely on his substance use is going to succeed, and therefore engagement with Barrie will need to focus on support in other areas of his life and this may be the 'way in' to engaging with him.

Similar reasons for substance use have been found in qualitative studies of injecting older drug users. Isolation resulting from the death of drug-using friends or isolation from families who have long since rejected their loved one is a key factor (Levy and Anderson 2005). In Michael's case, he wants to develop social networks, he's lost the company of his brother and has only sporadic contact with a younger woman, about whom we know little.

Reasons for continued use include the difficulties of changing habits at a later age and not seeing any alternative, the like of which was available to them when younger – for example, beginning a new career. The ageing process can lead to the marginalisation of older injecting users even within drug-using cultures. Some older users reported feeling uncomfortable in the new drug scene and were afraid of the tougher, more violent younger users (Anderson and Levy 2003). Levy and Anderson (2005: 252) cite one research participant who stated:

> "I feel out of place. I feel like I'm an old man playing a game that has got too fast for me, too dangerous. It doesn't have no honor about it no more."

Witnessing violent acts has also been explored in relation to older people's use of alcohol and experiences of depression, in a national sample from North America. Compared with older people who had not experienced acts of violence, Colbert and Krause (2009) found that older women had higher rates of depression as a response, whereas older men were more likely to abuse alcohol. This suggests potentially different ways of coping with, or responding to, having witnessed violent behaviour. However, the authors did not include people's own experiences of violence and abuse as opposed to witnessing violence to others, so some caution is needed in interpreting their results.

Levy and Anderson (2005) found that the way injecting drug users financed their drug use needed to change in older age. Due to their physical ageing, younger and more energetic ways of getting money, such as theft, robbery and physical threats, were no longer viable, nor did users want to face prison in older age. They therefore had to resort to what was considered the 'socially lowest work within the drug using world', that is, running errands, serving as lookout, bagging the drugs or doing without. Levy and Anderson also found that for older women the 'sex for drugs' exchanges were no longer an option and they too had to find alternative ways of getting their drugs, either through working on drug production or by selling medical prescriptions that they had obtained. The older users with histories of drug dealing also found a loss of status with ageing, in that the younger drug dealers were invariably related to gangs and were tougher and more violent.

This change in financial position appears not to pose the same challenges for older drinkers as it does for older illicit drug users. Alcohol is still readily available and, as Harding (2009) found, can easily be delivered by local suppliers such as off-licences or supermarkets. Further, the IAS (2010) suggests that many older people have more disposable income in their retirement, and therefore financing their alcohol use is not as problematic as financing illicit drug use because there is no requirement for illegal activity in order to generate money.

Health impact

A number of health benefits from alcohol use have been suggested by research in recent years. These health benefits are particular to older people who drink moderate amounts of alcohol only, particularly older men and post-menopausal women. Rapuri et al (2000) found that the bone marrow density of post-menopausal women was higher among those who drank moderately rather than abstained. In a review of alcohol and health research among older people, Hallgren et al (2009) pointed to evidence that moderate drinking can offer some protection against cardiovascular (heart) and cerebrovascular disease (stroke). Laing et al (2007) reported improved cognitive health, subjective well-being and lower levels of depression in middle-aged and older men and women who drank moderately than among abstainers. McCaul et al (2010) found lower mortality risk among men and women over the age of 65 who had four and two standard alcoholic drinks a day respectively.

However, these findings need to be interpreted with care and concerns have been raised about the methodological weaknesses surrounding research into the cardiovascular benefits of alcohol, in particular (see Hallgren et al 2009). Further, the improvements in cognitive health could well be explained by other factors – for example, the social interaction that often accompanies moderate drinking.

It is important to note, however, that even the researchers point out that the health benefits that may be demonstrated do not outweigh the health risks of alcohol consumption, particularly heavier use. Further, individuals will differ in their pre-existing health status, medication regimes and even unknown health problems, and therefore it is not safe to present a message that drinking in moderation can be healthy without taking all other individual health and social factors into account.

As might be expected, little is documented about the potential health benefits of illicit drug use, in spite of the fact that legal drugs such as alcohol and tobacco are seen to be far more harmful to health than some illicit drugs. Cannabis has been reported as helping to ease chronic pain, particularly that from illnesses such as multiple sclerosis and arthritis (Ware et al 2005).

Regardless of alcohol or other drug use, health problems tend to occur more often in later life as the natural ageing process begins to affect both mind and body. For older substance users, particularly those using to excess, the health risks are high. Gossop (2008: 1) highlights how the combined use of alcohol and other drugs leads to a range of problems:

> Ageing may lead to psychological, social and health problems which serve both as risk factors for substance misuse, and which may also be aggravated by substance use.

Physiologically, the ageing process results in the body's being less able to metabolise alcohol or other drugs in the same way that it did when younger. When people combine prescribed drugs, illicit drugs and alcohol use, the pressures on the body increase (Hallgren et al 2009).

Older alcohol users have been found to be at greater risk of ulcers, many forms of cancer, stroke, pancreatitis, hepatitis, cirrhosis, as well as chronic diarrhoea, heart problems, high blood pressure, peripheral neuropathy and loss of muscle mass (see Cummings et al 2006 for a review).

One of the difficulties in assessing Barrie's needs (in Practice Example 1) is to unpick which health problems are related to his drinking and which are pre-existing. Given the longevity of his drinking, it appears that this may never be established, but medical interventions will need to address the health problems concurrently with social care addressing his social needs.

The challenge for Barrie and others like him is that the combination of alcohol and medication can negate or accentuate the effects of prescribed medication. Common combinations that can lead to health problems include alcohol and medication to help with sleep, anxiety or depression. The interaction of these substances can lead to increased sedation, confusion, anxiety, feelings of light-headedness which, in turn, can lead to falls (Broadway undated; Hallgren et al 2009). Falls are among the top three causes of death due to injury for older people across Europe, although research on the association with alcohol consumption is equivocal (Hallgren et al 2009). In their summary of negative alcohol/drug interactions, Moore et al (2007) found increases of risk for hypertension, gastrointestinal bleeding, decreased drug metabolism, sedation, impaired motor function, insomnia, depression, liver disease, seizures and breast cancer. O'Connell et al (2003) reported negative interactions between the anti-coagulant Warfarin and alcohol consumption in older people. There is also evidence that alcohol problems are associated with suicide among older people (Waern 2003).

Levy and Anderson (2005) found that older injecting drug users struggled with the combination of physical ageing and their drug use. Like non-drug users, older drug users found that their bodies were no longer able to cope as well as they did when younger, affecting their enjoyment of their drug use and their tolerance of withdrawal symptoms. In other words, it was harder to get the same effects from the drugs and they experienced worse withdrawal symptoms. Levy and Anderson found no evidence, among the 40 older injecting drug users whom they interviewed, of increasing physical tolerance with longevity of use; rather, the process of physically ageing plus the reported lesser quality of the street drugs affected their experience of the drugs. As with younger drug users, seeking medical attention was avoided by older users for fear of separation from their drug supply and also fear of stigma, discrimination, hospitalisation or contact with law enforcement.

Beynon (2009) reported how the impact of illicit drug use on the brain can exacerbate some of the natural processes of ageing as well as increase the risk of liver, heart and kidney problems. The long-term impact of alcohol use on the brain can result in alcohol-related dementia, which presents with similar symptoms to Alzheimer's disease (Hallgren et al 2009). Other degenerative brain disorders resulting from alcohol use include Wernicke's encephalopathy and Korsakoff's amnesic syndrome. Wernicke's includes symptoms such as confusion, visual problems and hypotension, while Korsakoff's includes memory problems, both for past and newly acquired information, and disorientation (National Institute of Neurological Disorders and Stroke 2007). While they are separate disorders, they are generally considered to be different points on the spectrum of alcohol-related brain damage and will often be written as 'Wernicke-Korsakoff syndrome'.

As well as physical health problems, mental health problems can either lead to or stem from the use of alcohol and other drugs. Choi and Mayer (2000) found that older people who 'abused' alcohol or other drugs were at greater risk of self-neglect, due to the the the effect of substance use on their ability to self-care.

Harding (2009) reported that 83 of 105 older people with alcohol problems with whom she worked during a 12-month period suffered from mild to moderate depression and were receiving medication from a GP. A further 15 were receiving medication from their GP for anxiety, with only 6 having a 'clinical diagnosis' of mental health problems. She raised questions about the lack of concurrent psychological interventions when people were in receipt of GP attention only, and the impact that this would have on improving the mental health of the older people with whom she worked.

The challenges for people of whatever age who use substances and have mental health problems are considerable (see Chapter Nine). Often they are bounced back and forth between substance use and mental health services. For older people there is the additional challenge of mental health problems specific to older age. Thus, professionals supporting people like Barrie and Michael have to be tenacious in their contact with services and may need to advocate hard on their behalf for appropriate joined-up health and social care.

Policy context

Older people's substance use has not been a priority politically in the UK. There has been little recognition that older people may have different support needs from their younger counterparts, and their exclusion from national research adds weight to arguments that older people's use is not important. In the UK, recent drugs policy focus has been on younger people, crime and health. In the current national drugs strategy for England, families and communities are mentioned as requiring support (HM Government 2010a) but the needs of older people are not considered. While the previous national alcohol strategy was equally exclusive of older people's use (DH et al 2007), the related alcohol strategy local implementation toolkit published a year later (Home Office et al 2008) made one mention of the need to assess whether services were needed for a range of people from diverse groups, and included older people.

In terms of national health and social care policies for older people there is little mention of alcohol or other drug use. Even though alcohol-related dementia is a risk for older people, there is only one fleeting mention in the National Dementia Strategy, alongside a list of other activities that might help to reduce the risk of dementia (DH 2009a). The National Service Framework for Older People does better, making a number of references to alcohol as a risk factor for a number of health problems (DH 2001a), although there is no evidence in subsequent related policy publications of any resources being allocated or actions being taken to address this (Philp 2006).

For practice to change, it is helpful for policy drivers to be in place. Where policy does not exist but there is a need at practice level, it is important that practice does not wait and begins to implement change from the bottom up.

Improving practice

A failure to consider older people's alcohol or drug use in health and social care settings is a common theme emerging from the literature. Assumptions that older people's substance use is minimal or not a concern underpins the apparent lack of recognition of the increasing number of older people with alcohol and other drug problems. Good social work practice needs to buck this trend and reject these assumptions.

What research suggests is that most health and social care services that work with older people usually do not screen or assess for alcohol or other drug use. One study of UK social workers working with older people found that they did not see supporting older people with alcohol problems as part of their role, recommending instead the introduction of a specialist alcohol support worker (Shaw and Palattiyil 2008).

Klein and Jess (2002), in a study of 111 nursing homes in the US, found that nearly half did not ask about alcohol use during intake procedures. They also had a range of policies and practice relating to alcohol use that Klein and Jess felt reflected the ambiguous relationship with alcohol in wider society. On the one hand, staff were aware that alcohol does not mix with many medications; on the other hand, they felt that people had a right to self-determination. As is the case with most social workers in the UK, Klein and Jess found a lack of training among staff in the nursing homes they studied, and that the majority had not received alcohol training. Similarly, a study by Galvani et al (2011) found that social care professionals in England who specialised in work with older people were significantly more likely to 'rarely' or 'never' ask their service users about their substance use, as compared with colleagues working with children and families or people with mental health problems.

Social workers are trained to ask questions on a range of issues and are best placed to support people with a range of needs. Failure to ask the questions at practice level means that we are not truly aware of the extent of older people's substance use, nor are we aware of their needs in relation to support services.

Assessment

What the research evidence suggests is that these questions need to be underpinned by an awareness of the specific needs of older people. Sensitive enquiry is paramount, not only because of the shame and stigma of substance use, but also out of respect for the reasons why many people will have started or continued to use substances.

Ward's (2008: 4) research on older people in Brighton emphasised this need for sensitivity and offered suggestions of how to approach the subject:

> Professionals who have contact with older people who may be drinking heavily need to explore whether this is something the person is comfortable with and feels in control of, or whether there are changes they might like to make in their lives that would obviate their experienced need to drink heavily.

Ward further stated the importance of enabling people 'to tell their own stories about the place of alcohol in their lives', as many older people to whom she spoke had set their own rules about their consumption of alcohol, such as not drinking before a particular time of day or not drinking at home. This could be a good way for social workers to start discussions with older people about how they drink and whether they could decide on more rules that might minimise any health risks.

Chapter Two provides some examples of assessment questions, including an assessment of where the person is in terms of their readiness or willingness to change. Barrie, in Practice Example 1, appears to be unwilling to change much at the moment, so discussing with him referrals to specialist services would not be the way forward. As he has said, he is willing to cut down, and that may be a point for discussion. However, it may be his other needs, personal and practical, may need to be addressed first. This can establish trust and facilitate discussions on more sensitive matters. Michael, in Practice Example 2, on the other hand, has been attending services sporadically, although he still uses. With Michael, discussions can more easily focus on what it was about services that worked for him previously, what he sees as his goals, and what other support he might need to achieve them.

As well as the principle of sensitive questioning, practitioners also need to look at both risk and protective factors, based in knowledge of older people's substance use and precursors to it. For example, suggesting that someone reduces or stops their substance use while not considering their reasons for using is naive and unhelpful.

The questions you need to ask yourself prior to assessment include:

- What is the level of harm stemming from the person's substance use?
- If it is causing harm, are they aware of it and/or open to discussing either reducing or stopping their use?
- Will they need medical advice and assistance before making significant changes to their use?
- What will fill the void left by removing or reducing their substance use?
- What do I need to do to help the person fill that void?

Assessment of older people's substance use is confounded by the fact that the consequences of alcohol or other drug use can mimic the signs of ageing. Thus, questioning that is broadly related to all their use of substances, illegal or licit, is important. While some people will be cognisant of their excessive use of alcohol and prescribed or illicit drugs, others will be unaware of the negative effects that the combination of alcohol and other drug use can have on their health.

When alcohol use has been assessed through specific older people projects, the extent of people's use has been surprisingly high. Harding (2009) reported on the work of a pilot alcohol project for older people in the London Borough of Kensington and Chelsea. In the previous 12 months she had assessed 99 of 105 older people in their own homes. Half (n=53/105) were drinking more than 70 units of alcohol per week, 43 were drinking 50–70 units, 4 were drinking 30–50 units and 5 between 20–30 units.

A number of specific alcohol assessment tools have been found to be effective with older adults, but the most widely used appear to be the AUDIT (Babor et al 1992) or a shorter version of it (AUDIT C; see Figure 7.1) (Gomez et al 2006) and MAST-G, the geriatric version of the MAST (Michigan Alcohol Screening Test) (Blow 1991) or the shorter version of it, Short Mast-G (see Figure 7.2).

As highlighted above, the sensitive inclusion of questions such as these is key to a good assessment. Reeling off a list of questions without consideration for the tone or context in which they are asked is not good practice. Sensitive

Figure 7.1: AUDIT C

Questions	Scoring system					Your
	0	1	2	3	4	score
How often do you have a drink containing alcohol?	Never	Monthly or less	2–4 times per month	2–3 times per week	4+ times per week	
How many units of alcohol do you drink on a typical day when you are drinking?	1–2	3–4	5–6	7–9	10+	
How often have you had 6 or more units (if female), or 8 or more (if male), on a single occasion in the last year?	Never	Less than monthly	Monthly	Weekly	Daily or almost daily	

Scoring:
A total of 5+ indicates increasing or higher risk drinking.
An overall total score of 5 or above is AUDIT-C positive.

Figure 7.2: Short MAST-G

Questions
When talking with others, do you ever underestimate how much you actually drink?
After a few drinks, have you sometimes not eaten or been able to skip a meal because you didn't feel hungry?
Does having a few drinks help decrease your shakiness or tremors?
Does alcohol sometimes make it hard for you to remember parts of the day or night?
Do you usually take a drink to relax or calm your nerves?
Do you drink to take your mind off your problems?
Have you ever increased your drinking after experiencing a loss in your life?
Has a doctor or nurse ever said they were worried or concerned about your drinking?
Have you ever made rules to manage your drinking?
When you feel lonely, does having a drink help?

Scoring:
If the person answered 'yes' to two or more questions, encourage a talk with the doctor or other specialist.

questioning also entails discretion and ensuring that discussions happen in private, particularly in contexts where someone is living with family or in residential care.

Given the apparent absence of assessment of older people for alcohol use in health and social care services, it is highly unlikely that any assessment of illicit substance use is taking place. Beynon et al (2007: 808) call for 'detailed assessments of drug-taking experiences and histories across the lifecourse

… along with more information about the impacts on families and social networks'. However, current drug assessment tools do not appear to have catered for the older user in the same way that alcohol tools have. A range of assessment tools used with adults are accessible to download through the *Treatment Evaluation Instruments* list online at the EMCDDA (www.emcdda.europa.eu).

An important step in assessing either alcohol or other drug problems is contacting your local specialist services to see which tools they use or recommend. Not only can they provide copies of their assessment tools, but such contact can help to forge partnerships and create better understandings of each other's roles. These services will also be able to guide you on which questions to ask and what is more appropriate for specialist interventions.

The BASW pocket guide for social workers on working with alcohol and drugs (McCarthy and Galvani 2010) suggests the following basic questions in relation to drug use – the order in which they are used can vary according to the individual situation:

- What are the effects – positive and negative – of your use of drugs?
- What are you using?
- How much are you using?
- How often do you use?
- How do you use (smoke, swallow, inject)?
- What happens if you stop using?
- What do you want from your drug use?
- Do you always get it?
- Are there other ways you could get the same things?
- Would you like to change your drug use?
- What help do you think you might need?

As with younger drinkers and drug users, older people will have family and friendship networks that are affected by their use. Consideration needs to be given to:

- assessing the needs of family members or others negatively affected by the older person's substance use
- the extent to which the older person may be negatively affected by a family member's or carer's substance use
- the extent to which existing family and friendship networks support changes to the older person's substance use or, wittingly or unwittingly, support it.

In the practice examples at the start of the chapter Barrie's wife, Anne, is likely to need an assessment of her needs. Assessing the level of abuse that she receives from Barrie is important to ensuring her own safety and well-being (see Chapter Six on substance use and domestic violence). With a history of illness herself and the additional pressure of looking after Barrie, Anne is likely to need additional support for her own health and social care needs, and may even require respite care or a personal care arrangement for Barrie. It may also be worth exploring whether the sons can offer Anne any support or whether the one son who has contact with Barrie can offer some support or respite to allow Anne some of her own time. In Michael's case, further discussion about the woman he sees occasionally may help him to determine whether she is likely to be a positive or negative social support in any attempts he makes to change his substance use.

Intervention

Formal treatment for complex alcohol and other drug problems is the remit of specialist services. Statistics from the National Alcohol Treatment Monitoring System (NATMS) (DH/NTA 2010a) show that 6% of people in treatment for alcohol problems during the previous 12 months were aged 60 or over. The equivalent drug treatment statistics, unhelpfully, put all people aged over 40 in the same category, with an estimated 24% of people in treatment falling into this group (DH/NTA 2010b). People over the age of 75 were excluded from both sets of statistics and therefore the figures are likely to be slight underestimates. These figures will be based primarily on people in treatment at a community service or in hospital. However, given the discussion above about the needs of older people and the appropriateness of services for them, particularly in terms of accessibility, these statistics probably present only the very tip of the iceberg.

Substance use interventions are not just about specialist treatment, however. The assessment process alone needs to be considered as an intervention; done well, it raises the subject and helps the person to think about the pros and cons of their substance use. In addition, the provision of factual health information in a motivational approach and brief advice about substance use can also be effective (Conigliaro et al 2003; Gossop 2006; Raistrick et al 2006).

Social workers are often in the position of having an established relationship with the person and a remit that goes beyond focusing on one single issue. This puts the social worker in an ideal position to begin an intervention in the context of general discussions about health and well-being, isolation and social support, loss and coping mechanisms, opening the way for discussion of substance use. Social workers are also one of the few professions that will visit older people regularly at home and can therefore pick up on signs of substance use, be these bottles, cans, needles, the smell of alcohol or drugs, around the home.

Social workers will also be able to pick up more easily on the types of information discovered by Harding (2009) in her practice with older people. She found that all the older people had their alcohol delivered by either the off-licence or the supermarket delivery service. Importantly, she pointed out that 96 of the 105 people she worked with in a 12-month period had mobility problems, and thus getting public transport to attend specialist community services was not possible.

Thus, the types of intervention a social worker can provide include:

- sensitive home-based discussion about substance use located in a broader context of the person's health and well-being;
- discussion of the advantages and disadvantages of substance use in the person's life and the reasons for it;
- sensitive discussion about what other support would help the person reduce their substance use, for example, social activities, re-engaging with family or friends;
- provision of factual information about the negative interactions between substance use and prescribed medication. Take advice from pharmacists or look online for information on the interactions between prescribed medication and other substance use;
- for alcohol, provision of factual information about the units the person is drinking and current benchmarks (emphasising that these are possibly too high for people who are older, given the physiological differences resulting from age);
- provision of information about harm minimisation and reducing substance use;
- discussion of specialist services, where necessary, in an informed and supportive way, after checking whether the service can visit people at home;
- ensuring strong links with the person's GP and mental health services (where appropriate) to maximise sharing of information (with permission) and to ensure that medication and alcohol/drug interactions are considered by all and a punitive approach avoided;
- discussion of friend and family networks, particularly those who do not use alcohol or other drugs.

Harding (2009), describing the interventions used in her pilot project with older people with alcohol problems, found that many of the 'usual' tools or interventions, for example drink diaries, did not work because people did not want to complete them. She found that it was more effective to discuss drinking in relation to general health and 'structuring drinking around medication times and meal times' (p 6). Her practice experience was that the older drinkers appeared more concerned about having a healthier lifestyle than did other drinkers, in terms of motivation to change behaviours. She also used MI techniques to discuss drinking and possible change with older people.

As Gossop (2008) points out, there is a dearth of evidence relating to the treatment of older drug users, but what is emerging from the limited research is that older people tend to stick to 'treatment regimes' better, particularly in relation to alcohol interventions. Satre et al (2004) found that older people had higher levels of abstinence when they had a longer time in treatment and had no close family or friends who encouraged their substance use. This was particularly the case for older women. Cummings et al (2006), in a review of empirical studies relating to alcohol interventions, found that cognitive behaviour approaches as well as less confrontational approaches resulted in better retention and substance use outcomes for older people. This is a similar finding to successful interventions for other age groups of drinkers. Thus, provided that older people's substance use is recognised and assessed, the prospect for subsequent interventions appears good.

Barriers to practice with older substance users

There are a number of barriers to effective practice with older substance users. Some are individual, while others are more systemic:

1. *Lack of recognition*: Many social workers and other social and healthcare staff fail to consider alcohol or other drug use in their assessment of an older person's needs. Until this changes, people will slip through the net.
2. *Lack of policy attention*: As stated earlier in the chapter, older people's substance use receives very little, if any, national or local political attention.
3. *Inappropriate treatment services*: Most specialist services do not consider the different needs of older drinkers or drug users. This can range from lack of accessibility in terms of the service location or a building without lifts or disabled access, to lack of consideration of the particular context of older people's substance use.
4. *GPs* are likely to be the first port of call for many older people (Ward 2008) – yet many GPs, like social workers, do not ask questions about substance use or fail to recognise the signs.
5. *Resistance to help seeking*: There are many reasons why people won't seek help. Some of these are fear of the unknown, the stigma and shame of substance use, fear of police involvement or simply because they do not

feel that they have a problem. Harding (2009) also found that a number of people did not want to attend a service if it meant leaving a partner who was unwell, or leaving their pets.

6. *Lack of motivation*: Levy and Anderson (2005) found that many older drug users felt too old to make a fresh start and were so socially isolated from family and friends that there seemed little point. Neither were they of an age when they could look forward to starting a new family or career (Beynon et al 2007).

While these are not insignificant barriers, social workers are trained to work with people who are resistant to receiving their interventions, and are experienced in communicating well with people. Establishing trust and providing support for other needs may well be the way to overcome many of these barriers, including seeking permission to talk to health colleagues and/or family members.

Ultimately, a person may decide not to change their substance-using behaviours and it is important that social workers respect the person's right to self-determination and continue to support them as far as possible in relation to their health and social well-being. What makes social work a distinct profession is its ability to continue working with people in need, in spite of what we may see as unhealthy choices. Within drug and alcohol services people are unlikely to receive the same on-going support and they will be often be excluded from services for non-attendance or failure to change their substance-using behaviours.

Summary

Older people's alcohol and drug use is little recognised, in spite of evidence that older people with substance problems, particularly with alcohol, are growing in number. In the alcohol field there are some pockets of good practice, but there is no evidence of this happening in relation to drugs.

The health consequences of substance use in older age can place older people at particular risk of harm. The practice evidence earlier demonstrates the need for sensitive exploration of older people's substance use that both respects the person and identifies the reasons behind their use in, the context of their other support needs. Substance problems tend to be seen in policy and practice as a 'young person's game', so the additional stigma and shame should not be overlooked. Ensuring that people can retain their pride and dignity at the same time as discussing their substance use will mean that there is a better chance of facilitating good working relationships.

In spite of the gap in specialist substance use services for older people, social workers are among those best placed to identify and address substance use.

It is not about becoming a specialist in substance use, but it is about having enough knowledge to recognise the issue and being prepared to ask about it.

Discussion questions/exercises

1   What are some of the reasons why older people in particular may use alcohol and other drugs?
2   When talking to an older person about their substance use, how might you raise the subject with them?
3   What might be the differences between working with someone with early onset substance use and working with someone with late onset substance use?
4   What are the recommended alcohol unit levels for older people?
5   What are some of the prescribed drugs that you commonly encounter when working with older people? Can they be taken alongside alcohol or other drugs?

Further learning resources

A number of pamphlets and other types of information are available to download and can be given to older people:

■   *Alcohol, Medication and Older People* – www.broadwaylodge. co.uk/store/files/Alcohol,-Medication-and-Older-People.pdf.

■   *Alcohol and Older People* – www.apas.org.uk/docs/older.pdf.

■   There appears to be no equivalent information on drugs and older people in the UK. General leaflets on various types of drugs, their effects and risks are available a number of sources (see Chapter Two).

■   Nicholls, A. (2006) *Assessing the mental health needs of older people*. Adults' services: SCIE Guide 03. Available online at: www.scie.org.uk/publications/guides/guide03/files/guide03. pdf.

■   Royal College of Psychiatrists (2011) *Our invisible addicts*. London: RCP. Available online at: www.rcpsych.ac.uk/files/ pdfversion/CR165.pdf.

1. Christopher (17)

Christopher has been using alcohol and other drugs since the age of 12. He was belatedly taken into care, aged 14, when he lived with his mother, who uses heroin, and a grandmother who drinks heavily. He repeatedly ran away from the care home and is now living in supported independent accommodation. He is estranged from his father, who was also a heavy drinker. Christopher has not had any positive adult family role models in his life. He has some mental health problems, including a history of self-harm and suicide attempts. He was repeatedly raped and sexually abused when younger as a result of relatives' 'exchanging' him for drugs. There is also a suspicion that he has a brain injury or other learning difficulties. He is gay, has two older siblings, both in prison, and few interests outside his drug use, although has expressed an interest in a college course and joining a church group.

2. Kirsty (16)

Kirsty lives with a friend who is 17 years old. She has a two-year-old child who lives with her mother and stepfather, against her wishes. They claim benefits for both Kirsty and her daughter, so Kirsty has no income. She has starting drinking regularly and becomes very emotional and upset when she talks about her child. She reports that her mother and stepfather drink heavily and that her stepfather is violent and abusive. She was in and out of care herself, when she was younger, because of their abuse and neglect. She is afraid to talk to them about sole custody of her daughter and doesn't know what to do. She is no longer in touch with her own father or with her daughter's father.

Introduction

A great deal of political attention in the UK has been given to the increasing use of alcohol and other drugs by young people. Services targeting young people who use substances have blossomed. Alongside the attention to drug-related crime and treatment services, young people's substance use has been a key focus of national alcohol and drug policies for nearly two decades (see Galvani and Thurnham 2012). It appears that this investment is beginning to pay off. Annual data on young people's use of substances shows that substance use is decreasing (Fuller 2011), although concerns remain about high levels of alcohol use by some young people (Bremner et al 2011; Fuller 2011).

This chapter provides a brief overview of the patterns of young people's substance use, the policy response and what is known about specific risks and protective factors for young people's use. It will then explore assessment and intervention and good practice for social workers working with young people who may be using alcohol and other drugs.

> **Box 8.1: Who counts as a young person?**
>
> The literature pertaining to young people's substance use is vast. What counts as 'young' varies between specialist services and across the research literature. The range of ages covered is 10 years to 30 years. Young people, for the purposes of this chapter, are defined as those below the age of adulthood, that is, under 18 years. Thus, research evidence and services that include 18- to 24-year-olds in their definition will be included only if they are particularly pertinent.

Patterns and perceptions of drug use

In England, the most reliable source of data on the prevalence of drinking, drug use and smoking among 11- to 15-year-olds is an annual survey conducted by the National Centre for Social Research and the National Foundation for Educational Research. The most recent survey found that overall *drug use* among this age group had fallen since the last survey in terms of 'ever' having used drugs, 'previous 12 month' and 'last month' use (Fuller 2011). It reported that less than a fifth of young people in this age group had ever taken drugs (18%), although 28% had been offered drugs at some point.

In terms of ethnicity, young people of Asian ethnic origin were more likely than those of mixed heritage, White or Black ethnicity to have taken drugs (Fuller 2011). This is particularly important to note, given that in current adult populations of alcohol and other drug users it is far more common to find White and Mixed ethnicity people experiencing substance problems, or at least attending specialist services, than those from other ethnic backgrounds (see Chapter Four). Whether this suggests that the adult treatment population of tomorrow will see a higher proportion of Asian people, or whether it is further evidence that the needs of Asian adults are not being met by current specialist services, is an important issue that needs further exploration.

In a qualitative study by Miller-Day and Barnett (2004) exploring Black and White youths' use of, and attitudes towards, drug use, they found that the majority of young Black people (59%) believed that Black youths used more drugs than did White people. This rose to 100% for young Black people who used drugs. By way of contrast, only 16% of young White people thought that Whites used more.

Fuller (2011) found that age was also a determining factor in young people's use of substances. Only 5% of 11-year-olds had used drugs in the last year, compared to 25% of 15-year-olds. Hoare and Moon (2010) explored the age of first use of substances, reporting that the last figures available came from the 2003/04 British Crime Survey for England and Wales. It showed that 18 was the most common age at that time for first cannabis use, and that first use of powder cocaine was at 20 years. However, in 2009/10 these ages had decreased to 16 and 18 years respectively. Hoare and Moon also reported that ecstasy was most commonly used for the first time at age 18 in both the 2003/04 and 2009/10 surveys.

Unsurprisingly, cannabis was the most-used substance, followed by glue, gas and solvents (Fuller 2011). Gallup's research (2011) found that those who had used cannabis in the last 12 months were less likely to think that it posed a high risk to their health. Perceptions of high risk increased for those who had used cannabis, but not in the last 12 months, and for those who never used. Generally, regular use of any drug, including alcohol, was seen as a higher risk than occasional use.

Fuller (2011) found only 2.4% of young people surveyed reported using Class A drugs, for example, crack-cocaine or ecstasy. The frequency of substance use varied according to substance and age, with most of those who had used gas, aerosols, glue and solvents only being at the younger end of the age group. They were also more likely to have used substances only once.

In relation to *alcohol use*, less than half the pupils surveyed (45%) had ever drunk alcohol (Fuller 2011). This continues the fall in numbers from the previous survey, where 51% reported ever having had an alcoholic drink. Only 13% of pupils reported drinking once a week, and again the frequency increased with age, as might be expected. Bremner et al (2011: 1) found that the most common age for a first drink was 12 to 13 years and this was usually when the young person was with an adult and celebrating a special occasion. They also found that the frequency of drinking increased with age. Talbot and Crabbe's (2008) research concurs with this. Based on a survey of over 1,200 young people in deprived areas of England, they found that

13 years appears to be that age at which most young people start drinking. Of the young people who took part in the survey, 42% stated that they knew someone with a drinking problem.

Fuller (2011) also reported that more young people were abstinent from alcohol than in previous surveys (54%). Unlike with drugs, where boys' consumption was far higher than girls', girls' and boys' alcohol consumption was similar, and Asian pupils were less likely to have drunk than their White counterparts. No other ethnicity differences were significant.

While the reduction in drinking among these young people appears to be a positive message, it remains the case that alcohol consumption is far higher than drug use or smoking among this age group. Overall, beer, lager and cider were drunk most often, followed by spirits and alcopops (Gunning and Nicholson 2010; Fuller 2011), with girls less likely to drink beer, lager and cider and preferring spirits, alcopops and wine (Fuller 2011).

Concern about alcohol consumption is not to be underestimated. As the national charity Alcohol Concern highlights, alcohol is often implicated in accidents, suicide and violence, which are 'significant causes of death in the 16–25 age groups' (Alcohol Concern 2011: 6). Further, it states that 'the Chief Medical Officer's report for 2007 states that adolescent binge-drinkers are 50% more likely than their peers to be dependent on alcohol (or taking illicit drugs) when they reach 30 years of age'.

Box 8.2: Smoking among 11- to 15-year-olds

A national survey of 11- to 15-year-olds in England found that smoking was at its lowest levels since the survey started in 1982 (Fuller 2011). Girls were more likely to smoke than boys. No patterns emerged relating to ethnicity, but regular smoking was associated with other risk factors, including exclusion and truanting, drinking and other drug use and family deprivation.

Policy framework

Young people's illicit drug use and, latterly, alcohol use have been slow to move up the political agenda. However, since the publication of the national drugs strategy in 1995 (Home Office 1995), *The substance of young needs* in 1996 (NHS Health Advisory Service 1996) and the first national alcohol strategy in 2004 (Cabinet Office 2004), they have appeared to be a primary concern.

Substance use, particularly illicit drug consumption, was considered in the raft of policy documents that formed the Every Child Matters agenda. In 2005, the Department for Education and Skills published *Every Child*

Matters: Change for children. Young people and drugs. It set out the various existing policy initiatives and key performance indicators that a range of services had to meet relating to young people's drug use.

In 2008, the government produced a *Youth Alcohol Action Plan* (DCSF et al 2008) in response to concerns that young people who were drinking alcohol were drinking a lot of it. Broad objectives were:

- stopping young people from drinking in public places, including behaviour orders, arrest referral, police confiscation powers and new legislation;
- taking action with industry on young people and alcohol, including proof-of-age schemes and stricter monitoring of alcohol retailers;
- developing a national consensus on young people and drinking;
- establishing a new partnership with parents, including consultation and family-based interventions;
- supporting young people to make sensible decisions, including a campaign on the risks of alcohol and a review of treatment services for young people, with implications for local service commissioning.

These concerns over young people's substance use and the need to address it continued with the 2010 drugs strategy, which highlighted that rates of cannabis use and binge drinking by young people in the UK are among the highest in Europe (HM Government 2010a). Further, it states concern about young people's use of new 'legal highs'. One of the strategy's three core policy strands is to reduce demand for drugs, and young people are mentioned within it twice: first, in terms of the need for better information and education for young people and their parents, to ensure that they can 'actively resist substance misuse' (p 9); second, young people and young adults are seen to be a focus for early intervention.

Much of the strand's 'information and education' focus is centred around school initiatives and further education programmes to ensure that young people remain in education up to the age of 18 (HM Government 2010a). The significance of this is that those young people at higher risk of substance use are the ones who have higher levels of school truancy or leave school early (Fuller 2011). Drug and alcohol education may therefore not be reaching those most at risk and the protective role of full-time education will be limited. Further, these young people's absence from school may also indicate substance problems. In the current strategy 'early intervention' is to be passed down to local government, which is tasked with determining the needs of young people in its region.

The Drug Strategy 2010 also suggests that directors of public health and children's social care should adopt integrated approaches and sharing of resources in order to fund appropriate initiatives, and that this be extended to joint working with substance use, youth offending and mental health services. The extent to which this policy is put into practice remains to be seen, as partnership working and multi-disciplinary cooperation have been at the core of policies relating to both substance use and child welfare for many years. If funding for services becomes contingent upon multi-agency working, there may well be a greater chance of integrated working of the type that the policy proposes.

The economic argument for ensuring that services for young people are funded is supported by a cost-benefit analysis for young people in treatment published by the Department for Education (DfE) (Frontier Economics 2011). By way of context, it stated that 24,000 under-18s, primarily 16- to 17-years-olds, had been in formal treatment services in the 12 months preceding the report period (2008–09). The primary drug of choice for young people was alcohol (37%) or cannabis (53%), with the remaining 10% in treatment for Class A drug use. The report concluded:

> Overall, the study has shown that the immediate and long-term benefits of specialist substance misuse treatment for young people are likely to significantly outweigh the cost of providing this treatment. In particular, we have estimated a benefit of £4.66–£8.38 for every £1 spent on young people's drug and alcohol treatment. Furthermore, our central case estimates are based on a conservative set of assumptions. Therefore, the benefit of specialist drug and alcohol treatment for young people may be larger than we report here. (Frontier Economics 2011: 9)

Additional mention of young people's susceptibility to the use of alcohol and drugs as a policy focus has appeared in the government's White Paper, *Healthy Lives, Healthy People: Our strategy for public health in England* (HM Government 2010c), alongside other policy initiatives tackling young people's alcohol use as part of public health initiatives (Fuller 2011).

Box 8.3: The impact of advertising on young people

Alcohol advertising has been found to have an im[pact on young people's] alcohol use. NICE called for a review of alcohol adve[rtising in the media and] suggested a possible ban on it in order to stop or [reduce the exposure of] young people to alcohol advertising (NICE 2010). The [government has not done] this so far. It has been suggested that the government does not wish to sour relationships with the alcohol industry, in particular because of the revenue it brings in to central government through taxation.

The law

A number of resources are readily available on the internet in relation to the law and young people's substance use. While the illicit nature of drug use sends a clear message to parents and young people about not using or possessing drugs, and the repercussions if they do, the messages relating to alcohol can be ambivalent. Table 8.1 comes from Alcohol Concern's factsheet on young people and alcohol (Alcohol Concern 2011: 3).

Table 8.1: The law relating to young people's alcohol consumption

Age	Key message	Relevant legislation
Under 5 years	It is illegal to give an alcoholic drink to a child under 5, except under medical supervision in an emergency.	Children and Young Person's Act 1933
Under 16 years	Children under 16 are allowed on licensed premises as long as they are supervised by an adult, but cannot have any alcoholic drinks. However, some premises may be subject to licensing conditions that prevent children from entering, such as pubs that have experienced problems with under-age drinking.	Licensing Act 2003
Under 18 years	It is illegal for anyone under 18 to buy alcohol in a pub, off-licence, supermarket or other outlet or for anyone to buy alcohol for someone under 18 to consume in a pub or public place. The only exception is where young people aged 16 or 17 can drink beer, wine or cider with a table meal if it is bought by an adult and they are accompanied by an adult.	Licensing Act 2003
Under 18 years	Police have powers to confiscate alcohol from a) under-18s in possession of alcohol in a public place; b) someone (in a public place) who intends that alcohol in their possession should be consumed by a person under the age of 18 in a public place.	Confiscation of Alcohol (Young Persons) Act 1997

The law in relation to the possession or use of illicit drugs by those under the age of 17 is limited. The police will inform a parent or guardian and subsequent actions will depend on the extent to which the young person has previously been in trouble over drug use. Custodial sentences can be passed on young people for drug offences, depending on the seriousness of the crime, the risk that the young person poses to others and previous offending history (DirectGov 2011).

One criminal justice option is to refer the young person to a Youth Offending Team (YOT) which seeks to supervise and monitor the young person in the community. Under the Criminal Justice and Immigration Act 2008 there is also a Drug Treatment Requirement, a Drug Testing Requirement and Intoxicating Substance Treatment Requirement that the courts can impose as part of a Youth Rehabilitation Order, and these are often imposed alongside a Supervision Requirement (Youth Justice Board 2010). In order to qualify for it, drugs need to be part of offending behaviour and accepted as such by the young person who is willing to take part in the drug treatment regime. The orders are managed by YOTs but should be administered in close liaison with specialist substance use services (Youth Justice Board 2010).

A number of other legal frameworks that underpin social work practice and duties of care will also apply to young people's use of alcohol and other drugs and the environment in which it takes place, including childcare and community care law (Preston-Shoot 2012). Duties of care extend to young people's use of alcohol and drugs, particularly where young people are at risk of harm or where parental substance use is also placing them at risk.

Reasons for substance use

A number of studies have explored the motivations of young people to drink alcohol or use drugs. The reasons, explanations or motivations for starting to drink or use are many and varied. Usually there is no single reason for it; rather, it involves several overlapping reasons. Further, as people age, the reasons why they continue drinking or using evolve and are not always the same as the reasons why they first started.

In a survey of 1,250 young people by Talbot and Crabbe (2008: 2) the three main reasons that people gave for starting to drink included:

- that friends did it and it looked like fun (40%)
- a desire to experiment and see what it was like (19%)
- following the example of family members and relatives (17%).

For young people using drugs, the reasons for using for the first time were very similar but in different proportions (Jotangia et al 2010: 26):

- to see what it was like (56%)
- to get high or feel good (22%)
- because my friends were doing it (18%).

In Talbot and Crabbe's (2008: 2) survey, the reasons given for continuing to drink included:

- 69% said that they enjoyed drinking
- 29% said getting drunk for the sake of it
- 29% said socialising with friends and having fun.

Similar motivations were found in a study by Coleman and Cater (2005) (cited by Alcohol Concern 2011: 3). 'Social facilitation', including an increase in confidence both socially and sexually, was cited as a key reason for drinking. 'Individual benefits' were also reported, which ranged from a feeling of escape to a way to counter boredom. Finally 'social norms and influences' played an important role, involving perceptions that drinking to excess was an acceptable part of social behaviour, often influenced by peer pressure, and that to be accepted into a social group meant conforming with such norms.

On-going use of illicit drugs suggests slightly different motivations. In Jotangia et al (2010) the reasons young people gave for their most recent use of drugs were:

- to get high or feel good (47%).
- to see what it was like (25%)
- I had nothing better to do (21%).

Important differences emerged here from the reasons that people gave for using for the first time, in that more people were using drugs for their effects as opposed to experimenting, plus a fifth were using as an apparent response to boredom.

Having some understanding of why young people start and continue using may provide some clues as to how to intervene, with whom and what the risks and protective factors are. These, in turn, provide some information to consider in terms of building on strengths and taking action where risks are too great.

Risks and protective factors

It is clear from the research that a number of risk and protective factors for young people's substance use stand out above all others.

Risk factors

Role of parents in condoning alcohol or other drug use

Evidence shows that parents play a major role in the messages and behaviour that young people learn about substance use. Where there is greater parental supervision and monitoring of substance use and parental disapproval of substance use, this serves as a protective factor against young people's use (Talbot and Crabbe 2008; Fuller 2011). Where this is not the case and where parents' own use of alcohol or other drugs conveys a 'norm' or condones substance use, young people are at greater risk of using and developing problems (Burkhart et al 2008; Haase and Pratschke 2010; Bremner et al 2011; Fuller 2011). Further, those living with high levels of parental conflict are also at greater risk of substance use (Burkhart et al 2008).

School attendance

School attendance and education is a significant factor on a number of levels:

- Evidence shows far higher levels of drug use among those who leave school early (Haase and Pratschke 2010).
- Young people excluded from school are at greater risk (Burkhart et al 2008, Fuller 2011).
- Those who truant are also at greater risk (Fuller 2011).

Influence of friends and older siblings

As with parental influence, friends and older siblings pay an important role in young people's decisions about substance use (Talbot and Crabbe 2008; Haase and Pratschke 2010). In their research with young people, Bremner et al (2011) found that young people who spent more than two evenings each week with friends and/or had friends who drank alcohol were more likely to drink and to do so more frequently and to excess.

Access to substances

The ease with which young people can access alcohol or other drugs also has an impact on the likelihood that they will use them. A number of studies have found that where alcohol was easy to access, buy or steal (Bremner et al 2011) and where other drugs were more accessible (Gallup Organization 2011), particularly cannabis and tobacco, there were high rates of young people using. In a survey of 27 European Union states the UK and Ireland were among the countries where young people also had easier access to so-called 'legal highs' – often bought from friends or at a pub or a party.

Additional vulnerabilities

A number of additional vulnerabilities among young people have been found to place them at greater risk of substance use. These include:

- mental health or psychological health issues, for example Attention Deficit Hyperactivity Disorder or depression (Burkhart et al 2008) or low self-concept or self-esteem (Haase and Pratschke 2010)
- homelessness (Burkhart et al 2008)
- offending (Burkhart et al 2008) or 'acting out' behaviours (Haase and Pratschke 2010)
- having lived in institutional or foster care (Burkhart et al 2008).

From what is known about the backgrounds of both Christopher and Kirsty in the practice examples at the start of the chapter, their exposure to a number of these risks demonstrates the challenges they have to face in changing their own substance use. Given the abuse and trauma they both received when younger, using drugs or drinking alcohol would seem like a reasonable way to escape the memories of such experiences, albeit one that ultimately may be harmful to them. Their own substance use may not be the most pressing issue for them; listening to them and supporting them in other areas of need may be the best starting-point. This is particularly important where people have experienced abuse. Ensuring that how you work with people is enabling and provides them with choices and control is important in ensuring that the controlling behaviours of their parents and abusers are not replicated. Working with Christopher and Kirsty will require huge amounts of patience, time and support on practical and emotional levels.

Protective factors

Clearly, the opposites of the risk factors also act as protective factors, and therefore discussion of the risks with young people and/or their families can also offer opportunities for discussing how any risks can be addressed. In addition, the following protective factors have been identified:

- negative expectations of the effect of the substance (Bremner et al 2011)
- fears about consequences, in terms of health/addiction, career aspirations, legal consequences (Dillon et al 2007)
- strong ethnic identity and religious beliefs (see Chapter Four)
- positive school experience (Haase and Pratschke 2010)
- alternative ways of getting support (Dillon et al 2007).

In their study of young people's risk and protective factors, Dillon et al (2007) also explored the ways in which young people who did not want to use drugs achieved this. They summarised their findings into three refusal strategies:

1. **Actively saying 'no':** At times this needed to be more assertive if offers were persistent. This was sometimes found to be difficult if it meant marginalisation from the group and if people felt pressured to join in.
2. **Avoiding drug-related situations or offers:** People and places associated with drugs were avoided; other strategies were just leaving a situation or ignoring offers.
3. **Faking acceptance:** This was a theoretical response by the participants in the study, who stated they could accept a drug but not necessarily use it.

Assessment

Assessment of young people's substance use must not focus on substance use alone. It is clear from the evidence that young people at risk of developing substance problems are more likely to be those who are experiencing a number of problems, ranging from difficulties at home to intrapersonal difficulties and other issues (NTA 2010c) that make them more vulnerable to becoming involved with alcohol and other drug use.

Gilvarry and Britton (2009) point out how it is important to be clear about a young person's psychological or behavioural issues apart from the substance use, in order to not confuse what is resulting from substance use with what was there beforehand.

Thus, the assessment of a young person, while asking appropriate questions related to their substance use (see Chapter Two), should also focus on other needs and ensure that it prioritises those situations where an individual's safety is at risk or safeguarding actions may be needed.

Britton (2007) emphasises the importance of involving parents and carers in the assessment process, in particular of listening to their views about the young person's behaviour, any mental, emotional or behavioural problems and medical and developmental history. Information should be sought about relationships with school, friends and family, including any significant changes (Britton 2007). However, it is important to involve parents only when this does not place the person at risk of harm through expulsion from the home or from domestic violence and abuse. Initial discussion with the young person should establish this early on and you should continue to check this with them throughout the assessment and intervention process. Similarly, where parental substance use is putting the young person at risk, parents' involvement will need careful consideration.

Britton (2007: 10–11) highlights some of the issues that may be identified in risk assessment and are likely to indicate high risk of harm to the young person. These include:

- a history of overdose, self-harm and attempted suicide
- using substances with those whose substance use is far more established, for example, parents, older siblings or friends/partners
- situations where drug or alcohol use is related to sexual exploitation or sexual risk
- a relationship between the substance use and offending behaviour
- where use of the substance is in dangerous places, for example, near railway lines or while driving.

Clearly Christopher, in the practice example, is at high risk and the social and healthcare system appears to have failed him in not picking up earlier on his vulnerability and abuse. Kirsty is also at high risk, but appears to have fewer of what Britton refers to as high-risk factors.

Where referral to specialist services is appropriate, care needs to be taken to ensure that the young person is aware of what to expect and that the service is aware of the young person's needs and to find out what support it does or does not have available. In a study exploring the barriers to young people accessing specialist services, Duff and McNab (2004: 14–15) found that young people reported facing a number of barriers, including:

- lack of family and peer support to address their problems
- lack of awareness of the likely consequences of their actions (particularly of substance misuse)

- lack of knowledge of who to approach for help or how to get help
- distrust or fear of official agencies and staff, including social workers
- an assumption that they are disapproved of by most other social groups
- danger of victimisation or exploitation by others (including dealers and pimps)
- difficulty envisaging and committing to a positive course of action to help themselves.

Referrals to specialist substance use services should always be supported referrals; in other words, greater support will be needed beyond simply arranging an appointment and providing the young person (or adult, for that matter) with the referral information. Attending an alcohol or drug service is daunting and people need support to make that first step. Further, where the person does not attend or does not engage with the service the social worker needs to be on hand to pick up the pieces, to review what worked and what didn't and to offer further choices and support.

Intervention

Britton (2007: 6) points out that many needs related to low-level substance use do not require specialist intervention and can be met by the person undertaking an assessment of other needs, for example, the CAF. The use of Brief Interventions (BI) is found to have some evidence among young people and provide an easy and accessible tool for social workers. Details of BI and other methods of intervention are provided in Chapter Three. In sum, BI is an umbrella term that covers brief, structured interventions. One iteration uses the acronym FRAMES and entails:

- **F**eedback of personal risk or impairment (in relation to current advice and guidance on alcohol or other drug use, what is the person's risk?)
- **R**esponsibility for change (emphasising the person's choice to make their own decisions)
- **A**dvice to change (with reference to risks and so on discussed above)
- **M**enu of alternative change options (for example, self-help, where to go for formal help, online sources, other resources available)

- **E**mpathy on behalf of the practitioner (it is important that empathy is expressed throughout, so as to maintain engagement)
- **S**elf-efficacy or optimism in client facilitated by the practitioner (expressing a belief that the person is wholly capable of change if they choose to do so – drawing on other successes).

(Miller and Sanchez 1994 in Rollnick and Miller 1995)

It is possible that for Kirsty, BI plus advocacy and legal support regarding her child may be adequate. Only assessment will establish how heavy her drinking is. Given the extent of Christopher's substance use, BI is unlikely to be enough, but the principles of providing information, being empathic and promoting self-efficacy will still be important in establishing a positive, helping relationship.

Tone of voice is important when discussing and feeding back risk and responsibility. A paternalistic or lecturing tone is unlikely to succeed in establishing a good relationship or encouraging the person to hear what you're saying. The discussion needs to be judgement free and based on factual information that the social worker has to hand. In addition, discussions with the young person and/or their family can include:

- *The provision of advice and information* to the young person and to their parents. This may be on substances and the risks they pose, harm minimisation, what to do if they are concerned and whom to contact for specialist help.
- *Discussion about how to reduce the risk* of substance use and of harm relating to it. This may include a discussion of risk and protective factors and what family members can do to support their loved one and each other and best protect other family members from harm.

There are a number of other methods of working with young people that have been found to be effective in relation to substance use, some of which will be familiar to social workers and used in social work practice. Increasingly, calls are being heard for more community-focused interventions for young people (Calabria et al 2011), methods that move away from individually focused interventions and include, where it is safe to do so, families and communities. This leaves social workers well placed to draw on their knowledge of such methods when working with people with substance problems. Methods include:

- behaviour therapy (Burniston et al 2002) or cognitive behavioural therapy (Calabria et al 2011)
- Motivational Interviewing techniques (Britton 2007)
- family therapy (Burniston et al 2002; Calabria et al 2011)

- case management or coordinating other agencies involved in the person's care (Britton 2007; Galvani and Forrester 2011b)
- Community Reinforcement Approach (Calabria et al 2011)
- culturally sensitive counselling (Burniston et al 2002)
- the Minnesota 12-Step Programme (Burniston et al 2002)
- therapeutic community and residential care (Burniston et al 2002).

Calabria et al (2011) caution against a one-size-fits-all approach to working with young people and suggest that different methods of intervention may be more appropriate for some children and young people than others. They state that those who have fewer additional problems and have good social support are likely to benefit from individual cognitive behavioural interventions, whereas those who have less support and more additional problems will be more likely to benefit from 'multi-component programmes (such as multidimensional family therapy, brief strategic family therapy, functional family therapy or multisystemic therapy)' (p 2).

Elliott et al (2002) highlight a range of factors that can maximise the chances of success for young people receiving drug interventions. Unsurprisingly, many are congruent with the protective factors identified earlier. These include:

- peer and parental support
- self-motivation and completing the programme or intervention
- increased school attendance
- improved coping and relapse skills
- holistic support for the young person, that is, not just focusing on the substance intervention
- in the longer term, well-planned interventions with clear aims and objectives and booster sessions
- experienced staff and multi-agency working.

The NTA (2010c) states that, unlike many adults in need of specialist interventions, the majority of young people have not been using for many years. However, they can still experience withdrawal – both physiological and psychological. In addition, many will have overlapping problems relating to their families, education or offending and will thus require a multi-agency coordinated response (NTA 2010c). The NTA states that most of the young people in treatment are there for cannabis or alcohol use and receive psychological or behavioural therapies and that very few receive pharmacological treatment.

Box 8.4: Substitute prescribing

Young people who use substances are often not physically dependent on them in the same way that adults who have been using over a longer period or more heavily can be. The evidence suggests that younger people are less likely to be users of Class A drugs and therefore medically supervised detoxification and substitute prescribing is likely to be a rare necessity for most young people. Gilvarry and Britton (2009: 18–19) provide a list of medications licensed for the management of substance problems and clarify the ages for which they are licensed:

- Acamprosate – used to inhibit craving for alcohol – 18+ years
- Buprenorphine – substitute drug in tablet form for those with opioid dependence, age 16+
- Lofexidine – prescribed to help withdrawal symptoms from heroin opioid dependence – 18+ years
- Methadone – 'not licensed for children', which is 'generally recognised to mean those aged 13 and younger'
- Naltrexone – used for blocking sensation of opioids, is used post-detox for people aged 18+
- Nicotine replacement therapies – 18+ years.

Gilvarry and Britton (2009) state that substance specialists must provide a care plan and liaise with other professionals, including social workers, prior to any pharmacological treatment, as well as with the young person, and their parents where appropriate.

Services can offer specialist interventions without parental consent if a young person is aged under 16 years (Gilvarry and Britton 2009); however, the service must first have assessed the young person's competence and understanding of the intervention.[1] Gilvarry and Britton advise that only when 'strong encouragement' for the involvement of parents and carers has failed or where involving them may put the young person at risk should staff provide intervention without parental consent. For 16- to 17-year-olds, they state that consent is presumed but that good practice suggests that parents should be involved wherever it is possible and safe to do so.

Good practice

What is clear from the evidence presented is that good practice for working with young people with alcohol or other drug problems requires the same types of communication skills, empathic approach and holistic assessment processes as any other work with young people, whatever their presenting issue. These are core social work values and skills; there is not a new set of skills needed for good practice with young people's substance use.

The first step is focusing on engagement and listening to the young person, while being conscious of what concerns they might have about social workers, family involvement or the involvement of other friends and professionals. An overly questioning, lecturing or analysing style will put young people off immediately.

The additional component is to know how to conduct an assessment of the young person's substance use as part of a wider assessment and how to conduct a BI, together with having the knowledge base about substance use that is required to inform it. This is well within the ability and remit of social workers.

Many of the evidence-based risks and protective factors relating to substance use are the same or very similar to the risks and protective factors that support young people, or place them at risk of harm, from other behaviours or parental neglect or abuse. Thus there is no particular mystery to working with young people on this issue.

What specialist youth substance workers report is that most of their time is spent focusing on other issues rather than on the substance use (personal communication 2011). The substance use is only a small part of the young person's problems and is often a coping mechanism.

It is also clear that parental involvement can be key. Establishing the role and presence of a parent in the young person's life, if these are not immediately apparent, will be important early in the process. It may help explore the risks and protective factors in the young person's life, or establish the factors that will promote or prevent successful interventions for young people. Engaging with the parents or the young person's relationship with the parents is vital providing it is safe to do so. The evidence also suggests that it is crucial to work with parents on how they can support their child and on the importance of understanding how what they do will influence their child's decisions. In relation to alcohol in particular, Bremner et al (2011: 4) note:

> Parents strongly influence young people's alcohol-related behaviour through supervision and monitoring, as well as playing a role in modelling this behaviour. Being with a parent suggests an element of supervision and monitoring, which can reduce the likelihood of drinking, frequent drinking, and higher levels of alcohol consumption or drunkenness. Witnessing family members drinking and perceptions of drunkenness among family members in the home can make this kind of drinking appear normal.

In a study comprising discussions with both parents/carers and young people (DCSF 2008), the authors concluded that young people were not particularly interested in learning the risks of alcohol, as they enjoyed drinking, and that parents did not understand the importance of their role in facilitating or preventing alcohol use by their children. Therefore, while part of the social worker's role is to educate and inform young people and parents/carers about substance use, the timing of this needs to be considered. It may be that discussions with the parents/carers need to take place first, using what is known about what presents risks or helps to protect young people in relation to substance use.

> ### Box 8.5: Young people's sources of information on substances
>
> A Gallup Organization (2011) survey of young people in Europe asked where they would go for information on substances. The internet was the primary source of information about drugs (55% for UK respondents), followed by parents and relatives (49%), then friends and health professionals (each 45%). Only 16% of young people in the UK said that they would approach specialists, and even fewer (only 8%) would contact a social worker. Importantly, however, when they were asked from where they had received their information in the previous 12 months, most said they had got it through their school, followed by the media, then the internet. The school was particularly important for those below the age of 18 years.

For Kirsty and Christopher, the involvement of parents is unlikely to be helpful, given the parents' excessive substance use and histories of perpetrating abuse. However, it is not impossible, if Kirsty or Christopher wanted them to be involved in some way. Establishing whether there are other adult family members in their lives who can offer more positive support is an alternative approach.

Work also needs to focus on supporting Christopher and Kirsty to consider their own wishes in relation to both their substance use and other areas of their lives and on discussing with them what can be done to make the changes they want, with support from professionals.

Where referrals are needed, specialist services can be found by using the directories of services that are available through regional DAATs or via the online databases of services provided by national charities such as Drugscope and Alcohol Concern.

- Drugscope's 'Helpfinder' service: www.drugscope.org.uk/resources/databases/helpfinder.htm
- Alcohol Concern – link to alcohol services directory: www.alcoholconcern.org.uk/concerned-about-alcohol/alcohol-services
- Adfam's 'Find a local support group' service: www.adfam.org.uk/find_help/find_a_local_support_group

Britton (2007) highlights that aftercare is vitally important for young people leaving specialist treatment, particularly if there is a transition from young people's to adults' services. They stress the need for planning and that young people will need both information and support, alongside an agreed care plan.

Summary

Young people's substance use in the UK is decreasing. However, it remains among the highest in Europe and there is still a minority of young people whose substance use is problematic and causing them harm. Political attention has focused on young people's use, with school programmes targeting prevention and young people's services targeting those at risk or already experiencing problems. However, as the evidence shows, the risk factors for young people's problematic use are far more about the social and familial context in which they live than about any wish to experiment or try something new.

For those experiencing problems, it is clear that solutions focused only on the substance use are likely to fail. Social work is a profession that sees people within their environment and social workers are therefore particularly well placed to work well with young people who use, or who have problems with substance use. But this need not be alone. The evidence suggests that responding to young people's use involves joint working between social care, specialist alcohol and drug services, educational provision and youth justice. The work should comprise information and education, prevention work and specialist treatment services for young people who use, or are at risk of having problems with, illicit drugs. It also involves working with both the individual young person and their parent or carer, wherever it is safe to do so. First and foremost, it involves listening to the young person, hearing their views and experience and their priorities for change.

Note
[1] '... the young person understands the advice and has the maturity to understand what is involved; their physical and/or mental health will suffer if they do not have treatment; it is in their best interest to be given

such advice/treatment without parental consent; they will continue to put themselves at risk of harm if they do not have advice/treatment; they cannot be persuaded by the doctor/health professional to inform parental responsibility holder(s), nor allow the doctor/health professional to inform them' (Gilvarry and Britton 2009: 11).

Discussion questions/exercises

1   What are the substances most commonly used by young people?
2   Name three risk factors for problematic substance use among young people.
3   What would be your priority in supporting young people who have substance problems?
4   Find two local services for young people in your area.

Further learning resources

■ D-World (Drugscope site for 11- to14-year-olds): www. drugscope-dworld.org.uk/wip/24/index.htm.

■ Direct.gov – government website on young people and substance use:

• www.direct.gov.uk/en/YoungPeople/ HealthAndRelationships/ConcernedAbout/DG_10030639
• www.direct.gov.uk/en/Parents/Yourchildshealthandsafety/ Youngpeopleandalcohol/index.htm.

■ Drinkaware – advice on young people and alcohol: www.drinkaware.co.uk/talking-to-under-18s/parents/ govemment-advice-on-young-people-and-alcohol?gclid=CK SBjbjZj6oCFQJO4QodGGNpzA.

■ In-volve – national organisation providing information and training and other resources designed to support young people using substances: www.in-volve.org.uk/index.html.

■ Re-solv – website on solvent and volatile substance use: www.re-solv.org/.

- Talk about alcohol – website targeting young people, parents and teachers in relation to young people's use of alcohol: http://talkaboutalcohol.com/AboutUs/location-21.aspx.

Coexisting mental distress and substance use

Practice examples

1. Andrew (38)

Andrew is a man of Jamaican descent who has a diagnosis of paranoid schizophrenia. He has been in and out of prison for a range of offences, including assault and possession. He has engaged with mental health and other support services on an erratic basis, usually when his mental health is stable after leaving prison. He is currently homeless and living in a direct access hostel for homeless men. He smokes cannabis on a regular basis and has some history of other drug use. As his illicit drug use increases, he reduces or stops taking his medication and becomes increasingly mentally unwell. He is eventually arrested for committing an offence, which sometimes involves violence.

2. Mary (54)

Mary is of Irish descent and has an 11-year-old son. She has a history of depression and anxiety, for which she has previously received medication through her GP. She doesn't like the effect of the drugs, as they make her feel drowsy in the morning. Her husband works long hours and she has no close friends. She has a strained relationship with her older children from a previous marriage, seeing them only occasionally. They believe that she has an alcohol problem, but she denies it. She had been having her alcohol delivered by the local supermarket and the local off-licence until a recent visit to hospital, when she became very ill and eventually admitted that she drank daily – and possibly a little too much.

Introduction

Substance use and mental health are inextricably linked. For many people the whole point of using alcohol or drugs is to create an altered perception of reality, be it short term or longer term, and an experience that is physical, mental and emotional. In the UK we have an ambivalent relationship with substances that supports this end while at the same time disapproves of it. Alcohol, for example, is often seen as a reward – an aid to relaxation at the end of the working day/week. For some it symbolises a 'time out' from the reality of everyday pressures and worries, combined with the social environment within which it is often consumed. Yet drinking to excess, such that it becomes problematic to our health and or the well-being of those around us, is stigmatised and shameful. Cannabis is used in the same way. Its illegal status creates greater secrecy and discretion around its use, but among particular groups of people – particularly among young people – its use is much more commonplace (see Chapter Eight). It is the illicit drug most commonly used in British society, yet its potential for causing harm, in particular its impact on people's mental health, has caused great debate among scientists and mental health advocates.

So, on the one hand, we seek a range of ways to alter our psychological consciousness, whether through alcohol, tobacco, other drugs, food, spiritual rituals or extreme sports, to name a few; on the other, this altered state is frowned upon when the very thing we seek has the desired effect and we continue to want to achieve that state through the same means. We are expected to have learned and accepted the temporary nature of this altered state, and not to seek to make it longer lasting. Further, when this use becomes problematic, society rejects the motivations for continued use and distances itself from the people concerned, who, become marginalised and stigmatised.

One of the ways in which society has attempted to address the phenomenon of problematic substance use is to define it as a mental illness. However, when such substance use is combined with a coexisting mental health problem, it becomes difficult to unravel how and whether the two are linked, the impact the one has on the other and how to assess and intervene.

This chapter will provide an overview of some of these issues, describing the nature of the links between them, the evidence in relation to assessment and intervention and the policy frameworks within which they sit. This is a huge topic area and some areas will not be covered at all, or not covered in any great depth. The further learning resources at the end of the chapter are a resource for readers wanting to find out more.

Terminology

One of the first things we learn about in social work education is the importance of language. Language, and the jargon each profession uses, can serve to either engage or alienate service users, carers and other professionals. We learn that, underpinning language, there is often a set of assumptions or particular models of thinking or constructing various phenomena. This holds equally in the field of substance use (see Box 3.2).

In addition to the substance use terminology, the terms used in the world of specialist mental health services and among service users and carers vary enormously. A range of terms are used, including mental disorder, mental illness, mental ill-health, mental health problems, to name a few. In this chapter the term 'mental health' is used as a broad term focusing on the health of the mind rather than the body. The term 'mental distress' will be used to refer specifically to people who experience, either episodically or on an on-going basis, distress of the mind. This term has been chosen because some people who have what professionals may call 'mental health problems' or 'mental illness' may never feel that they have an illness or problem; thus, 'mental distress' more accurately reflects the subjective nature and interpretation of their experiences. Where other terms are used, this will be to reflect the use of a term by a particular author on whose work this chapter is drawing, or will be related to health-dominated constructs of mental distress.

Various shorthand terms have been used to describe people who use substances and experience mental distress. The one that is most succinct and often used is 'dual diagnosis'. The use of the term 'diagnosis' suggests formal medical intervention, and 'dual' that there have been two such diagnoses. However, this term is strongly criticised, including by medics themselves, for a number of reasons:

1. The two diagnoses could be diagnoses of anything; for example, they could refer to people with learning difficulties and experiencing mental distress.
2. The term is unhelpful because formal diagnosis of the coexisting issues will not always be appropriate or necessary. People can still have both substance use and mental health issues without one or both either being formally diagnosed or needing to be.
3. There can be more than two issues coexisting, and relying on diagnosis can result in overlooking the others. Banerjee et al (2002) suggest that the appropriate phrase is 'complex needs', rather than two problems as is suggested by the term 'dual diagnosis'.

Velleman and Baker (2008) also argue against the use of medicalised terms such as 'dual diagnosis' and 'co-morbidity'. They advocate the more inclusive and accurate 'coexisting mental health and substance use problems'. In relation to social work practice, the language of coexistence is far more appropriate for social work and social care than language that is underpinned by medical models. Kvaternik and Grebenc (2009) concur. They suggest that using medical terminology in the field of social work is often a strategy to exclude people from accessing help.

Ultimately, the key to choice of terminology is one of values and ability to communicate clearly and appropriately. If a service user or carer is comfortable with the term 'dual diagnosis', then it is not our remit to correct people. However, being clear about preferred language and the reasons for using it is important and serves to ensure that language is non-stigmatising and inclusive, rather than marginalising and exclusive. At times, service users may refer to themselves using negative terminology. While it is respectful to acknowledge the terms that service users employ to describe themselves, social workers need to avoid using negative and critical terms.

Is it a mental illness or not?

A second debate is whether problematic substance use is a mental illness. Few would disagree that moderate alcohol or other drug use should not be defined this way, in spite of its effects on the central nervous system and subsequent functioning – but when that use becomes problematic, the picture changes. Is it a medical or a social problem? Is it a symptom of mental distress, an individual behaviour over which control can be exercised or an illness beyond the person's control? What adds to the complexity is the negative effects the problematic substance use can have on many aspects of the individual's mental and physical health and their social circumstances and well-being.

Health professionals worldwide have sought to classify problematic substance use as a mental illness. Both the *International statistical classification of diseases and related health problems, 10th revision* (ICD-10) (WHO 2006) and the *Diagnostic and statistical manual of mental disorders, 4th revision* (DSM-IV) (APA 2000) have classified alcohol and drug problems using a range of criteria by which people can be diagnosed (Box 9.1).

Box 9.1: Diagnostic criteria for substance use

ICD-10   Codes F10 to F19 cover 'Mental and behavioural disorders due to psychoactive substance use'. As well as the more obvious substances, for example, cocaine, cannabis and opioids, the categories also include alcohol, tobacco and stimulants, including caffeine.

DSM-IV-TR   Currently, the DSM differentiates between substance abuse and substance dependence. It then breaks each of these down into the specific substances, including nicotine and caffeine. The revised DSM-V is due to be published in 2013 and it is expected that gambling problems and internet addiction may be included.

Of course, not everyone who uses alcohol or drugs will meet diagnostic criteria, and not all those who do not meet diagnostic criteria will be free from substance-related problems. Indeed, many people will be drinking or using to levels that are hazardous or harmful. In the practice examples, Mary has been diagnosed and medicated by her GP for anxiety and depression, but it appears that her drinking has not been assessed and no formal diagnosis has been made. This is also likely to be the case with Andrew, although, because his cannabis use has appeared to be significant in the pattern of his deteriorating mental health, it is more likely than in Mary's case that this will have been medically assessed.

The difficulty in focusing on medical diagnostic criteria is that services may determine on the basis of such criteria, or at very least, the severity of the problems they assess, whether or not to work with someone. Both mental health and substance use diagnoses are transient, however, and people can move in and out of them during their lives. This raises the crucial question that has, arguably, hindered effective working with people experiencing dual issues, which is: whose responsibility is it to support people if they do not meet the service criteria? Many substance use services will focus on 'heavier' end substance use, while mental health services may have criteria that allow only people with more 'severe' mental health problems to access services. Who is working with those people who do not meet these criteria and who, if they do not receive help, may experience worsening mental health or substance use? Mary may well fall into this gap in services, although she does have some contact with primary care. She may not qualify for specialist mental health care, nor for substance use services, particularly if she believes that her alcohol use is not problematic. Partnership working and advocacy is therefore vital.

Policy frameworks (see later) and service user feedback (Hughes 2006) suggest that mental health services are better placed to lead on work with people who have coexisting problems because they are usually more able to work with people for longer. Substance use services often work with people for a limited length of time. Thus, where there are multiple needs, it is argued that mental health services are better positioned to engage and work with people over the long term, but partnership working with substance use services will be required for specialist expertise and advice. Trippier and Parker (2008: 19) state:

> Unfortunately, the assessment and intervention around substance misuse and its effects on an individual's physical, psychological and social health appears to have become a specialist career, rather than part of the core work of a mental health professional.

Thus, while medical aspects have a place, particularly in medical settings, they are perhaps less helpful to social workers and others who also focus on the social lives and circumstances of the people affected.

The relationship between substance use and mental health

People who experience mental distress are no different from the rest of the population with regard to their propensity to experiment with or use alcohol and other drugs. There is no single way that substance use impacts on mental health, and vice versa. People experience both issues in completely different ways, depending on the nature, severity and intensity of their mental distress and the type, quantity, and mix of substances they use, not to mention their physical tolerance of them.

Crome et al (2009: 4) set out four ways in which the two issues can be related:

1. A primary psychiatric illness may precipitate or lead to substance use, misuse, harmful use and dependent use, which may also be associated with physical illness and affect social ability.
2. Substance use, misuse, harmful use and dependent use may exacerbate a mental health problem and physical health problem, for example, painful conditions, and any associated social functioning.
3. Substance use, for example, intoxication, misuse, harmful use and dependent use may lead to psychological symptomatology not amounting to a diagnosis, and to social problems.
4. Substance use, misuse, harmful use and dependent use may lead to psychiatric illnesses, physical illness and social dysfunction.

There are some common 'couplings' of particular substances with particular experiences of mental distress. Alcohol use and depression commonly co-occur, sometimes coupled with prescribed medication. For Mary, these overlapping issues are compounded by an apparent sense of isolation. Bartels et al (2006), in their review of research on older people and mental ill-health, found that depression and alcohol were frequently linked. In particular, this older age group were at higher risk of 'increased suicidality' and were more likely to use out-patient services.

Manning et al (2002) found that depression and 'social phobias' were common among people attending services for support with alcohol problems. Crawford and Crome (2001) report strong links between substance use and number of mental health disorders, particularly personality disorders, bi-polar disorder, schizophrenia and post-traumatic stress disorder, as well as much higher rates of substance use among people who go on to commit suicide.

However Crome et al (2009) *caution against spending too much time trying to assess what comes first* with the result that people can be excluded from services. Trying to focus on whether the substance use or the mental distress is the primary issue and which is the secondary issue takes up time that could otherwise be spent supporting the person concerned. Such a focus may result from a professional's lack of understanding of the coexisting issues or from systemic concerns to ensure that caseloads are kept manageable and that other professionals take the lead where appropriate. Some negative attitudes and values on the part of professionals with regard to substance use may also be part of this desire to identify the 'main' problem – in particular, the view that people who suffer from both issues are far more difficult to work with.

The impact of cannabis on people's mental health is also an on-going high-profile debate (Box 9.2) and scenarios such as Andrew's are not uncommon. There is a long-standing tradition of cannabis use in Jamaica, particularly by the Rastafari, who use it as part of their religious celebrations (Chevannes et al 2001).

Box 9.2: The cannabis debate

The debate about the reclassification of cannabis has been heated and controversial. Cannabis was downgraded from a Class B to a Class C drug in 2004. As discussed in Chapter One, the classification of drugs is supposed to be based on the degree of harm the drug may cause when misused. Tied to these classifications are penalties for possession, supply and other related offences. The higher the classification of a drug, the stiffer the penalties will be. Classification of harmfulness cannot be an exact science because it cannot account for each individual's pre-existing physical health problems or experiences of mental distress. However, this is not well understood either by politicians or by the general public. In addition to public perceptions that downgrading cannabis would give the wrong message regarding its use, there were also concerns about the impact of cannabis on people's mental health, in particular, its ability to worsen existing mental distress and its potential to trigger schizophrenia-type illness. Some mental health charities were very outspoken about their opposition to downgrading the classification of cannabis. On 8 May 2008, the Home Secretary announced in the House of Commons that cannabis would be reclassified as a Class B drug, in spite of scientific evidence presented by the government's own advisory body (the Advisory Council on the Misuse of Drugs) that this was not necessary. This demonstrates the difficulties of separating scientific expert evidence, opinion and advice from the social and political environment in which the debate occurs. The change of classification came into force in January 2009.

Crawford and Crome (2001) highlight the importance of differentiating between psychiatric *symptoms* and *disorders* because the two will require different responses.

Withdrawal from substances can also involve mental distress, including visual hallucinations. Much of this is only temporary and should not be confused with on-going mental distress. However, it highlights the importance of conducting a good assessment grounded in people's experiences and of understanding the broad impact of substances and possible withdrawal symptoms.

Service users' experiences

The findings of the Rethink Dual Diagnosis Research Group (2004) illustrate the importance of assessing the role and function that substance use plays in the lives and experiences of people with coexisting problems. It identified four 'explanatory frameworks' for alcohol and other drug use, following research with both service users and carers. These were:

- self-medication to deal with the effects of mental health problems;
- mental health service user lifestyles including boredom;
- external triggers e.g. relationship breakdowns;
- drug culture and the attraction of substance use.

(Rethink Dual Diagnosis Research Group 2004: 5)

Further, the Group identified that substance use 'can enhance well-being in the short term', which becomes a disincentive to stopping. Such insights are vital considerations when supporting someone to change their substance use. It is clear that these explanations echo the explanations that people without mental distress give for starting and continuing to use substances (see Chapter Two). Professionals must acknowledge and discuss these issues with people early in their intervention, in order to demonstrate understanding and remain client centred.

From the information that we have on Mary, it is possible that her reasons for drinking include self-medication for her anxiety and depression, or that she feels socially isolated, as well as lack of contact with her partner because of his long working hours. Finding out how the alcohol helps her is the first step to understanding what additional support and services she may need. Similarly with Andrew, he may be smoking either as a religious experience or to minimise the side-effects of medication, or perhaps because he is bored or finding it difficult to escape the culture of drug use and drug users of which he has become a part.

The Rethink Dual Diagnosis Research Group (2004) also explored the impact of living with dual diagnosis on service users' and carers' lives. A common theme from the responses was one of loss, be it loss of 'normality', life chances, family relationships, work, income, motivation and purpose, self-esteem and self-confidence, or losing the ability to be as active as they would wish to be. Other qualitative studies looking at service users' experiences have also found separation from family members to be characteristic of service users' histories, as well as frequent stays in hospital and 'educational problems' (Warfa et al 2006).

Crome et al (2009: 3) point out that among people with coexisting issues, experiences of 'social isolation, stigmatisation and social exclusion are likely to be common'. People will, no doubt, be facing a double helping of such stigmatisation, both as a person experiencing mental distress and as a person using substances.

How much overlap is there?

The most reliable prevalence data are drawn primarily from studies within either substance use or mental health settings. National household surveys of psychiatric morbidity are regularly carried out and do not suggest that coexisting mental health and substance use problems are as prevalent as is suggested by the studies of specific populations (see later) (McManus et al 2009). However, the household surveys are of a sample of the general population and only cover people in private households, thus excluding those in any type of residential or institutional care or those with insecure housing – for example, homeless people. Given the stigma attached to mental health problems, alcohol and other drug use, it is almost certain that respondents will not volunteer such information fully, if at all. The survey's authors also point out that people with, for example, severe mental health problems or alcohol dependence 'may be less available, able or willing to respond to surveys' (p 22).

Needham (2007) studied four specialist NHS mental health trusts and four DAATs in the North West of England. Among the mental health trusts, prevalence of substance use ranged from 16% to 51% of service users. The primary substance used was cannabis, with smaller numbers of people using amphetamines and even fewer using heroin. Needham reported that polydrug use was common, particularly in combination with alcohol, as well as misuse or mismanagement of prescription medication. The rate of prevalence was similar among the four DAATs in the study. Mental distress among service users ranged from 15% to 47% for 'common mental health problems', from 2% to 13% for 'complex mental health problems' and from 0.5% to 3% for 'serious mental health problems'. In a review of research on older adults and 'dual diagnosis', Bartels et al (2006) also found variation depending on the population studied. They found that prevalence rates for substance use ranged from 7% to 38% among people with mental health problems and that rates of mental ill-health were higher among people with substance problems (21% to 66%). This is supported by the research of Menezes et al (1996), who studied 171 people with psychotic conditions in South London. Of these, 36.3% were found to have had a substance problem in the last 12 months, with the rate of alcohol problems far higher in comparison to drug problems (31.6% and 15.8%, respectively).

Other studies put the figures far higher. Manning et al (2002) studied 50 people attending a substance use service and 50 people attending a mental health service. Using a screening tool, they found that 64% of the whole sample reported 'any psychiatric disorder and either a drug or alcohol problem'. Rates were remarkably high in the alcohol sample, followed by the drug sample and then the community mental health sample (92.3%, 87.5% and 38% respectively). Moselhy (2009), in a study of 70 people attending a substance use service, found high levels of post-traumatic stress disorder, including intrusive (45%) and avoidant (65.7%) symptoms. People reported a history of childhood sexual abuse, physical abuse and witnessing parental domestic abuse, as well as physical abuse and injuries in adulthood and adult rape. A holistic assessment of Mary's and Andrew's needs would also need to ask about previous and current abuse.

It is clear that the rate of coexisting problems among people using substances or experiencing mental distress, while varied, is at a level that services need to be able to respond to. With an ageing population, notice must also be taken of the increase in numbers of people with coexisting issues in older age. Arguably, people with both problematic substance use and mental distress are potentially more vulnerable, and yet also more likely to fall into the gap between services.

Policy framework

The policy framework for working with people experiencing coexisting substance use and mental distress is a complex one. It reflects the confusion over where substance use sits and whether it should be addressed within mental health services. On the one hand, the Mental Health Act 2007 very clearly states that 'dependence on alcohol and drugs is not considered to be a disorder or disability of the mind' (Box 9.3), but on the other hand, services that prescribe medication and provide psychosocial interventions to people who are considered to be substance 'dependent' often sit firmly within mental health services.

Box 9.3: Code of Practice – Mental Health Act (MHA) 1983 (amended 2007)

Dependence on alcohol or drugs

3.8 Section 1(3) of the Act states that dependence on alcohol or drugs is not considered to be a disorder or disability of the mind for the purposes of the definition of mental disorder in the Act.

3.9 This means that there are no grounds under the Act for detaining a person in hospital (or using other compulsory measures) on the basis of alcohol or drug dependence alone. Drugs for these purposes may be taken to include solvents and similar substances with a psychoactive effect.

3.10 Alcohol or drug dependence may be accompanied by, or associated with, a mental disorder which does fall within the Act's definition. If the relevant criteria are met, it is therefore possible (for example) to detain people who are suffering from mental disorder, even though they are also dependent on alcohol or drugs. This is true even if the mental disorder in question results from the person's alcohol or drug dependence.

3.11 The Act does not exclude other disorders or disabilities of the mind related to the use of alcohol or drugs. These disorders – for example, withdrawal state with delirium or associated psychotic disorder, acute intoxication and organic mental disorders associated with prolonged abuse of drugs or alcohol – remain mental disorders for the purposes of the Act.

3.12 Medical treatment for mental disorder under the Act (including treatment with consent) can include measures to address alcohol or drug dependence if that is an appropriate part of treating the mental disorder which is the primary focus of the treatment.

(DH 2008a: 21)

Thus, for Andrew, while his substance use alone would not be considered a reason for detention under the MHA 1983, the fact that he has a diagnosed 'disorder or disability of the mind' means that he could be detained when appropriate, in spite of the fact that the substance use appears to have led to the deterioration of his mental health.

In 1999, the National Service Framework for Mental Health (NSF) (DH 1999: 31) identified people experiencing coexisting substance use and mental distress as a 'particularly vulnerable population' requiring careful assessment and possibly requiring specialist services. In 2004, Appleby reported on the progress of the NSF five years on, and demonstrated that little progress had been made. He stated that providing services for people with coexisting issues was 'the most challenging clinical problem that we face' (p 1).

This lack of progress clearly reflects how services struggle to work with coexisting issues. Services are predominantly set up to work with one specific issue, be it mental distress or substance use. Where there are coexisting issues, service users are referred on to other teams to address those issues. This tendency for people with coexisting needs to fall between the cracks and be left to run between services, or to be passed back and forth during differences over the main presenting problem, resulted in the publication of guidance on good practice when working with 'dual diagnosis' (DH 2002). It states:

> Individuals with these dual problems deserve high quality, patient focused and integrated care. *This should be delivered within mental health services.* This policy is referred to as 'mainstreaming'. Patients should not be shunted between different sets of services or put at risk of dropping out of care completely. Unless people with a dual diagnosis are dealt with effectively by mental health and substance misuse services these services as a whole will fail to work effectively. (p 4)

In addition to 'mainstreaming', the guidance called for a definition of 'dual diagnosis' to be agreed between local services, for mapping of local service need, and for improvement of joint planning between mental health and substance use services. It also suggested the appointment of lead clinicians, and that staff training needed to be implemented.

Appleby (2004), however, found that in spite of support from organisations such as the National Institute for Mental Health (England) (NIMHE) to implement changes suggested by the good practice guidance, there was only 'modest' progress. He reported that only 17% of Local Implementation Teams (LITs) had specific strategies in place and that improvements were needed in the planning and commissioning process. He also reported that while assertive outreach teams were often providing support to people with alcohol or other drug problems, they often did so without any training. Appleby made clear recommendations for change, including dedicated services for 'dual diagnosis', better collaboration across mental health and substance use teams, training for mental health staff on substance use, and prevention initiatives targeting people with 'severe mental illness' and those in hospital.

Four years later, the Care Services Improvement Partnership (CSIP) (2008a) undertook a further review of progress on the implementation of the 2002 good practice guidance. CSIP surveyed all mental health LITs in England and received an 80% return rate (n=131). While there had clearly been some improvement since Appleby's (2004) review, 40% still had no local strategy to address coexisting mental health and substance use issues, and while some progress had been made in relation to mainstreaming provision for coexisting issues, only 20% had dual diagnosis leaders or champions.

CSIP also reported that LITs' monitoring of service use and attention to local needs assessment planning was variable and that only 40% collected user feedback on services. Fewer than half of the LITs that responded looked at local training needs, in spite of this being a frequent recommendation in earlier policy documents and reviews, and in spite of the publication of comprehensive guidance on training for staff working with coexisting issues (Hughes 2006). The guidance drew on existing National Occupational Standards in mental health, substance misuse and other fields to bring together one set of competencies for working with people with a dual diagnosis, split into values, knowledge and skills, and practice development.

In its review of, and amendments to, the Care Programme Approach (CPA)[1] (DH 2008b: 22), the Department of Health again reinforced the need for substance use to be taken into account in 'all assessments undertaken by mental health services'. It emphasised the need for routine questions to be put to all service users about their drug use, as well as planning for the management of risk. It once again emphasised the need for local strategies and agreed definitions of dual diagnosis, as well as developing care pathways and service models.

The importance of planning across agencies and departments was reflected in the mental health strategy, *New Horizons: A shared vision for mental health* (HM Government 2009), and in its successor, *No health without mental health* (HM Government 2011c). The latter, in particular, emphasises the importance of partnerships within and across health and social care and also within government departments, as well as partnerships with the community, families and carers. Importantly, the strategy acknowledged the need for services to support people with coexisting substance use and experiencing mental distress (HM Government 2011c: 41):

> Dual diagnosis (coexisting mental health and drug and alcohol problems) covers a wide range of problems. It is important that the appropriate services are available locally in the right settings including the provision of fully integrated care, when this is appropriate, to meet this breadth of need. The Government will continue to actively promote and support improvements in commissioning and service provision for this group, their families and carers.

From the substance use perspective, key policy documents such as the *Models of care for treatment of adult drug misusers: Update 2006* (NTA 2006) and the *Models of care for alcohol misuse* (MoCAM) (DH/NTA 2006)[2] both mention the need to coordinate and plan care where people have mental health issues. However, the national drugs strategy (HM Government 2010a), while acknowledging that the issues overlapped, included little on the need for an integrated or developed service response.

What has emerged is national guidance on working with severe mental distress and substance use (NICE 2011b). *Psychosis with coexisting substance misuse* provides guidelines for assessing and managing these overlapping issues and sets out requirements for each of the professions that may be involved in caring for someone with both issues, including substance use services, mental health services, primary and secondary care. Its key messages appear, once again, to be predicated on close partnership working between service providers as well as client–centred care and involvement of service users and families in assessing need and planning care. It also stresses the importance of good communication and information for service users, ensuring that they take account of those with specific communication needs, for example, those who have sensory or learning disabilities or do not speak English.

What remains to be seen is whether the more recent policy documents have a greater impact than their predecessors on service delivery and joint working. Only if these policy statements, recommendations and guidance are operationalised and monitored will the good intentions expressed within them become a consistent reality and better support the individuals and families living with both issues.

Working with both issues

In spite of the policy emphasis on interagency working and planning, service users and carers have been very critical of services' lack of response to their coexisting issues; in particular, they have been critical of mental health services' inability to engage with substance use (Rethink Dual Diagnosis Research Group 2004; Warfa et al 2006). Lawrence-Jones (2010), in a small study of mental health service users' experiences, also reported a lack of integration between services and that even when someone was receiving input from two services, the services did not talk to each other. Crome et al (2009) cite research that suggests the result is that people do not seek help for one of their coexisting issues. This means that people will have to choose which service to go to or have professionals decide this for them.

However, while integrated response to the needs of service users with coexisting issues appears to be a better way of responding, evidence suggests that integrating teams is not necessarily the solution (Galvani and Forrester 2010). Whether teams are integrated or not, a review of research indicates that the key characteristics of building effective integrated working are strong leadership and an agreed vision, high-quality staff, good communication across professional boundaries and between levels of the organisation, and time to allow integrated services to develop understanding, processes and procedures (Galvani and Forrester 2010).

Donald et al (2005) concur. In a systematic review comparing integrated and non-integrated interventions for people with coexisting problems, they found no clear evidence to support integrated practice as a better way of working. However, partnership working is key and to support this work a number of dual diagnosis professional networks have developed around the UK, for example, in the West Midlands, Croydon and the East Midlands (CSIP 2008b).

Effective partnership working does take time and commitment. Often agencies will have different philosophies and different powers. Banerjee et al (2002) point out that mental health services are able to intervene in a person's life without consent if certain criteria are met. Substance use services cannot. On the contrary, their approaches are usually underpinned by the expectation that the person has some motivation to seek help, be it internal or external motivation. Banerjee et al (2002) state that partnerships require good on-going communication and must seek to understand each other's work. The motivation for overcoming any differences that do occur should be the goal of delivering the best care possible to the service user. Watson et al (2007) state that service managers also have a role to play. They state that commitment is needed from senior management, who also need to establish formal communication channels and ensure role clarity for their team members.

Models for practice

In their review of research and practice, Banerjee et al (2002) highlight three slightly different models of practice within the UK: specialist teams, specialist worker within a team, and a mainstream response. The specialist team is trained to work specifically with people with both issues; the specialist worker works within a more generic team, undertaking direct work and also advising and training staff; and in the mainstream response all team members are trained to a minimal level in good practice with people who are experiencing mental health and substance use issues.

Trippier and Parker (2008) state that the idea of placing an expert within a more general team in order to advise them does not work. They give the example of the complexity of the care coordination role in a mental health team, stating that the specialist nature of the person's knowledge will be subsumed by the wider demands of their role, thus not allowing for the training or 'modelling' part of the role to be fulfilled. They state that a 'critical mass' of trained and knowledgeable staff is needed.

In a similar way, the DH (2002) identified three models of service provision: serial, parallel and integrated. As the terms suggest, the serial model 'implies treatment of one condition before progressing to treatment of the other condition' (DH 2002: 22). Clearly, the disadvantage of this is the potential to overlook the relationship and interaction between the coexisting issues. The parallel model is where a person receives both services at the same time. While this model may result in attention to both issues, it is possible that the two services will be working in different, potentially contradictory ways. However, the DH suggests that where there are good liaison and shared knowledge and skills between specialists this can work well. Finally, the integrated model also offers interventions for both issues concurrently, except that it is offered in one setting and both issues are addressed by the same person.

Banerjee et al (2002: 90) list a number of important characteristics that services can self-assess against in order to determine their readiness to support people with coexisting problems:

- team working
- shared supervision
- range of professional skills, specialist and generic: mental health, drug services, social care, resettlement
- reflective practice that engages with conflict constructively
- flexibility of referral criteria whilst retaining clarity of target group
- communicating effectively with individuals
- communicating effectively with organisations that are unfamiliar with working with people with dual diagnosis
- working with communities so local resources and local problems are understood
- managing expectations of stakeholders
- a clear theoretical basis to the work to which the team can sign up
- clarity about the range of interventions offered
- skills to meet the range of needs that emerge from people with dual diagnosis
- capacity to respond to crises
- coherence and seamless delivery of a range of services.

Hodges et al (2006) sought service users' perspectives on the characteristics of service providers and services, finding that people wanted flexible and consistent services that helped them with more than their 'diagnosis'. People also wanted to be able to access services when they needed them, rather than being placed on a waiting list or being cut off without support once their service involvement had ended. They wanted 'warm, friendly, empowering services usually provided by one individual on a continuous basis', and services that engaged with both substance use and mental health issues not just one or the other (Hodges et al 2006: 4). Both service users and service providers felt that specialist knowledge and workers would be beneficial, as would be specific training and support for staff on working with both issues.

Assessment and risk assessment

When people experience coexisting mental distress and substance use, the chances are high that they have been assessed by various professionals on a number of occasions. The chances that they will have received the services they want or need are not so high, and often people will feel excluded from decisions about their care (Hodges et al 2006), as well as feeling stigmatised and excluded by the labels that their diagnosis places upon them (Rethink Dual Diagnosis Research Group 2004). Indeed, some research shows that either issue alone can result in lower levels of medical care (Mitchell et al 2009).

The values of the professionals and their approach to assessment are therefore vital to building a good relationship with the person, avoiding the replication of previous negative assessment experiences and creating an environment where worker and service user emerge feeling that the experience was positive and helpful. Jargon and medicalisation must be avoided. There needs to be recognition of the person's wider social and cultural needs alongside any healthcare needs (Hodges et al 2006), plus a commitment to accessing resources to meet those additional needs. For example, given Mary's reticence about her alcohol use, using terminology like 'alcoholic', in whatever context, (for example, 'I'm not suggesting you're an alcoholic or anything') and language that has very negative images is likely to damage any chance of engaging with her and exploring her alcohol use further. Similarly, while her ill-health provides a good opportunity to discuss it, sensitive questioning will be needed about her social circumstances, relationship stresses and her possible sense of isolation. Given the positive relationship between people having good social support and their attempts to reduce alcohol or drug use (Dobkin et al 2002, Tracy et al 2005, Copello et al 2006), attention to these issues is just as important as discussing her alcohol use.

One of the values underpinning the assessment process has to be a non-judgemental approach, which can be a challenge for some professionals where people are using substances to problematic levels. The professional has to understand and accept that substance use brings positives, not just negatives, and that these positives need to be acknowledged and explored. Findings from discussions with service users in Scotland showed that their use of substances provided them with short-term gains, making it harder for them to give it up (Hodges et al 2006). However, users also recognised the negative impact of longer-term use on the quality of their lives and their financial circumstances, in particular. Exploring the positives facilitates a more open discussion of the negatives. For Andrew, this discussion about positives and negatives is a good place to start.

Banerjee et al (2002) suggest the following principles for assessment:

- Take time to establish a relationship – good engagement is vital to good assessment.
- Avoid form filling and tick boxes.
- Do not get caught up in seeking to determine which is the primary problem.
- Establish and record the person's view – avoiding disagreements.
- Include strengths-based assessment, for example, previous coping strategies, achievements and motivation.
- Ensure that assessment seeks information from a range of sources:
  (a) because of stigma and understandable reluctance to disclose and
  (b) where the coexisting issues may have affected memory recall or accurate perceptions.
- Consider cultural stereotypes. Watson et al (2007) point out that different cultures can have different views about the origins of mental health issues and these need to be understood.
- Ensure that interpreters are offered where appropriate.

Crawford and Crome (2001) add that it is important to address immediate concerns or needs prior to embarking on an in-depth assessment. Banerjee et al (2002) state that people experiencing mental distress and using substances have higher risks of self-harm, harm to others and neglect. They list a number of risks and factors that people living with coexisting issues are more likely to face (p 3):

- increased likelihood of suicide
- more severe mental health problems [Andrew]
- homelessness and unstable housing [Andrew]
- increased risk of being violent [Andrew]
- increased risk of victimisation
- more contact with the criminal justice system [Andrew]
- family problems [Mary]
- history of childhood abuse (sexual/physical) (particularly among women [Crawford and Crome 2001])

■ more likely to slip through net of care

■ less likely to be compliant with medication and other treatment [Andrew, ?Mary].

In addition risk assessment processes for substance use will include questions about overdose, polydrug use, unsafe injecting, unsafe sex, self-harm and harm to others, including dependent children or adults.

Box 9.4: Assessment of intoxicated people

The Code of Practice for assessing people under the Mental Health Act 1983 addresses the question of whether to assess people who may be intoxicated at the time of the interview or assessment. It states (DH 2008a: 37):

4.55 Where patients are subject to the short-term effects of alcohol or drugs (whether prescribed or self-administered) which make interviewing them difficult, the AMHP[3] should either wait until the effects have abated before interviewing the patient or arrange to return later. If it is not realistic to wait, because of the patient's disturbed behaviour and the urgency of the case, the assessment will have to be based on whatever information the AMHP can obtain from reliable sources. This should be made clear in the AMHP's record of the assessment.

Subsequent assessment for substance use can be split into screening and full or comprehensive assessment. Screening will focus on the substance use alone, whereas a full assessment, akin to comprehensive assessments undertaken by social workers, will focus on four key domains: drug and alcohol use; physical and psychological health; offending and social functioning, followed by goal setting (NTA 2007). In the substance use field this underpins a 'care planning process' that is similar to the care management and care planning process familiar to social workers.

An alcohol screening tool that has been validated for use with people experiencing mental distress and alcohol use is AUDIT (Alcohol Use Disorders Identification Test) (O'Hare et al 2004). Screening instruments for other drug use are not so easy to find. There are many tools available that focus on different drugs or stages in the drug-using process. The guidance offered by NICE (2011b: 8) is to ask the following questions:

■ particular substance(s) used

■ quantity, frequency and pattern of use

- route of administration
- duration of current level of use.

However, seeking this information is only helpful if it is set within the context of the impact that it has on the user's health and well-being. Understanding what, how much and how often means very little, and certainly does not seek to identify the views of or impact on the individual, nor establish their needs.

The Severity of Dependence Scale (SDS) is a brief, five-item questionnaire for assessing dependence rather than lower levels of use (Gossop et al 1995). The professional needs to specify a time-scale prior to asking the questions, for example, 'In the last month/6 months/12 months/...':

- Did you think your use of [named drug] was out of control?
- Did the prospect of missing a fix (or dose) or not chasing make you anxious or worried?
- Did you worry about your use of [named drug]?
- Did you wish you could stop?
- How difficult did you find it to stop, or go without [named drug]?

(Gossop et al 1995: 609)

The SDS has not been validated with people experiencing mental distress, although it is a far better way of seeking the experience of the service user and eliciting their responses. NICE recommends for those delivering secondary mental health care that an assessment should include:

- personal history
- mental, physical and sexual health
- social, family and economic situation
- accommodation, including history of homelessness and stability of current living arrangements
- current and past substance misuse and its impact upon their life, health and response to treatment
- criminal justice history and current status
- personal strengths and weaknesses and readiness to change their substance use and other aspects of their lives.

(NICE 2011b: 19–20)

This holistic approach to assessment will be familiar to most social workers, particularly those working within care management frameworks. Watson et al (2007) suggest focusing assessment on what the service user wants to prioritise. In the spirit of client-centred and empowering assessment, this is a good place to start. Ultimately the goal is to establish the person's needs and then formulate the best package of care possible (Banerjee et al 2002). This may require a joint assessment with specialists from both mental health and substance use services, but in the interim assessment should focus on engaging the person and discussing positives and negatives of their substance use and the extent to which it affects their lives, in particular their mental health. From this point, conversation can develop that is located in the experience of the person, while at the same time demonstrating an empathic response.

Interventions

While there are no one-size-fits-all solutions to working with people with coexisting issues, the importance of engaging them and retaining them in services is paramount, due to their increased vulnerability. Like any other group, those experiencing mental distress and using substances will respond to different people and different approaches and have different intervention needs.

Kvaternik and Grebenc (2009) state: 'The planning of a social work intervention should be based on an operational definition of everyday life, for example, how people live through the day, what are the important and valued roles they play in life, what are their wishes and needs.' While this seems an obvious point, it is often overlooked in favour of 'doing' an intervention with someone rather than its being moulded around their individual needs. Crome et al (2009) concur, stating that the focus of any intervention needs to be on recovery, not on adherence to a particular form of treatment. Further, they point out that change will take time, thus patience and persistence are needed in supporting people as their needs fluctuate.

Empathy is at the core of social work interventions and it is a vital ingredient of interventions working with people who are experiencing mental distress and substance use. The risk of not keeping it central is that the professional will fall into blaming the service user for being 'non-compliant', rather than understanding changing needs and responding to them. Watson et al (2007: 7) state: 'Treatment needs to focus on the "long haul". Services should tolerate and continue to work with service users who have poor attendance records and who do not comply with their medication.' This may be a challenge to some social care systems and structures, and advocacy has an important role to play in supporting people with coexisting issues.

Crome et al (2009) point out the need to adopt a motivational approach. Indeed the most evidence-based intervention with people with alcohol and drug problems is MI and related approaches (see Chapter Three). In the spirit of MI, Banerjee et al (2002) state that what does not work is pushing people into doing something they are reluctant to do; rather, it is important to explore why they are reluctant to do it. Telling Mary and Andrew that they must get help for their substance use or that their substance use is the problem is going to be far less effective than discussing it in a motivational way that results in their deciding to make some changes or to seek advice or help.

Setting realistic and achievable goals with, rather than for, the person is more likely to engender success and motivation, and will evidence that the social worker is concerned about the person rather than imposing their own agenda. At the same time practical and social issues need to be addressed. Given that Andrew is homeless and living in a hostel, this is likely to be the first issue that needs to be addressed. Crawford and Crome (2001) point out that financial, emotional and relationship issues all need to be considered, as these can be a barrier to a person's progress to change.

Warfa et al (2006), in a small study of service users, reported that their impressions of the effectiveness of the service varied, depending on whether the services considered their social and cultural needs. This reinforces the fact that what doesn't appear to help is the focus solely on medical issues. The service users in Hodges et al's (2006) study also wanted support with social contact, requesting access to peer support groups. Further, social support may not necessarily be perceived as family and friends only; it may be that the professional is a key contact of social support for some service users, particularly in the early stages of interventions (MacDonald et al 2004), or for people like Andrew, who does not appear to have family and friends around him.

The Rethink Dual Diagnosis Research Group (2004: 7) reported a number of difficulties that service users faced in getting support, including:

- getting timely and appropriate help
- not being listened to by professionals
- inadequacy of services at first contact
- gaps in services for black and minority ethnic communities
- lack of crisis support
- the impact of 'double' stigma
- lack of continuity of care
- lack of information and understanding of dual diagnosis
- lack of specific services for dual diagnosis carers.

Studies have explored the effectiveness of different approaches to intervention with people experiencing mental distress and using substances. Haddock et al (2003) found evidence that, compared with 'routine' treatment, those who received motivational interventions, cognitive behavioural treatment and family interventions had better outcomes in relation to service use and 'illness'.

Mueser et al (2005) reviewed evidence for a range of individual and group interventions for people with 'severe mental illness and co-occurring substance use disorders'. They also found particular success for individual motivational approaches, and also success for CBT and MI as well as education work in groups.

Particular approaches for younger people and older people with coexisting issues have also been reviewed. Bender et al (2006) reviewed randomised controlled trials of interventions for 'dually diagnosed adolescents'. They found evidence that family behaviour therapy and individual cognitive problem-solving were most effective. D'Agostino et al (2006) evaluated a North American model of working with older people who experienced substance problems and coexisting mental distress, the Geriatric Addictions Program (GAP). The community-based programme included care management, motivational counselling and links to both substance use and geriatric specialist services. The authors found that the combination of addressing physical and psychological problems was more likely to improve outcomes and lead to recovery.

Davidson et al (2008) took a different, more client-centred approach. They reviewed the literature exploring service users' views from the fields of both mental health and substance use. From this they drew up a summative list of core components of recovery and distributed it through advocacy networks for consultation with service user groups. The result was a refined list demonstrating many areas of overlap between the two fields. From this they integrated the responses and developed the Hopscotch Model of Dual Recovery (Figure 9.1).

This model provides a helpful overview of service users' defined needs and goals in their quest for recovery. It also provides clues as to how social workers should respond in combination with the methods or approaches outlined above. In order to help people gain a sense of empowerment, approaches that focus on strengths and motivation are required; to 'assume control', approaches that are truly client-centred need to be adopted.

What is without doubt is that the skills of the social worker to engage with the person will be at the core of successful interventions with service users experiencing coexisting substance use and mental distress. Effective engagement allows professionals to offer support that is meaningful, and not just medically focused but focused on the person in their environment and with a range of needs and desires.

Figure 9.1: Hopscotch Model of Dual Recovery (Davidson et al 2008)

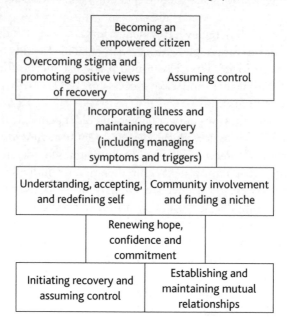

Supporting families and carers

For many people experiencing mental distress, partners and other family members are their primary source of support and yet, many people who use substances to problematic levels can become increasingly isolated from family and friends. When the two experiences are combined it is easy to see how pressures can develop within relationships and how carers and family members need information and support in their own right.

In the current climate of the government's 'Big Society' there has been an increase in policy initiatives focusing on support for carers. The government's mental health strategy (HM Government 2011c) states that family members and carers should also have choices about the support they receive and should be involved in decisions about their loved one's care. The Carers Strategy (HM Government 2008a) and the subsequent updated strategy (HM Government 2010d) signalled overdue recognition of families and carers supporting the needs of their loved ones. Importantly, the two documents reinforced the rights of carers to be involved in decision-making processes, ensuring they and their family have personalised support to allow them to lead a family and personal life and have support to maintain their own physical and mental well-being and to seek education and employment as they wish. While these policy provisions apply to adults, the needs of children whose parents use substances are also a key consideration. Some children and young people may be carers and/or may be at risk of harm through their parent's substance use and mental ill-health (see Chapter Five).

The Rethink Dual Diagnosis Research Group (2004) found that carers often felt that the label of 'dual diagnosis' led to the user's increased dependence on their care, while at the same time reducing their loved one's motivation to take care of themselves. They also identified the following pressures on different aspects of their lives:

- *Financial:* This often included finding money to fund the person's substance use or paying for private treatment in an attempt to get help.
- *Family relationships:* Carers reported the whole family being affected and finding the substance use difficult to cope with.
- *Fear of domestic abuse:* Partner abuse and child abuse is common in relationships where one person has a substance problem (Galvani 2010a) and there is growing evidence of adolescent/adult child to parent abuse also, where the 'child' is using substances (Galvani 2010b).
- *Loss of personal freedom.*
- *Personal impact:* 'stress, powerlessness, anxiety and pessimism for the future' (p 5).
- *Feeling under-valued and under-supported* by services that were often inappropriate, difficult to access and whose quality varied along with the continuity of care (p 6).

Thus, the involvement of family and carers in any assessment and intervention is good practice as well as offering them assessment and support in their own right. Banerjee et al (2002) point out that families can both help and hinder care, so family perspectives must be considered but must not be allowed to become detrimental to the care of the service user. One way to do this is to seek agreement with carers or family members on shared goals and on what support will be provided.

In Mary's situation, there are two key considerations: (a) how is her son affected, and does he need some support? He may also feel responsible in some way for Mary's not being well and this will need to be discussed with him; (b) what role does Mary think her partner can play in supporting her (provided that his drinking is not problematic too), and what is his view about involvement in changes that she decides to make?

Watson et al (2007) suggest the involvement of families and carers must be on-going and not a tokenistic gesture. Richards et al (2009), in their review of family interventions for people experiencing both mental distress and substance problems in forensic services, found evidence to suggest that family interventions benefited family members as well as service users. Further, evidence has been found that using methods such as the five-step method for supporting family members of people with substance problems (Orford et al 2007) can have a positive impact on the substance user, irrespective of whether or not they are in treatment.

Thus, social workers clearly have a role to play not only in supporting service users but also in ensuring that family members and carers are supported and provided with information and help in their own right.

Summary

Coexisting substance use and mental health issues cut cross all areas of social work practice. For some people, one or the other will bring them into contact with health and social services; for others, their substance use may be undetected and their mental health issues may not reach crisis point. Alternatively, they may receive primary care support from their GP with prescriptions for anti-depressants or sleeping pills, but never have contact with specialist mental health services. Social workers will come into contact with a range of people with differing levels of need in relation to these overlapping issues. In an environment of service delivery provided to those at greatest risk, those with lesser levels of need can often be overlooked. Given the additional vulnerabilities that people with these coexisting issues face, advocacy and tenacity on the part of those involved in their care will often be required.

Importantly, effective working with people presenting with both issues is not about addressing first one and then the other or trying to work out which came first. This approach keeps people bouncing between services and does not provide the necessary support. The evidence shows that good communication and partnership working between specialists is required and is more likely to meet the overlapping needs of these service users. Overcoming initial barriers to joint working, and differences in service focus, is essential to providing an informed service. Consider the better experience for a service user of a single initial joint visit that includes a discussion between the two professionals and the service user (and family or carers where appropriate) about the support options, as compared with a series of assessments at different agencies, followed by a number of conversations between different professionals and different combinations of professionals and family or carers and service users, before agreement can be reached on the support plan.

Social workers excel at assessing people holistically within their environment, coordinating care and providing support in many aspects of people's lives. Working with people with coexisting substance problems who are experiencing mental distress presents two main issues where often other issues may be more pressing. However, careful professional assessment will often highlight the issues to be dealt with more immediately. Social workers are used to identifying risk and prioritising interventions. Remaining empathic, listening to service users and meeting a range of practical and social or healthcare needs will be crucial in providing concurrent support for their mental health and substance use needs.

This is a group of people who clearly live with a double dose of stigma, and service provision that still appears to be struggling to respond. Involving service users and carers in decisions about their care is not only good practice but also ensures that they begin to develop a greater sense of self-determination and to regain the control they want over their lives.

Notes

[1] The CPA was introduced to ensure that health and social care services collaborate to provide a programme of care for people experiencing mental distress. It contains four key elements: assessment, care plan, an allocated keyworker and regular review processes.

[2] Under review at the time of writing.

[3] Approved Mental Health Professional (formerly Approved Social Worker). The 2007 amendments to the Mental Health Act 1983 enabled other professionals, in addition to social workers, to be approved under the Act, following the successful completion of appropriate training.

Discussion questions/exercises

1   To what extent do you think terminology is important in the context of working with people with coexisting mental health and substance problems?

2   How would you begin a discussion with Mary and Andrew about their substance use? Presuming that they were willing to talk to you about it, what types of open questions might you ask them?

3   Name four of the principles for assessing people with coexisting substance use and mental health problems.

4   What do service users and carers say is important to them in terms of service delivery?

Further learning resources

■ Banerjee, S., Clancy, C. and Crome, I. (2002) *Co-existing problems of mental disorder and substance misuse (dual diagnosis). An information manual.* Available from www.rcpsych.ac.uk/cru. This is an excellent source of information and case studies, although some of the language is now dated (for example, ASWs as opposed to AMHPs) and it is quite medically oriented in places. However, it provides a wealth of information.

■ Mind – the website of this national charity contains information and resources for people living with mental distress and substance use: www.mind.org.uk/help/diagnoses_and_conditions/addiction_and_dependency.

■ NICE (2011b) *Psychosis with co-existing substance misuse.* The NICE guidance for the assessment and management of people with coexisting mental health and substance problems. While it is largely focused on those in the health professions, it provides some good practice guidance and useful information and links to other resources: www.nice.org.uk/nicemedia/live/13414/53729/53729.pdf.

■ Watson, S., Hawkings, C. and Aram, L. (2007) *Dual diagnosis: good practice handbook.* London: Turning Point. As well as good practice tips, the book contains case studies of agencies, groups and approaches to use with people experiencing mental distress and using substances.

Mind the gap: people with disabilities and substance use

10

Introduction

The move from institutional care to community care that took hold in the UK in the 1980s raised concerns about the increase in the number of potentially vulnerable and/or disabled people exposed to the risks and opportunities of community living. Among these was the concern that substance use, and problematic use in particular, would increase.

Whether these concerns were realised is still to be determined. In 2010, the UKDPC (Beddoes et al 2010) highlighted the gap in research evidence, stating that more information was needed on the 'nature and extent of drug use' among people with disabilities. However, it stated that what evidence was available suggested that substance use by people with a range of disabilities was generally low and that where problematic use was identified it tended to be alcohol use rather than illicit drug use.

In the US, where more research has been conducted, researchers report high levels of substance use among people with disabilities. West et al (2009a) reported consistently high levels of problematic alcohol and illicit drug use – higher than the rates of problematic use in the general population. They drew on evidence across a range of physical and learning disabilities; however, they also pointed out that some research demonstrates that the problematic use of substances 'predates the disabling condition' (p 243), which reinforces the importance of establishing the temporal relationship between the two.

In the UK, people with disabilities who have problems with alcohol and other drugs have undoubtedly been overlooked in research, policy and practice. For many, their substance use brings with it a second dose of exclusion, additional to that which they are already experiencing as a result of their disability. This chapter explores the evidence base, and the practice issues for social workers working with people with disabilities who use substances. It will discuss both physical disabilities and learning disabilities in two separate parts and draw out the similarities and differences between the two in terms of service response.

Definitions

Definitions of disability vary hugely both across research studies and between service providers. Definitions between different countries also emerge. In North American literature, for example, People with Disabilities (PWDs) is a commonly used phrase that includes acquired and congenital physical disabilities as well as mental distress, behavioural problems and developmental and learning difficulties. Other authors focus on 'mental retardation', as distinct from learning difficulties or conduct disorders or mental health problems. In the UK it is different again (Box 10.1).

Box 10.1: Definition of disability

The Equality Act 2010 defines a disabled person as someone who has:

- a physical or mental impairment and the impairment has a substantial and long-term adverse effect on his or her ability to carry out normal day-to-day activities.

(HM Government 2011b: 7)

It goes on to be more specific about the nature of these impairments, as follows:

- sensory impairments, such as those affecting sight or hearing;
- impairments with fluctuating or recurring effects such as rheumatoid arthritis, myalgic encephalitis (ME), chronic fatigue syndrome (CFS), fibromyalgia, depression and epilepsy;
- progressive, such as motor neurone disease, muscular dystrophy, and forms of dementia;
- auto-immune conditions such as systemic lupus erythematosis (SLE);
- organ specific, including respiratory conditions, such as asthma, and cardiovascular diseases, including thrombosis, stroke and heart disease;
- developmental, such as autistic spectrum disorders (ASD), dyslexia and dyspraxia;
- learning disabilities;
- mental health conditions with symptoms such as anxiety, low mood, panic attacks, phobias, or unshared perceptions; eating disorders; bipolar affective disorders; obsessive compulsive disorders; personality disorders; post traumatic stress disorder, and some self-harming behaviour;
- mental illnesses, such as depression and schizophrenia;
- produced by injury to the body, including to the brain.

(HM Government 2011b: 8–9)

This variation in what count as disabilities suggests that the evidence base needs to be carefully considered within its geographical and cultural context. The various definitions used in the evidence base and wider literature make interpreting the limited evidence that exists particularly challenging, and this should be borne in mind in reading this chapter.[1]

Policy framework

In 2011 the Law Commission, as part of a reform of adult social care policy in England and Wales, reviewed Adult Social Care law at the request of the government. The Law Commission's final report contains 75 recommendations on many aspects of adult social care, including assessments (service users' and carers'), adult protection, eligibility criteria and the provision of services (Law Commission 2011). Key proposals include the introduction of a single adult social care statute (rather than the range of policies that currently exist and some of which date back more than 60 years – for example, the National Assistance Act 1948) and the placing of adult safeguarding boards on a statutory footing. At the time of writing, the government proposes to introduce new legislation in spring 2012. Clearly, such changes will affect all adults in need of or in receipt of social care. What remains unclear is whether adults with substance problems will be included.

Much of the debate will centre on definitions of what counts as a need and whether some people are to be excluded where needs are seen to be self-inflicted, as is often the case with substance use. The Equality Act 2010 (HM Government 2010b) defines a disabled person in terms of the adverse effect that their physical or mental impairment has on their ability to carry out daily routine activities. Under this definition, people with chronic problems relating to substance use would qualify.

The key policies underpinning the delivery of services to people with learning disabilities make no mention of alcohol and drug use. The White Paper *Valuing People* (DH 2001b) set out a new vision for people with learning disabilities that focused on rights, independence, choice and inclusion. It set out a plan to ensure that adults and children with learning disabilities had improved choices over participation in employment, education and training. It extended direct payments so as to include people with learning disabilities and pledged to develop advocacy services. Person-centred planning was, it stated, at the core of support and service delivery. Of particular relevance was its promise to support people to develop leisure opportunities and to ensure equality of access to mainstream health services. This was also strengthened in the White Paper's successor, *Valuing People Now: A new three-year strategy for people with learning disabilities* (DH 2009b). The importance of building new relationships of all kinds and increasing independence through choice about services and housing were also key tenets of the policy. In theory, this planned increase in independence and the personalisation agenda could, potentially, impact on the substance use of people who previously had little access. Further, it highlighted additional groups of learning-disabled people who required inclusion in the strategy. These included people with 'complex needs' and 'offenders in custody and the community' (p 9), two groups whose use of substances in the general population is often higher than most.

The key policies in relation to supporting people with physical disabilities are not so easily identifiable. A raft of legislation dating back decades influences service delivery, including the NHS and Community Care Act 1990, the Chronically Sick and Disabled Persons Act 1970, the National Assistance Act 1948 and legislation pertaining to carers such as the Carers (Recognition and Services) Act 1995, the Carers and Disabled Children Act 2000 and the Disabled Persons (Services, Consultation and Representation) Act 1986.

Relevant to both learning and physical disabilities, and to all adult social care service users, was the publication of two policies, *Fair Access to Care Services* (FACS) (DH 2003) and *Putting People First* (HM Government 2007; DH 2010a). The former was designed to ensure that the 'postcode lottery' of service receipt in different parts of the country was minimised and established a single process and set of eligibility criteria for accessing services. *Putting People First* superseded FACS, with the initial 2007 vision statement setting out the intention for an adult's care system based on personalised needs and values that promoted maximising independence. The subsequent eligibility criteria, published in 2010, responded to concerns that only people who met the highest criteria for eligibility under FACS were being provided a service and stated that councils had to consider 'universal services' and 'early intervention and prevention', as well as maximising the control people had over where they spent their allocated funding.

In 2010, the government also published *A Vision for Adult Social Care: Capable communities and active citizens* (DH 2010b), which outlined its intent to focus more on preventing people from needing state health and social care support by doing more to support their carers at home and within the community. It also highlighted the government's intention to move the purchasing of services to a local and individual level by building on the personalisation agenda through the expansion and reinforcement of the direct payments and personal budgets schemes. How this will impact on the support and care of people with alcohol and other drug problems remains to be seen once the vision has been translated into practice. Where someone has both a disability and a substance problem there is less likely to be a debate; however, if the substance problem *is* the disability or 'impairment' it may be viewed differently by both communities and professionals. There is on-going debate among professionals and service users regarding the extent to which people with drug and alcohol problems are provided with individualised budgets and will benefit from the personalisation agenda (Daddow and Broome 2010).

The raft of policy that exists and that does, or could, apply to the care of someone with substance problems and a disability demonstrates the complexity of providing services for people with overlapping needs.

Links between substance use and disabilities

This additional level of complexity stems from the various relationships that can exist between substance use and disabilities. There are five key relationships between the two, as follows:

- *Disabilities stemming directly from substance use*: for example, brain damage as a result of substance use, or loss of a limb due to infected injection sites.
- *Disabilities stemming indirectly from substance use*: for example, accidents that occur while someone is under the influence of substances and result in a disability.
- *Disabilities prior to substance use*: for example, someone who is born deaf or with muscular dystrophy and who chooses to use substances.
- *Substance use as a way of coping with disabilities*: for example, people with mental distress, trauma or physical disabilities whose use of substances serves to temporarily ease difficult feelings and experiences
- *Disabilities stemming from someone else's substance use*: for example, children born with foetal alcohol spectrum disorder (FASD).

The position of substances in each of these relationships is quite different and thus is likely to need a different approach in practice. Establishing the nature of the relationship between the disability and substances, wherever possible, is an important step.

This chapter will now be split into two parts: the first part will provide a brief overview of the evidence base and practice issues in relation to substance use and learning disabilities; to the second part will do the same for physical disabilities.

Part 1 – Learning difficulties or disabilities

Practice example

Jo is a 40-year-old woman with mild learning disabilities. She has been living in her own flat for five years since leaving supported accommodation. Her father lives in the same area and she has some contact with him. During the last seven years her drinking has steadily increased and it appears to have slowly worsened since she moved into independent accommodation. Jo is a sociable person but, as a result of her drinking, she has started to be excluded from a number of community events that she used to attend. She has become more socially isolated and now her circle of friends consists mainly of heavy drinkers. Jo's vulnerability to abuse and exploitation increases when she is drinking. She has accepted that she has needs and the alcohol service is arranging for a detox programme for her, but she does not want follow-up respite care and support; she wants to return to her flat, go on holiday as planned with her father and relatives, and return ready to take on paid work. Jo also suffers from anxiety and possible mental health problems, which are exacerbated when she is withdrawing from alcohol.

Under the governing eye of the National Treatment Agency for Substance Misuse (NTA), services must ensure equality of access. A report by the NTA in 2009 revealed that the area of disability was the least developed in terms of service provision, in comparison to developments around gender and ethnicity. Further, the NTA's interpretation of disability appeared to focus on physical disability and physical access to buildings rather than the accessibility of services and methods of intervention to people with learning difficulties or disabilities.

Box 10.2: Terminology – learning difficulties and learning disabilities

- A 'learning difficulty' generally refers to one of a range of difficulties people can face when processing and learning new information, for example, dyslexia, dyspraxia and attention deficit disorders.
- A 'learning disability' is used most often to describe people who have some organic disability that impairs their intellectual capacity or cognitive functioning. According to the DH (2001b), a learning disability includes: significantly impaired intelligence, impaired social functioning so that a person's ability to cope independently is reduced. Learning disabilities can be developed during pregnancy, for example, in cases

of FASD, or through genetic transmission. Learning disabilities are thought to occur in childhood and have a lasting effect on a person's development, although adults who suffer disability through brain injury might be included under this definition. The lack of clarity about terminology is further complicated by attempts to describe the severity of the learning difficulty or disability, for example, mild, moderate, severe.

Prevalence

Data on the extent of substance use among people with disabilities are limited; however, prevalence is an important consideration in determining policy and practice responses and in monitoring change over time. For learning disabilities and difficulties, a confusing picture emerges.

The UKDPC's (2010) view that the evidence suggests fairly low levels of substance use by people with learning disabilities is supported by the work of Clarke and Wilson (1999) and Cosden (2001). In reviews of the available research evidence, both authors found similar or lower rates of substance problems among people with 'intellectual' or 'learning' disabilities, respectively, as compared to people without learning difficulties.

McGuire et al (2007) studied the 'lifestyle and health behaviours' of people with intellectual disabilities (IQ-based definition) in the West of Ireland. They surveyed 157 carers of people with intellectual disabilities and found that both smoking and alcohol consumption were comparatively low when set against general population data. However, some data pertaining to choice about these behaviours were missing, and the authors therefore suggest caution in interpreting their results.

However, other research has demonstrated higher levels of substance use among people with learning disabilities, although again the difference may be between people with learning disabilities and those with learning difficulties. Cosden (2001) found that among people in treatment for substance problems there was a disproportionately high number of people with learning disabilities [not defined]. Hassiotis et al (2008) also found elevated substance use in a UK-wide survey. In a secondary analysis of data from 8,450 adults living in private households, Hassiotis et al found that approximately 12.3% had 'borderline intelligence' (according to the criteria in the *Diagnostic and statistical manual of mental disorders, 4th edition*) and that they were more likely to be excessive users of substances, particularly alcohol, than those of 'normal' intelligence.

Research in Australia with a sample of 30 adults with 'mild intellectual disability' (not specified) who were involved with the criminal justice system

(McGillivray and Moore 2001) found that 60% were under the influence of substances prior to their offence. The authors state:

> Although interpretation is limited by the small numbers in each offence category, substance use was associated with offending by all the individuals who had been charged with assault, property damage and endangering life and by 75%, 67% and 50% of those charged with sexual assault/rape, burglary and murder, respectively. Substance use was associated with only two of the eight individuals charged with sexual assault against children. (pp 305–6)

The authors found that people with learning disabilities in the criminal justice system had higher rates of substance use than non-offenders, but less knowledge about the impact of alcohol on their behaviour (McGillivray and Moore 2001).

Young people have also been a focus of research in this area. The general trend has been for young people with learning difficulties or disabilities to be at greater risk for problematic substance use and to have greater levels of use than their counterparts without learning difficulties or disabilities. However, much of the research also states that, in spite of these elevated risks and rates of use, their levels of substance use still remain below the national or general population rates (Maag et al 1994).

Molina and Pelham (2001) studied 109 adolescents aged 13–18 with ADHD (attention deficit/hyperactivity disorder) using four different methods of calculating learning disabilities, based on maths and reading tests. They found no statistically significant differences for any substance use variable based on the IQ and academic achievement tests on which learning disabilities were assessed. In fact, the young people with higher IQs were more likely to drink at an earlier age and to use cigarettes

Maag et al (1994) compared 123 pupils with learning disabilities (IQ level only) aged 14 years in North America with a comparison group (n=138). They found no statistically significant differences in alcohol use between the two groups. However, they found that for marijuana and tobacco use, the pupils with learning disabilities scored higher than the comparison group. Thus, there is some indication that substance use could vary by type of substance as well as by severity of learning difficulty/disability. Particular groups of young people showing higher rates of substance use and co-occurring learning difficulties or disabilities include those in the youth justice system (Mallett 2009).

In sum, the prevalence research presents a confusing picture. This is perhaps understandable, given the huge variation in the definitions of disability, the range of needs of the population being studied and the different methodologies used by researchers to 'measure' as well as to define learning difficulties or learning disabilities. Most of this evidence focuses on learning difficulties and suggests that some people, like their counterparts with no learning difficulties, will develop problems. While we await clear research evidence about the scale of the problem, however, it is important to ensure that social work practice is able to identify and respond to substance use issues and to do so at the earliest opportunity.

Impact of substance use

The evidence is clearer about the potential negative impact of substance use on people with learning disabilities than it is about any benefits of substance use. Following a review of the literature on substance use and learning disabilities ('a clinically significant learning disability (or mental retardation)'), Huxley et al (2005) drew up a list of potential negative impacts:

- Cognitive deficits associated with substance misuse which mask the individual's real ability level, leading to inappropriate work placements, accommodation and even health services
- The associated physical and psychiatric difficulties associated with substance misuse
- Exclusion from services due to behavioural problems
- Exacerbation of existing impairments
- Experience of additional marginalization and exclusion
- Experiencing greater barriers to accessing services
- Greater risk of experiencing unemployment, poverty and crime.

(Huxley et al 2005: 15)

For young people in particular, research suggests that there are also higher levels of dropout from school, lower academic achievements and higher rates of engagement in sexual activity at a young age, among people with a range of disabilities (Hollar and Moore 2004).

As with Huxley et al's (2005) findings, the potential for increased risks was also highlighted by Cosden (2001) in a review of the literature on substance-using adolescents with learning disabilities (not defined). Cosden (2001: 355) drew up a table of possible risk and protective factors for substance use (Table 10.1).

Many of these risk factors will overlap. Low self-esteem can lead to lower confidence in self-determination and/or acceptance of company and friendship when it is offered without the internal vetting process of the individuals concerned. This clearly overlaps with poor peer relationships and a lack of positive social support. One extreme example is the tragic case of Raymond Atherton, a 40-year-old man who was tortured and murdered by two teenagers in 2007. Raymond had a long-standing alcohol problem and a learning disability and was taken advantage of by people who 'abused his kind, gentle nature and exploited his vulnerability' (Carter 2007). Although he was in touch with social services because of his learning disability, he was not able to remember the names of his abusers, nor was he willing to report their attacks and abuse to the police (Carter 2007). Subsequent reports of people with learning disabilities being abused by friends, housemates or professionals have increasingly come to light in the media and are highlighted by charitable organisations campaigning for better rights and recognition of people with learning disabilities (Brindle 2011; Mencap 2011). While this type of abuse occurs without people experiencing alcohol or other drug problems, the additional vulnerability that problematic substance use poses can increase the risks.

Table 10.1: Possible risk and protective factors for substance use

Risk/protective factors	Special considerations
Low self-esteem	Poor understanding of strengths and weaknesses associated with LD [learning disability] may hamper self-esteem
Poor peer relationships	Impulsiveness and inability to read social cues may interfere with the development of sober peer relationships
Depression	Depressed affect may be associated with real losses not cognitive distortions
Social support	Prolonged period of dependence may result in greater need for social support and mentorship
Hyperactivity	Neurological factors may affect aforementioned problems

While the negative impact of substance use needs to be identified and recognised in policy and practice, Snow et al (2001: 270) point out the importance of also understanding the benefits of substance use to people with learning disabilities or difficulties. They call for a better understanding of the harms and benefits to young people with disabilities and for a distinction between harms from the substance use itself and harms stemming from the people in their environments.

Ultimately, understanding the harms and benefits facing a vulnerable person should be part of a skilled assessment of their needs. In the practice example, Jo's socialising is positive and has involved drinking alcohol; however, the level of her use appears to be creating problems. Discussions with Jo therefore need to look at the positives and negatives of her use, set in the context of the life-style she would like to lead and the people she would like in her life.

Role of the social worker in practice

What commentators agree on is the importance of social work, health and other social care staff adopting a number of roles in relation to supporting people with learning disabilities who use substances.

Education and prevention

Among these roles is prevention and awareness-raising through provision of appropriate education about substance use and its risks, in a form that is clear and understandable for people with different levels of learning disability. A number of studies identified that knowledge and awareness of substance use was limited among people with learning disabilities, particularly those in hospital and community settings, and that education and support were important factors in supporting them (McCusker et al 1993; Jobling and Cuskelly 2006). A study by McCusker et al (1993) found that people with learning disabilities felt that it was embarrassing to refuse a drink when offered and they were more susceptible to pressures to drink, as compared to other groups. However, following an education programme that combined more traditional teaching methods with practical visits to the pub and role play, the group's knowledge and awareness improved, although it was not known whether this led to changes in alcohol consumption. Another study suggests that knowledge and awareness do not necessarily lead to changes in drinking. Following a survey of 122 people with 'mental retardation' from community agencies, McGillicuddy and Blane (1999) also found that those who had substance problems had 'poorer refusal skills' than those without problems who used. They also ran an education programme that enhanced refusal skills, assertiveness and other related skills. However, their study showed that the programme did not have an impact on the level of substance use or the group's attitudes to it.

For young people in particular, Hollar and Moore (2004: 933–4) state that education programmes should also target the unique risk factors faced by young people with learning disabilities, including 'isolation, discrimination, lack of personal adjustment to disability, health difficulties, pain, lack of social access, easier access to prescription drugs, and perceived entitlement to substance use based upon their disability'. Snow et al (2001) reviewed drug education issues for young people with special developmental needs and also found such elevated risks as were identified by Cosden and Hollar and Moore. However, they also highlighted evidence of 'sensation seeking behaviours' as an additional concern. They stated that for some people with learning disabilities there were 'fewer opportunities to engage in experiences likely to develop resilience' because of the 'emotional, communicative and behavioural challenges' they faced (Snow et al 2001: 267). They also stated that professionals and carers considered education about alcohol and drugs as a low priority for these young people because of their particular needs.

Thus, the role of education is important not only in enhancing people's knowledge of substances but also in supporting them to negotiate the environment of the pub or substance-using context as well as the people within it. It is also important in terms of educating professionals, parents and carers about alcohol and drug use. What these studies also suggest is that on-going work may be necessary to monitor and reinforce the messages learned and to determine what additional work can be done to reduce actual use where necessary, rather than simply enhance knowledge and awareness alone. Education may include media such as audio, or visual resources such as CDs, DVDs or websites.

In the practice example it is possible that Jo has received information on alcohol and its effects, or it may have been assumed that she doesn't need it. Either way, having a discussion with her about her use and what she gets from it can also include a discussion of some factual information about the risks of substance use and how others may have taken advantage of her when she is intoxicated. As the evidence suggests, this may need repeating at intervals, and others in Jo's social and community network, where appropriate, could assist in this. Furthermore, educating Jo about what to expect in the detoxification process will be important, as will be education about relapse and ensuring that she has information or support for how to avoid it. Given her hoped-for involvement with her father and family, it may also be worth having a family discussion, in conjunction with a substance specialist, about how they can support her, particularly on holiday and afterwards.

Identification

One of the key challenges identified in the literature is determining whether any cognitive and behavioural changes are a) a result of the impact of the substance use, b) related to the individual's personality or choices about how to behave or c) a manifestation of their learning disability or difficulty (Fox and Forbing 1991). This highlights the importance of ensuring that assessment processes adequately explore these various possibilities and that positive and supportive therapeutic relationships are established in order to allow this exploration to happen.

Asking routine questions about substance use in a manner that is appropriate to the communication skills of the service user is absolutely vital. For people who are not able to read or to read well, this means that questions about alcohol and other drugs or information about them need to be presented in a range of ways, including through easy-to-read/see leaflets containing pictures or symbols as well as words.

Working in partnership with substance use agencies will also be mutually beneficial in terms of exchanging expertise and supporting each other to work with people who have both a learning disability and problematic substance use. Substance use specialists can contribute the types of questions an assessment could ask, while learning disability specialists can contribute the expertise in how the questions could be asked and what types of responses or interventions are likely to work best. These will clearly be individually determined. There is currently a lack of tools to help professionals assess and intervene in substance use where someone has a learning disability. There is also a lack of information for people with learning disabilities about alcohol and other drugs.

Negotiating specialist service access

Advocating for access to substance use services is another role that social workers may need to adopt – or at least, advocacy for partnership working. The literature suggests that substance use services are ill prepared for working with people with learning disabilities, and social work services appear ill prepared for working with substance use (Slayter 2007, 2008; Taggart et al 2008; Galvani et al 2011). Taggart et al (2008) state that people are falling into the gap between the two services because of a lack of integration. A partnership approach is the obvious solution to overcoming this mutual ignorance.

Evidence from research with professionals shows that currently people with learning disabilities are more likely to present to learning disability services about their substance problem than to substance use services (McLaughlin et al 2007; Taggart et al 2007; Slayter and Steenrod 2009). In a recent survey in England social care practitioners working with people with learning disabilities reported feeling isolated and left to work alone with substance problems because alcohol and other drug services were not trained to work with people with learning difficulties (Galvani et al 2011). Both surveys found that the professionals lacked education for working with the needs of this group of people, and McLaughlin et al also found a lack of policies to guide any collaborative work.

There are a number of barriers to people's accessing substance use services. Campbell et al (1994 cited in Simpson 1998) identified five obstacles to people with 'learning differences' accessing services:

1. Given that many therapeutic approaches require some insight and reflective ability in the person with the substance problem, services will need to adapt to the lower levels of insight that are possible among people with learning disabilities.
2. Group therapies may not be beneficial if some people lack the social skills required for group work.
3. Discussions focusing on making different choices about their life-styles may not be the reality for people with learning disabilities. They may have fewer choices, due, for example, to their lesser academic ability or financial dependence on others.
4. Substance use professionals are not educated about interventions for people with learning disabilities and, if they do offer a service, they may base interventions on stereotypes.
5. There is a lack of joint working between learning disability and substance use services.

West et al (2009b: 299), in a small study of UK drug services (n=23), found that none of them had information in alternative formats that would suit the learning needs of people with 'varying degrees of cognitive ability'. It is clear that learning disability services and drug services need to work more closely together to support their own professional development and, importantly, the needs of people with learning disabilities and substance use problems.

In another small-scale study in Northern Ireland, Taggart et al (2007) interviewed 10 people (7 females, 3 males) with 'an intellectual disability and substance disorder' as defined by DSM-IV criteria. Nine had borderline/mild learning disabilities, the remaining person had a 'moderate' learning disability. Seven of the participants who had previously been referred to mainstream substance use services found it to be a negative experience and some found the group work particularly off-putting. They also reported that their reasons for use included a response to trauma, loss and violent or abusive experiences and social isolation within their community. Taggart et al reported that bullying and exploitation in childhood and adulthood was common. In spite of their reasons for using, the survey participants had only been offered advice and leaflets by their GPs and been told to reduce their drinking. No other services had been offered.

In a consultation report from Northern Ireland relating to its 2005 Alcohol and Substance Misuse Strategy, recommendations were included that sought to ensure that people with learning disabilities had equal access to services and health promotion (Taggart et al 2008). The recommendations included equal access, collaboration between learning disability and substance use services via a 'link expert', development of screening tools, the availability of appropriate interventions, school-based health promotion, establishing a specialist interest group for planning and evaluating practice and consideration of the effort needed to support people living independently (Taggart et al 2008: 19).

Thus, for Jo, the fact that she has accepted that she needs help and is willing to undergo detoxification is positive. However, it is likely that the specialist services will need support for how best to work with her, her communication needs, and tips and techniques for on-going work with her. Not providing this support runs the risk of Jo not liking or wanting the service, and the service providing a lesser service to her. Further, the service should be asked to involve and educate her family members, where it has her permission to do so. The whole experience for Jo and for the two sets of professionals involved is likely to be a far more positive and informed one where the professionals are helping each other out as well as supporting Jo.

Intervention

There is a dearth of evidence about 'what works' for people with learning disabilities who have substance problems. Interventions that work with people with substance problems who do not have learning disabilities contain a number of key elements, including positive social support, non-judgemental feedback and advice on the person's substance use, and a motivational and/or cognitive behavioural component (see Chapters Two and Three). It is possible that the cognitive behavioural element will not work for some people with learning difficulties, but it is likely that, for the other types of intervention, the same elements will work. They will need to be communicated appropriately, that is not just verbally, and may need repeating.

Taggart et al (2008: 17) summarises a number of interventions for people with learning disabilities and substance problems that combine biological, psychological and social components:

- Detoxification ensuring client safety (from, for example, seizure risk and risk of suicide), deterioration of mental health and management of withdrawal symptoms
- Use of psychopharmacology treatments (antabuse, naltrexone, methadone and serotonin specific re-uptake inhibitors (SSRIs))
- Individual education (including anger management, relaxation training, challenging negative statements)
- Modifications of AA & Twelve Step Programme

- Use of group therapy (including art therapy) to promote feelings of acceptance, belonging and peer support
- Use of social skills training (eg develop coping and refusal skills, self-monitoring skills, promote interpersonal communication, facilitate expression of emotions, respond appropriately to criticism, engage in realistic role plays)
- Behavioural and cognitive approaches (for example assertiveness skills, distinguishing between positive and negative role models in substance abuse situations)
- Motivational interviewing
- Relapse prevention programmes focusing on self-regulation of thinking and feeling, accepting past relapses, identifying the causes of relapse and learning to prevent and interrupt relapses
- Mainstream addiction and learning disability staff education on preventative programmes, identification of intra-personal and interpersonal risk factors, promoting early recognising/ screening and prompt referral
- Promotion of social support including family, friends, neighbours, social support groups, education, recreational opportunities and employment
- Environmental/milieu therapies such as diversional activities, learning new hobbies and developing new friendships.

As with interventions for people without learning disabilities, the therapeutic relationship is vital for an effective intervention. Focusing on engagement with the person is key and may at times require greater effort than usual from the professional where the person's social skills and behaviour impact on their ability to form relationships (Cosden 2001).

Snow et al (2001) and Huxley et al (2005) point out that some individuals with learning disabilities will not be able to absorb and process information in the way that substance use services require people to do. Snow et al suggest that 'language based support' may not be the most appropriate support and that professionals should not expect that learning in one context will be applied to another, as this is not always the case. This means that the approach to giving and discussing information needs to be adapted accordingly, perhaps adopting a clearer, more directive approach. Huxley et al also suggest that some people may not have the ability to comply with medication regimes and treatment times because of their particular disability. Seeking ways around this, including outreach work or the involvement of supportive others, may need to be considered so as to avoid people being considered obstructive or non-compliant when in actual fact the problem arises from the failure of the service to understand how best to work with an individual's needs.

In sum, people with learning disabilities who experience substance problems are as diverse in their needs as those who do not have substance problems. However, the extent of their disability needs to be considered in determining how to intervene in relation to the substance use, and appropriate support strategies developed accordingly.

Good practice

There is limited evidence of what constitutes good practice, as this is an area of practice that is as yet under-recognised and underdeveloped. In Taggart et al's (2007) study with service users, the users wanted future services to be individual rather than group focused and to support them to build more social activities or networks and involve their families in care packages. They also wanted opportunities for employment or education during day. This wish for more activities and employment is reflected in Jo's wishes in the practice example. It is also part of relapse prevention, as outlined in Chapter Two.

Drawing from the evidence available, some key messages for practice include:

1. Keep main messages clear but not patronising, and easy to assimilate (UKDPC 2010).
2. Communicate messages in a manner and through a medium that is appropriate to the user's level of communication, including visual means (Snow et al 2001; UKDPC 2010).
3. Repeat the key messages at intervals (Huxley et al 2005).
4. Focus on motivating people to change rather than telling them to stop (Taggart et al 2007).
5. Ensure close working with substance use professionals to facilitate mutual understanding and to maximise the best support possible for the person concerned (Huxley et al 2005; Slayter 2007).
6. Establish whether other medications are being taken alongside any alcohol or other drug use and assess the risks this may pose (Slayter and Steenrod 2009).
7. Marshal positive social support from those around the person (Clarke and Wilson 1999).
8. Ensure that attention is paid to developing skills and confidence in other aspects of the person's life that will support them to change their substance use, for example, assertiveness skills, finding new activities or friendship networks (Cosden 2001).

9. Provide practical support to the individual and offer practical advice to colleagues from substance use services, for example, scheduling appointments at particular times.
10. Provide some educational work for parents, carers or other professionals to ensure individuals are supported appropriately.
11. Determine whether family members or carers have any support needs in their own right in relation to their substance use and whether this poses any risk to the individual (Cosden 2001).
12. It will also be important to assess the impact of the person's substance use on family members or carers and to gather information about the nature, frequency and context of the individual's substance use from family members and close friends, as well as its impact on any employment or other activities (Slayter and Steenrod 2009).

Huxley et al (2005) state that integrated service provision, alongside adequate training, is vital in order to provide a needs-based service that is likely to require intensive one-to-one working rather than, for example, a weekly group. They suggest that the lead responsibility should remain with learning disability services, but ideally with substance use specialists on the staff.

> **Box 10.3: Keeping language clear**
>
> A key resource for people with learning disabilities in terms of translating existing literature or information on alcohol and drugs into clearer language is Mencap's (2000) *Am I making myself clear? Mencap's guidelines for accessible writing*.
>
> It contains clear guidance, with examples of bad practice followed by examples of good practice. It is downloadable at: www.mencap.org.uk.

Practice challenges

Balancing rights and responsibilities is the bread and butter of social work practice. Concepts of normalisation and efforts to maximise individual autonomy for people with learning disabilities will clash with organisational cultures that err on the side of caution and focus primarily on protection (Manthorpe et al 1997; Slayter 2007). Manthorpe et al (1997) point out that alcohol and other drug consumption may be an important social activity for people whose disability means that they may be more socially isolated. Thus while ensuring that problematic substance use is identified and addressed appropriately, it is all important to ensure people are not prohibited from their choice to use substances, if they wish to do so.

Slayter (2007: 652) concurs, stating: 'If social workers are to strive for the development of self-determination among their clients, then they need assistance in answering questions about how people with MR [mental retardation] can best be supported in balancing the risks and consequences associated with SA [substance abuse]'. Slayter (2007: 656) suggests that social workers ask themselves five questions in relation to the substance use of people with 'mental retardation':

- Is the person in question able to make informed decisions about substance use and SA?
- Does a family member or guardian ad litem hold a health proxy for this client?
- Who or what might influence this person's decision making around areas of risk?
- What settings and approaches are most conducive to learning for this person?
- How can this person be best engaged to consider these issues in a meaningful way for themselves?

In Jo's situation, she has accepted help but is clear that she wants neither respite nor follow-up support. These decisions have to be respected because she has capacity to make them. However, involving her father in discussions, given his importance to her, may provide leverage for her to accept support post-detoxification, as may talking to her about whether she thinks her drinking friends are likely to support her cessation of drinking.

What is important is that people with learning disabilities are given the education and information on alcohol and other drugs that will prepare them as much as possible for the consequences of that choice. As Manthorpe et al (1997: 76) state, 'Issues of judgment will always intrude if normalisation is being put into practice.'

Simpson (1998) goes further, stating that it is important to also explore whether or not the majority of people with learning difficulties who do not use alcohol is a problem. In other words, are carers or family members actively excluding people from alcohol consumption or are societal myths and stereotypes preventing people with learning disabilities from drinking – a behaviour that is a cultural norm for a large part of society. He is also critical of the assumptions inherent in the literature that learning disabilities are associated with anti-social behaviour and that people with learning difficulties are more likely to develop alcohol problems as a result.

In sum, Part 1 has explored the overlapping issues of learning disability or learning difficulty and substance use. The flaws and gaps in the evidence base are unhelpful for defining good practice in this area. However, enough literature exists to draw out key messages for practice. As with any relationship between service user and social care professional, good communication is fundamental to engagement and building a therapeutic relationship. For people with learning disabilities and learning difficulties, this may require communication other than verbal communication as well as a willingness to inform and educate other professionals about appropriate communication skills. While many of the broad principles of good practice apply to anyone with disabilities and substance problems, Part 2 will now explore the evidence relating to people with physical disabilities.

Part 2 – Physical disabilities

Practice examples

1. John (48)

John has been unemployed for more than 10 years, since leaving his job as an engineer. He is divorced and lives alone in a flat in the centre of town. He has lost most of his sight over recent years and consumes dangerous levels of alcohol – usually vodka. He has had eye surgery during the same period, but this has repeatedly failed. John's existence is an isolated one. He has no contact with his family and the few people around him appear torn between supporting him and exploiting his disability benefits, consequentially having higher levels of benefits to shore up their own habits. One of John's 'friends' once hit him, in an attempt to bully funds from him. His home is in a complete mess, with rubbish bags lying around the flat. The only service he receives is from a local housing official, who has helped with rubbish clearances. John has considerable debts that have built up over the years. Previous attempts to put in home care have failed, due to a variety factors – not least of all, health and safety. John shows signs of developing mental illness associated with prolonged drinking. He understands that alcohol is a main cause of his present condition, but doesn't have sufficient eyesight to get to the local treatment and structured day care service. He is therefore dependent on friends to assist him with this – yet it seems unlikely, given their conflicting interests. He has previously asked for in-patient detoxification.

2. Nancy (27)

Nancy has Huntingdon's Disease. She has used speed (amphetamine) for many years. Her long-term drug use has primarily resulted in her living in poverty and having few real friends. Because her condition is hereditary, she has seen its effects on other family members. Nancy says that using speed helps her to control aspects of her disability. However, her speed use is not constant and is more characteristic of a binge pattern. As is the case with many stimulant users, her relationship with the local drug treatment service has been fleeting. There is no input from social services. Nancy has debts with everyone – especially local dealers, who live just doors away. She is currently looking after a dealer's dog while he is in prison. Lately, it has been noticed that her health has taken a turn for the worse and her GP is concerned for her. However, services are unwilling to enter the property because it is risky, due to dog faeces and concerns about needles. Nancy is seeking an in-patient detoxification and professionals are concentrating on keeping her alive until this happens and planning for her aftercare following the detox. Nancy faces a bleak future, with the prospect of deteriorating physical and cognitive ability.

Prevalence

As with learning difficulties, the research evidence on the prevalence of substance use among people with physical disabilities is limited. However, contrary to the findings of the UKDPC's (2010) review of evidence, findings from the British Crime Survey of England and Wales found higher rates of substance use among people with disabilities. The survey records illicit drug use among people aged 16–59 years and collects data on whether or not someone has a 'longstanding illness or disability' that 'limits activities'. Some caution is needed in interpreting the findings, as survey respondents self-report and self-define whether or not this definition applies to them, and it therefore covers a potentially huge range of illnesses and disabilities. In spite of these limitations, the use of substances among people with disabilities was significantly higher than among those without disabilities, particularly in relation to polydrug use (Hoare and Moon 2010).

North American data are also very clear that people with disabilities have far higher rates of substance use and are more at risk of developing problematic use than are people without disabilities. In a North American study of almost 2,000 men by Turner et al (2006), they found a clear relationship between physical disability and lifetime occurrence of psychiatric and substance use problems, particularly among younger Hispanic men. Figures up to twice the rate for the general population have been cited (Krahn et al 2006).

Studies focusing on specific disabilities have found higher risks of substance use among participants.

Hearing impairments

Brunnberg et al (2008) focused on 15- to 16-year-olds with combined hearing loss and tinnitus, finding that those with both hearing problems were at comparatively higher risk of developing substance problems that those with either tinnitus or hearing loss or students with no hearing impairments. Titus and White (2008: 16) also focused on young people with hearing loss. They highlighted particular factors that were specific to these young people in comparison with those with no hearing loss:

1. lower age of onset of substance use
2. greater substance problem severity (dependence and withdrawal)
3. higher rates and greater severity of childhood victimisation
4. higher rates of co-occurring psychological problems (depression, traumatic stress, conduct problems)
5. social networks more dominated by substance users
6. greater likelihood of running away from home in the past or being homeless.

Traumatic Brain Injury (TBI)

Taylor et al (2003) found that pre-injury substance use was high among people with TBI; in particular high blood alcohol levels (BALs) were common among those involved in vehicle accidents or assaults or whose injuries were self-inflicted. Those who were intoxicated at the time of their injury also had less-positive outcomes in terms of neurological improvement, as well as complications resulting in longer hospital stays and other more negative outcomes. The authors point out that there is not the same evidence base on which to make any firm conclusions about illicit drug use preceding injury. After injury, however, the research literature suggests substance use declines, with some alcohol use increasing as time elapses post-injury (Taylor et al 2003). Perhaps unsurprisingly, those with fewer impairments resulting from the TBI were more likely to drink post-injury.

Additional risk factors

Violence and abuse

Research has also found important relationships between disability, substance use and being a victim of violence and abuse (Li et al 2000: Wolf-Branigin 2007). In a study of 1,876 people with disabilities (including people with physical and learning disabilities, mental health problems and substance problems), Li et al (2000) found that women with disabilities in particular were at higher risk of receiving substance-related violence than men or women without disabilities. Particular types of health problems were significantly associated with being a victim of substance-related violence, including disability onset, multiple disabilities and chronic pain.

Li et al also found that victims of violence were more likely than non-victims to have their own substance abuse problems. This was supported by the research of Wolf-Branigin (2007), who found that people with substance problems and a disability (defined as receiving disability benefits) were more likely to be victims of physical abuse and domestic violence, as compared to their non-disabled peers.

In the practice examples, John has already been subjected to violence and bullying. With Nancy's deteriorating disability increasing her vulnerability, violence and abuse are a risk for her too. What is positive for both of them is that, in spite of their multiple problems, they appear to have some willingness to receive help, which, if acted upon, may offer a way out of the negative social networks that they appear to be involved in at present.

Ethnicity

In an American study focusing on ethnic differences among people with disabilities and who drank alcohol, Sample et al (1997) found that specific disabilities were significantly related to alcohol problems. For Caucasians, they found a relationship between alcohol consumption and disability onset, multiple disability, acceptance of disability and 'entitlement to drink' attitudes. They also found that older African-American men and those who had lower levels of education were more likely than their Caucasian counterparts to drink more often.

A later study on lifetime and one-year prevalence of mental health problems (including substance use) among those with physical disabilities across age, gender and ethnicity also found an association between having a physical disability and an increased risk of substance use (Turner et al 2006). Unlike Sample et al (1997) above, Turner et al found higher levels of risk among Hispanic-heritage rather than African-Americans or non-Hispanic whites, and among younger rather than older men.

These American-based studies have limited application to the UK; however, they demonstrate the complexity of the potential relationships between substance use, ethnicity, age and disability.

Reasons for substance use

Disabled people were also the focus of one of the UKDPC's explorations of diversity in drug use (Beddoes et al 2010). In its review of the literature, a number of disabilities were searched for, including physical and learning difficulties but not mental ill-health. The review identified a number of factors that were believed to increase drug use among disabled people, including:

- *'Isolation' and 'exclusion'*: It suggests that the possible lack of participation in mainstream activities may lead to drug use as a coping mechanism for the isolation and frustration they feel, particularly if they are bullied too. This is particularly relevant for John who appears to have become increasingly isolated since he became unemployed and as his sight has deteriorated. It is possible that this is the case for Nancy too.
- *'Social pressure'*: to fit in with non-disabled peers.
- *'Mental health problems and poverty'*: both of which are associated with problematic drug use in the wider population. From the information we have about John, he is suffering from mental health problems and these may pre-date his increasing alcohol use. For both John and Nancy the implication is that their problematic substance use has left them living in poverty although some of this may be due to being financially abused by those around them.
- *'Communication difficulties and lack of accessible information'* potentially make it more difficult for people to seek help. John may not have been able to access information on alcohol or services that he can read, particularly if he doesn't read Braille. Nancy has clearly had some information as a result of her contact with services, but may feel that it is not as relevant to her as it could be, given her medical condition.
- *'Self-medication'*, for example, cannabis use to relieve pain. Nancy states that she is using substances to cope with various symptoms of her Huntingdon's Disease, although the information suggests that her use may pre-date the physical symptoms of

Huntingdon's. However, it may have helped her (and still be helping her) to cope with the emotional and psychological fears relating to her condition.
(Beddoes et al 2010: 2)

This recognition of the additional stress that may contribute towards the substance use of people with disabilities is not new. Boros (1989 in Helwig and Holicky 1994) identified a number of stress factors in addition to those identified above, including difficulties adjusting to their disability, boredom, easy access to prescription drugs, double stigma (substance use and their disability) and low self-esteem resulting from both the physical disability and the substance use.

Accessing services

The evidence about barriers to people with disabilities accessing substance use services is unequivocal. In spite of a higher need for services, entry to treatment is restricted (Krahn et al 2007). People with disabilities have to deal with:

- significantly lower chances of accessing residential and out-patient care, as compared to those without a disability (Wolf-Branigin 2007)
- services that present physical access barriers (West 2007; West et al 2009b)
- lack of resources for people with sensory impairments (West 2007)
- services declined for people with 'developmental disabilities' (West et al 2009a, b) or learning disabilities
- lack of support from their 'social environment' (Krahn et al 2006: 383)
- stigmatisation, and negative attitudes towards people with disabilities on the part of professionals (Krahn et al 2006).

Moore et al (2009) summarised the literature about barriers to accessing services for deaf people and found that services were unprepared for working with deaf people and some of the methods used within services, for example, group therapy, were too difficult for deaf people. They too found that key concepts used in substance treatment were not in the 'deaf lexicon' and could not easily be translated. They also reported that self-help was 'largely missing' for deaf people and that, as the deaf community was quite small, confidentiality was an issue. Alexander et al (2005) found that there were many items on alcohol assessment tools that some services use, for example the CAGE and AUDIT screening tools, that deaf people did not understand. They suggested that these tools would not be accurate or appropriate for deaf people.

Practical issues also need to be addressed. For example, West et al (2009b), in a study of 23 UK drug agencies, found that 15 (65%) did not have fire alarms with visual as well as auditory alarms. West (2007) points out that the widespread lack of services accessible to people with disabilities may be a factor in the low numbers attending services. In their study of 23 UK services, West et al (2009b) found that 16 (65%) had no accessible parking spaces, 6 (40%) did not have a ramp or lift to gain access to the building, 19 (83%) did not have automatic or power-assisted doors. They also found that, among those providing residential care, most (11/13) did not have accessible baths or showers. In comparison to similar surveys in the US and Canada, West et al (2009b) concluded that the UK sample were far worse in terms of service adaptations to people with disabilities

Krahn et al (2006) found that those with disabilities who were in treatment tended to be slightly older in age, suggesting that it might have taken them longer to find a service that catered for them. Indeed Krahn et al (2007) found that people with disabilities do just as well as their non-disabled counterparts in terms of treatment outcomes once they have been able to access a service.

Policy and practice implications

While the evidence base on what services are providing and how they are responding to people with a range of disabilities is limited, it is apparent that many drug and alcohol services are not meeting the needs of people with disabilities. The UKDPC suggests that the solution is two-fold: to ensure that disability services and those working in them are better equipped to respond to substance use, and to ensure that drug services are better equipped to respond to people with disabilities (Beddoes et al 2010: 3).

The literature is clear. First, staff in both disability services and substance use services need the professional training to ensure that they can recognise and respond appropriately to each issue, as well as overcome any attitudinal and/or ignorance barriers at an individual professional level (Helwig and Holicky 1994; NIAAA 2005; Krahn et al 2006). Second, those providing services at commissioning and operational levels need to be sensitive to the needs of people with disabilities and take steps to ensure that disability needs can be met and that their services are accessible to all (Krahn et al 2006).

However, as Krahn et al state, it is not just about substance use services improving their accessibility; social workers and social care staff specialising in disability services also have work to do, coordinating services from a range of professionals and supporting wider recognition of the needs of people with disabilities and substance problems:

> Provider sensitivity to treatment barriers (political, attitudinal, or physical) is crucial while devising evaluations and individual treatment plans. Leaders in the disability community have a role to play in informing their members about SA [substance abuse] and treatment, advocating for clean and sober accessible housing, and supporting training for PWDs [people with disabilities] and personal assistants to recognize and address SA. (Krahn et al 2006: 383)

The reality on the front line for service users like John and Nancy is that partnership working is likely to provide a far better and more holistic service. Sharing the care and support that John and Nancy need both in relation to their substance use and also for their practical living arrangements and financial difficulties will feel far more manageable where professionals are working together than for one professional alone. It will also provide for more informed interventions and some mutual professional support in what are clearly difficult living situations for John and Nancy.

Moore (1998) provided guidance for substance use services on how to improve services for people with disabilities; however, much is also relevant to social work and social care staff working with them. The following suggestions for good practice have been adapted from Moore (1998):

- Provide information on alcohol and drugs or service in a range of media suited to those with a range of disabilities.
- Meet with the person alone wherever possible so as to get their view, prior to meeting with those who care for or work with them.
- Do not focus immediately on their disability – adopt a strengths-based approach.
- Plan substance use interventions on a case-by-case basis, identifying needs and strengths; consider if a longer than usual time in services may be needed.
- Regularly review any care plans or treatment plans, as needs may change more often.
- Address the practicalities, for example, transportation difficulties and reimbursement for transport.
- Review physical access to the building, meeting rooms, toilets and so on. Is it possible for someone with mobility issues to access them?
- Ensure that additional needs or support are considered, for example, training or employment support.
- Interventions should include verbal and non-verbal cues, where needed.
- Collaborate with other professionals in specialist substance use or disability services to ensure good communication and joint working (with permission).

Specific disabilities will require consideration of specific services. For example, substance use services may need to use interpreters who use sign language to help them communicate with people who are hearing impaired (NIAAA 2005). The National Institute on Alcohol Abuse and Alcoholism (NIAAA) suggests these should not be family members or friends, due to the chances of their relationship inhibiting disclosure and discussion.

The NIAAA (2005) advises agencies and training programmes to contact service users or former service users as well as rehabilitation professionals for advice on how to work with people and the skills and sensitivities needed to work with someone with a disability and substance problem.

Good practice examples

Moore et al (2009:82) describe an e-therapy project for people with *hearing loss* called *Deaf Off Drugs and Alcohol*. Based in the US, the programme involves deaf people being supported in a combination of local services and through American Sign Language (ASL) based e-therapy. The programme uses both group and individual interventions and case management via video conferencing and video phone technology. However, this does rely on people having access to computers and the necessary equipment (including cameras and the internet). The programme chose to bring together two different staff, case managers for deaf people and substance use counsellors, rather than an interpreter, to ensure that the focus of the intervention was clearly on the individual and not 'diluted' by giving attention to the interpreter.

For people with *visual impairment* the NIAAA (2005) recommends that first the extent of the visual impairment needs to be established, but that other needs need to be considered, that is, a person may also need mobility support as well as resources such as large-print materials, audio or Braille information. However, such practical resources are only one part of the work. In a study of 20 professionals working with people with visual impairments, the majority felt that visually impaired and blind people would have less successful outcomes in relation to interventions for alcohol and drugs and be more difficult to work with (Davis et al 2009). This suggests that professionals' attitudes also need to change. West et al (2009b), in a survey of a small sample of 23 UK drug services, found that 19 of them (87%) did not have materials in Braille or large print.

There is also a small literature focusing on *brain damage* or *TBI* in relation to substance use, mainly alcohol. Cleak and Serr (1998), in their description of a service working with people with alcohol-related brain damage (ARBD), stated that memory problems and a lack of insight requires services to focus on building trusting relationships and that perseverance and on-going support and involvement by case managers are needed. Further, staff need to provide guidance and education to those caring for the person with ARBD and anyone else who may be working with the person, so as to enable them to offer appropriate and informed support. In a randomised trial comparing three different interventions for working with people with TBI, Corrigan et al (2005) explored 'treatment compliance' – early engagement in particular – for 195 people with TBI attending substance use treatment. All participants had acquired brain injury and a subsequent cognitive disability and were randomly assigned to one of three groups – barrier reduction, brief motivational interview and financial incentives. The financial incentives group was more able to move people from initial engagement to an 'individualized service plan' (ISP) than were the other two approaches. Retention in this group and in the barrier reduction group was also higher, suggesting that the initial intervention may also have had an impact on retention rates. However, the authors point out that what may have been most important was the reminder calls people received, given that some people with TBI had memory problems. People with mental health problems were less likely to engage within 30 days.

Box 10.4: Good practice – people with Traumatic Brain Injury (TBI) and substance problems

- Monitor and routinely assess substance use over time.
- Help people to recognise when they may have a substance problem and emphasise responsibility and choice over their next steps.
- Facilitate empathic discussion about the effects of substance use on themselves and their relationships.
- Involve family members and friends in the assessment and intervention process where appropriate, taking care not to breach confidentiality.
- Teach both individuals and their support network about substance use and its impact on people with TBI as well as about intervention. Help them to distinguish between behaviour that is substance related or TBI related.
- Teach individuals and support networks about relapse and how to avoid relapse or support someone who has relapsed.
- Ensure communication is appropriate to the person's needs, using repetition or other forms of communication, for example, role play, visual aids.
- Ensure good decisions and positive goal setting are given due credit.
- Put individual and family members/friends in touch with their own support networks including mutual aid groups.
- Support people to access substance-free social activities.

- Provide substance use services with information on TBI and how the service can best work with people with TBI.

(Adapted from Taylor et al 2003: 182)

Summary

Supporting people with a range of disabilities and substance problems is important in maximising their quality of life and opportunities for independence and in minimising the risk of self-harm. So too is understanding the additional impact and risk that people with disabilities can face when using substances, particularly to problematic levels. The reasons why people with disabilities use are likely to be the same as the reasons why people without disabilities use substances, but there are additional stresses and difficulties that emerge for people with disabilities. Overcoming the double dose of stigma faced by people living with both issues requires tenacity and excellent communication skills. Advocacy is likely to be a vital part of the social worker's role when supporting people with these overlapping issues, alongside a determination to facilitate partnership working. Substance use specialists do not specialise in working with people with disabilities, or vice versa. Pushing people back and forth between services is likely to be a negative and undignified experience for the person concerned, who will get the message that no one wants to help. There is a lack of evidence in all aspects of assessing and intervening with people with disabilities and substance problems. While we await the evidence, it behoves the individual practitioner to take what can be gleaned from the expertise of their service users, the research evidence, good practice guidance and useful policy frameworks and apply that to their practice.

Note

[1] In the review of the literature the terminology used by the original authors will be used throughout. Where an author has clarified their definition this will be summarised in parentheses alongside their terminology.

Discussion questions/exercises

1   What would be your initial question to Jo, John and Nancy about their substance use and disabilities?
2   What type of questions would you ask specialist substance use services when considering a referral for someone with (a) a learning disability, or (b) a physical disability?
3   What are three ways in which substance use and disabilities can be associated?
4   Name two recent pieces of policy that you could use to underpin your advocacy for access to specialist services for someone with a disability.
5   Find out if your local alcohol and drug service/s provide information on their services in picture form or in large print or Braille.

Further learning resources

■ Beddoes, D., Sheikh, S., Khanna, M. and Francis, R. (2010) *The impact of drugs on different minority groups: A Review of the UK Literature. Part 3: Disabled people.* Available online at: www.ukdpc.org.uk/resources/disabled_people.pdf.

■ Krahn, G., Deck, D., Gabriel, R. and Farrell, N. (2007) 'A population-based study on substance abuse treatment for adults with disabilities: access, utilization, and treatment outcomes', *The American Journal of Drug and Alcohol Abuse*, 33, 791–8.

■ Taggart, L., Huxley, A. and Baker, G. (2008) 'Alcohol and illicit drug misuse in people with learning disabilities: implications for research and service development', *Advances in Mental Health and Learning Disabilities*, 2 (1), 11–21.

■ Wolf-Branigin, M. (2007) 'Disability and abuse in relation to substance abuse: a descriptive analysis', *Journal of Social Work in Disability & Rehabilitation*, 6 (3), 65–74.

Conclusion

11

It is beyond doubt that substance use is a social issue. The evidence presented in the preceding chapters demonstrates how substance use stems from, and leads to, social harms. Social workers and other social care professionals are on the front line of work with people with problematic substance use and others affected by it.

Substance use cuts across areas of specialist practice and does not discriminate according to class, ethnicity, age or disability. However, those who are most negatively affected are often those who have neither the material nor the social resources that would offer them some degree of support or protection. People who are disadvantaged are more likely to come to the attention of statutory services than those whose income or social networks afford them greater choices about where they turn for help.

Substance use overlaps with issues at the core of social work practice, in particular adult and child safeguarding. Social workers are among the few community-based professionals who are in a position to identify and respond to these social harms, including identifying and engaging with substance use. Most importantly, those who are vulnerable because of their substance use are no less deserving of safeguarding and care.

Social work is not alone as a profession that has previously failed to intervene with substance use in its practice with adults and children. Nursing and medical colleagues have fared little better (see Galvani 2007). But it is social work that is particularly well equipped to respond and do better. Social work has the sound value base and underpinning principles of social justice, advocacy and critical reflection that make it ideally suited to working with people often deemed undeserving.

Social work is able to view the person's life as a whole and to intervene to meet practical, emotional and social needs. People experiencing problems from their substance use will often have all three needs. Social work recognises the interplay between the person and their environment and understands the impact this may have on their difficulties and their support needs.

Social work also allows for more than brief intervention. For many social workers working within a care management (or case management) framework, there is longevity to their involvement that supports longer-term change. This is among the key issues that service users identify on their wish list when changing their substance use – on-going, consistent care and support. Brief interventions with a rapid turnover of staff do little to address the significant social changes that users need to make in order to maintain an alcohol- or drug-free (or reduced) life-style.

The role of the social worker in working with substance use has never been so important as it is now, set within a political context that is focused on long-term recovery from substance problems and increasing community and family involvement to support it (HM Government 2010a). While the opportunities for social work to engage fully with substance use have not previously been realised (Galvani 2007), the tide is turning. Reviews of children and families social work repeatedly highlight the negative impact of substance use within the family environment, as well as the failure of services to address it (Laming 2009; Brandon et al 2010; Munro 2011).

But attention must be paid to the adults and parents within these families who need support beyond that resulting from the needs of their child. As the evidence shows, many adolescents and adults with problematic substance use have tragedies, trauma and abuse in their own lives. This needs to be recognised and addressed within social care. Tragic circumstances have brought substance use within children's lives to the political fore – this has yet to be recognised within adult social care. However, the evidence presented in previous chapters demonstrates that it is a growing issue among adult service user groups.

Good practice in working with people with substance problems is not rocket science. It begins with an honest appraisal of our own values and our attitudes towards substance use and the people who have problems with it. This is closely followed by acknowledging that it is a legitimate part of our role and that we are entitled to ask about it and intervene appropriately. The absence of these factors has been shown to negatively affect professionals' willingness to engage with their service users' substance use (Loughran et al 2010).

People's relationship with their substance use, be it alcohol or other drugs, is an intimate one. It is a reliable crutch on which they lean. They know where to get the substance, how much it will cost them and the risks and benefits of using it. The same cannot be said at present for social work interventions. In a review of the effectiveness of social work and social care interventions for substance use, Galvani and Forrester (2011a) found a shocking lack of interventions within the UK.

This needs to change. Social work interventions with people who use substances are in desperate need of development, implementation and evaluation. In the meantime, literature from North America provides some useful insights. Case management, in its various forms, emerged as having a strong evidence base when working with people with substance problems (Galvani and Forrester 2011a). In particular, the important features included:

- the ability to develop and sustain a good therapeutic relationship
- effort to engage the individuals that went beyond the office-based delivery of services, for example, out-of-hours contact or home-based interventions
- the provision of additional support services that addressed other needs in the lives of the service users
- a limited number of service users per worker.

At the core of this evidence a number of skills and qualities emerged. Chief among them were excellent communication skills and, through such skills, conveying respect and recognising people's strengths. In other words, the most successful interventions moved beyond care coordination, to the skilled involvement of social care staff combined with an ability to build strong, respectful and caring relationships. These are skills and roles that already have a strong foothold within social work practice. Yet there is room for improvement, particularly in the development or enhancement of communication skills (Forrester et al 2008a, b). Effective communication is a skill that is, arguably, taken for granted once qualifying training ends, and can be diluted by procedural approaches to care.

So while the skill base exists in social work, what is different for the profession is the development and application of those skills to interventions with people who have substance problems. Responding to individual substance use needs has been passed on to health colleagues rather than engaging with it as part of social work practice. However, engagement is not about becoming a substance use specialist, but it is about meeting a duty of care.

Evidence from social workers across the UK shows that those on the front line are already attempting to engage with substance use, albeit without the knowledge, education and training that will support them to do so effectively (Galvani and Forrester 2011b, Galvani et al 2011). In 2009 BASW responded to this gap by publishing a position statement that calls on individual social workers and their employers and educators to do better in terms of responding to substance use:

1. BASW recognises the difficulties faced by service users, their families and communities, as a result of alcohol and other drug problems.
2. BASW believes social work practice can and should respond effectively to people suffering from their own, or a loved one's, alcohol and other drug problems.
3. BASW believes that service users have the right to professional social work care, delivered by well-trained and well-supervised workers who are competent to deal with alcohol and other drug problems.

4. BASW believes that competence in working with alcohol and drug problems is an essential component of high-quality social care service provision for all service user groups.
5. BASW believes social workers must be able to intervene with confidence where they encounter alcohol and drug problems, and participate in active partnerships with specialist colleagues in the drug and alcohol fields.
6. BASW calls on social work educators and employers to take responsibility for enabling social workers to access the relevant education and training to meet their duty of care towards service users with alcohol and other drug problems.
7. BASW seeks to support individual social workers to take responsibility for ensuring their knowledge and skills meet the needs of service users with alcohol and other drug problems.
    (BASW Special Interest Group in Alcohol and Other Drugs 2009)

It followed this position statement with a workforce development statement targeting qualifying and post-qualifying social work educators and employers who should be providing substance use training and education in house (BASW Special Interest Group in Alcohol and Other Drugs 2010). The responsibility for improving the service we provide to people with substance problems is a shared one.

However, it is time for change. Social workers' professional codes of practice and their commitment to their profession means they are well placed to develop good practice in working with substance problems. For good practice with substance use, social workers need to:

■ feel confident in their knowledge and skills
■ be competent enough to identify, assess and intervene
■ be adequately supported by managers, systems and processes.

Service users have the right to a social work service that is prepared for and committed to supporting them to change their problematic substance use. Social workers can and should intervene with people's substance problems and be supported to do so. Social work remains a profession underpinned by a passion for giving support to those who need it and a commitment to social justice – people with substance problems are no exception.

References

Adams, P. (1999) 'Towards a family support approach with drug-using parents: the importance of social worker attitudes and knowledge', *Child Abuse Review*, 8, 15–28.

Adfam (2008) *We count too*. Good practice guide and quality standards for work with family members affected by someone else's drug use. 2nd edn. Available online at: www.adfam.org.uk/publications/publications_for_professionals_and_practitioners/we_count_too [accessed 17 August 2011].

ADSS (Association of Directors of Social Services) (2005) *Safeguarding adults: A national framework of standards for good practice and outcomes in adult protection work*. London: ADSS.

Afuwape, S.A., Johnson, S., Craig, T.J.K., Miles, H., Leese, M., Mohan, R. and Thornicroft, G. (2006) 'Ethnic differences among a community cohort of individuals with dual diagnosis in South London', *Journal of Mental Health*, 15 (5), 551–67.

Agic, B., Mann, R.E. and Kobus-Matthews, M. (2011) 'Alcohol use in seven ethnic communities in Ontario: a qualitative investigation', *Drugs: Education, Prevention and Policy*, 18, (2), 116–23.

Alcohol Concern (2011) 'Young people and alcohol'. Acquire factsheet. Available online at: www.alcoholconcern.org.uk [accessed 16 August 2011].

Alexander, T., DiNitto, D. and Tidblom, I. (2005) 'Screening for alcohol and other drug use problems among the deaf', *Alcoholism Treatment Quarterly*, 23 (1), 63–78.

Amaro, H., Dai, J., Arvalo, S., Acevedo, A., Matsumoto, A., Nieves, R. and Prado, G. (2007) 'Effects of integrated trauma treatment on outcomes in a racially/ethnically diverse sample of women in urban community-based substance abuse treatment', *Journal of Urban Health*, 84 (4), 508–22.

Anderson, T.L. and Levy, J.A. (2003) 'Marginality among older injectors in today's illicit drug culture: assessing the impact of ageing', *Addiction*, 98, 761–70.

APA (American Psychiatric Association) (2000) *Diagnostic and statistical manual of mental disorders*. 4th edn, text revised. Washington, DC: American Psychiatric Association.

Appleby, L. (2004) *The National Service Framework for Mental Health – five years on*. London: DH.

Austin, A. and Wagner, E.F. (2010) 'Treatment attrition among racial and ethnic minority youth', *Journal of Social Work Practice in the Addictions*, 10 (1), 63–80.

Azrin, N.H. (1976) 'Improvements in the community-reinforcement approach to alcoholism', *Behavioural Research and Therapy*, 14 (3), 339–48.

Babor, T.F., de la Fuente, J.R., Saunders, J. and Grant. M. (1992) *AUDIT. The Alcohol Use Disorders Identification Test: Guidelines for use in primary health care*. Geneva: World Health Organization.

Baird, J., Longabaugh, R., Lee, C.S., Nirenberg, T.D., Woolard, R., Mello, M.J., Becker, B., Carty, K., Minugh, P.A., Stein, L., Clifford, P.R. and Gogineni, A. (2007) 'Treatment completion in a brief motivational intervention in the emergency department: the effect of multiple interventions and therapists' behavior', *Alcoholism: Clinical and Experimental Research*, 31(Supplement 10), 71S–75S.

Banerjee, S., Clancy, C. and Crome, I. (2002) *Co-existing problems of mental disorder and substance misuse (dual diagnosis). An information manual*. Available online at: www.rcpsych.ac.uk/cru [accessed June 2010].

Barnard, M. (2005) *Drugs in the family. The impact on parents and siblings*. Final report. York: Joseph Rowntree Foundation.

Barnard, M. (2007) *Drug addiction and families*. London: Jessica Kingsley.

Barnett, O.W. and Fagan, R.W. (1993) 'Alcohol use in male spouse abusers and their female partners', *Journal of Family Violence*, 8, 1–25.

Bartels, S.J., Blow, F.C., Van Citters, A.D. and Brockmann, L.M. (2006) 'Dual diagnosis among older adults co-occurring substance abuse and psychiatric illness', *Journal of Dual Diagnosis*, 2 (3), 9–30.

Barter, C. (2009) 'In the name of love: exploitation and violence in teenage dating relationships', *British Journal of Social Work*, 39, 211–33.

Bashford, J. (2003) *Resources for use in drug education and prevention work with Black and minority ethnic community groups*. Report for DrugScope DEPIS. Final Draft. The Centre for Ethnicity and Health, University of Central Lancashire. Available online at: www.drugscope.org.uk/Resources/Drugscope/Documents/PDF/Good%20Practice/bashford.pdf [accessed 11 July 2011].

Bashford, J., Carpentier, C., Fountain, J., Khurana, J., Patel, K., Underwood, S. and Winters, M. (2004a) 'Drug use amongst black and minority ethnic communities in the European Union and Norway', *Probation Journal*, 51 (4), 362–78.

Bashford, J., Carpentier, C., Fountain, J., Khurana, J., Patel, K., Underwood, S. and Winters, M. (2004b) 'Laying the foundations of an evidence base on drug use amongst black and minority ethnic communities: the research methods used for an EMCDDA project', *Journal of Ethnicity in Substance Abuse*, 3 (1), 29–46.

BASW (2002) 'Code of Ethics for Social Work'. Available online at: www.basw.co.uk [accessed 8 August 2011].

BASW Special Interest Group in Alcohol and other Drugs (2009) *Position statement on alcohol and other drug problems.* Available online at: www.basw. co.uk/special-interest-groups/alcohol-and-other-drugs/.

BASW Special Interest Group in Alcohol and other Drugs (2010) *Position statement: Educating and enabling social workers to address alcohol and drug problems.* Available online at: www.basw.co.uk/special-interest-groups/ alcohol-and-other-drugs/.

Bear, Z., Griffiths, R. and Pearson, B. (2000) *Childhood sexual abuse and substance use.* London: The Centre for Research on Drugs and Health Behaviour.

Becker, J. and Duffy, C. (2002) *Women drug users and drugs service provision: Service-level responses to engagement and retention.* Report for the Home Office Drugs Strategy Directorate. DPAS paper 17. London: Home Office.

Beddoes, D., Sheikh, S., Khanna, M. and Francis, R. (2010) *The impact of drugs on different minority groups: A review of the UK literature. Part 3: Disabled people.* Available online at: www.ukdpc.org.uk/resources/disabled_people. pdf [accessed 21 June 2011].

Bender, K., Springer, D.W. and Kim, J.S. (2006) 'Treatment effectiveness with dually diagnosed adolescents: a systematic review', *Brief Treatment and Crisis Intervention*, 6 (3), 177–205.

Bennett, L. and O'Brien, P. (2007) 'Effects of coordinated services for drug-abusing women who are victims of intimate partner violence', *Violence Against Women*, 13 (4), 395–411.

Beynon, C.M. (2009) 'Drug use and ageing: older people do take drugs!' *Age and Ageing*, 38, 8–10.

Beynon, C.M., McVeigh, J. and Roe, B. (2007) 'Problematic drug use, ageing and older people: trends in the age of drug users in northwest England', *Ageing & Society*, 27, 799–810.

Bhopal, R., Vettini, A., Hunt, S., Wiebe, S., Hanna, L. and Amos, A. (2004) 'Review of prevalence data in, and evaluation of methods for cross cultural adaptation of, UK surveys on tobacco and alcohol in ethnic minority groups', *British Medical Journal*, 328, 76–80.

Birmingham Safeguarding Children Board (2011) 'Child protection procedures. Section 25. Substance misuse by parents or carers'. Available online at: www.lscbbirmingham.org.uk/child-protection-procedures/ downloads/section-25.pdf [accessed 17 August 2011].

Blair, P.S., Sidebotham, P., Evason-Coombe, C., Edmonds, M., Heckstall-Smith, E. and Fleming, P. (2009) 'Hazardous cosleeping environments and risk factors amenable to change: case-control study of SIDS in South West England', *British Medical Journal*, 339, b3666.

Blow, F.C. (1991) 'Michigan Alcoholism Screening Test – Geriatric Version (MAST-G)'. Available online at: www.ssc.wisc.edu/wlsresearch/pilot/P01-R01_info/aging_mind/Aging_AppB5_MAST-G.pdf [accessed 25 August 2011].

BMA (British Medical Association) Board of Science (2007) *Fetal alcohol spectrum disorders. A guide for healthcare professionals.* London: British Medical Association.

Brandon, M., Bailey, S. and Belderson, P. (2010) *Building on the learning from serious case reviews: A two-year analysis of child protection database notifications 2007–2009.* Available online at: https://www.education.gov.uk/publications/eOrderingDownload/DFE-RR040.pdf [accessed 18 August 2011].

Brecklin, L.R. (2002) 'The role of perpetrator alcohol use in the injury outcomes of intimate assaults', *Journal of Family Violence*, 17 (3), 185–97.

Bremner, P., Burnett, J., Nunney, F., Ravat, M. and Mistral, W. (2011) *Young people, alcohol and influences.* York: JRF.

Brennan, P.L., Schutte, K.K. and Moos, R.H. (2005) 'Pain and use of alcohol to manage pain: prevalence and 3-year outcomes among older problem and non-problem drinkers', *Addiction*, 100, 777–86.

Brindle, D. (2011) 'MPs call for guaranteed care for the vulnerable'. *Guardian*, 7 June. Available online at: www.guardian.co.uk/society/2011/jun/07/mps-guaranteed-care-vulnerable?INTCMP=SRCH [accessed 8 June 2011].

Britton, J. (2007) *Assessing young people for substance use.* London: NTA.

Broadway (undated) *Alcohol, medication and older people.* Available online at: www.broadwaylodge.co.uk/store/files/Alcohol,-Medication-and-Older-People.pdf [accessed 23 April 2010].

Brookoff, D., O'Brien, K.K., Cook, C.S., Thompson, T.D. and Williams, C. (1997) 'Characteristics of participants in domestic violence. Assessment at the scene of domestic assault', *Journal of the American Medical Association*, 277 (17), 1369–73.

Brown, T., Caplan, T., Werk, A. and Seraganian, P. (1999) 'The comparability of male violent substance abusers in violence or substance abuse treatment', *Journal of Family Violence*, 14, 297–314.

Brown, T.G., Werk, A., Caplan, T., Shields, N. and Seraganian, P. (1998) 'The incidence and characteristics of violent men in substance abuse treatment', *Addictive Behaviors*, 23 (5), 573–86.

Brunnberg, E., Lindén-Boström, M. and Berglund, M. (2008) 'Tinnitus and hearing loss in 15–16-year-old students: mental health symptoms, substance use, and exposure in school', *International Journal of Audiology*, 47 (11), 688–94.

Burkhart, G., Olszewski, D., Martel, C., Nilson, M. and Wallon, A. (2008) *Drug use amongst vulnerable young people.* Available online at: www.emcdda. eu.int [accessed 15 August 2008].

Burniston, S., Dodd, M., Elliott, L., Orr, L. and Watson, L. (2002) *Drug treatment services for young people: A research review.* Available online at: www. scotland.gov.uk/Resource/Doc/46746/0013989.pdf [accessed 11 August 2011].

Bury, C., Powis, B., Ofori-Wilson, F., Downer, L. and Griffiths, P. (1999) *An examination of the needs of women crack users with attention to the role of domestic violence and housing.* Report for Lambeth, Southwark and Lewisham Health Authority in collaboration with the National Addiction Centre and the Brixton Drug Project.

Cabinet Office (2004) *The National Alcohol Harm Reduction Strategy.* London: Cabinet Office.

Cabinet Office (2008) *Think family: Improving the life chances of families at risk.* London: Cabinet Office.

Calabria, B., Shakeshaft, A.P. and Havard, A. (2011) 'A systematic and methodological review of interventions for young people experiencing alcohol-related harm', *Addiction*, 106 (8), 1406–18.

Camden Safeguarding Children Board (2009) *Working with substance misusing parents. Multi-agency guidance.* Available online at: www.cscb.org.uk/ downloads/policies_guidance/local/Working%20with%20Substance%20 Misusing%20Parents%20guidance%202009.pdf [accessed 17 August 2011].

Care Quality Commission and National Mental Health Development Unit (2011) *Count me in 2010.* London: Care Quality Commission and National Mental Health Development Unit. Available online at: www.cqc. org.uk/_db/_documents/Count_me_in_2010_FINAL_%28tagged%29. pdf [accessed 15 August 2011].

Carter, H. (2007) 'He couldn't say no', *Guardian*, 15 August. Available online at: www.guardian.co.uk/society/2007/aug/15/guardiansocietysupplement. socialcare [accessed 21 June 2011].

Castro, F.G. and Alarcon, E.H. (2002) 'Integrating cultural variables into drug abuse prevention and treatment with racial/ethnic minorities', *Journal of Drug Issues*, 32 (3), 783–810.

Cawson, P. (2002) *Child maltreatment in the family: The experience of a national sample of young people.* London: NSPCC.

Central Council for Education and Training in Social Work (1992) *Substance misuse: Guidance notes for the diploma in social work.* London: CCETSW.

Chalder, M., Elgar, F.J. and Bennett, P. (2006) 'Drinking and motivations to drink among adolescent children of parents with alcohol problems', *Alcohol and Alcoholism*, 41 (1), 107–13.

Chartier, K.G., Hesselbrock, M.N. and Hesselbrock, V.M. (2009) 'Ethnicity and adolescent pathways to alcohol use', *Journal of Studies on Alcohol and Drugs*, 70 (3), 337–45.

Chermack, S.T., Murray, R.L., Walton, M.A., Booth, B.A., Wryobeck, J. and Blow, F.C. (2008) 'Partner aggression among men and women in substance use disorder treatment: correlates of psychological and physical aggression and injury', *Drug and Alcohol Dependence*, 98 (1–2), 35–44.

Chevannes, B., Edwards, W., Freckleton, A., Linton, N., McDowell, D., Standard-Goldson, A. and Smith, B. (2001) *A Report of the National Commission on Ganja to Rt. Hon. P.J. Patterson, Q.C., M.P. Prime Minister of Jamaica.* Available online at: www.cannabis-med.org/science/Jamaica.htm [accessed 30 August 2011].

Choi, N.G. and Mayer, J. (2000) 'Elder abuse, neglect, and exploitation: risk factors and prevention strategies', *Journal of Gerontological Social Work*, 33 (2), 5–25.

Clark, A.H. and Foy, D.W. (2000) 'Trauma exposure and alcohol use in battered women', *Violence against Women*, 6 (1), 37–48.

Clarke, J.J. and Wilson, D.N. (1999) 'Alcohol problems and intellectual disability', *Journal of Intellectual Disability Research*, 43 (2), 135–9.

Cleak, H. and Serr, K. (1998) 'Case management in action: an examination of two cases in the area of alcohol related brain damage', *Australian Social Work*, 51 (1), 33–8.

Cleaver, H., Unell, I. and Aldgate, J. (1999) *Children's needs: parenting capacity: The impact of parental mental illness, problem alcohol and drug use, and domestic violence on children's development.* London: The Stationery Office.

Cleaver, H., Nicholson, D., Tarr, S. and Cleaver, D. (2006) *The response of child protection practices and procedures to children exposed to domestic violence or parental substance misuse. Executive summary.* London: University of London/DfES.

Cleaver, H., Nicholson, D., Tarr, S. and Cleaver, D. (2007) *Child protection, domestic violence and parental substance misuse. Family experiences and effective practice.* London: Jessica Kingsley.

Colbert, S.J. and Krause, N. (2009) 'Alcohol use among older persons witnessing violence across the life course, depressive symptoms, and alcohol use among older persons', *Health Education & Behavior*, 36 (2), 259–77.

Coleman, K., Eder, S. and Smith, K. (2011) 'Homicide', in K. Smith (ed), K. Coleman, S. Eder and P. Hall, *Homicides, firearm offences and intimate violence 2009/10. Supplementary Volume 2 to Crime in England and Wales 2009/10.* Available online at: www.homeoffice.gov.uk/publications/science-research-statistics/research-statistics/crime-research/hosb0111/ [accessed 22 August 2011].

Conigliaro, J., Gordon, A.J., Kelley, M.E., Kraemer, K.L., McNeil, M. and Maisto, S.A. (2003) 'Comparison of consumption effects of brief interventions for hazardous drinking elderly', *Substance Use and Misuse*, 38 (8), 1017–35.

Copello, A., Williamson, E., Orford, J. and Day, E. (2006) Implementing and evaluating social behaviour and network therapy in drug treatment practice in the UK: a feasibility study', *Addictive Behaviors*, 31 (5), 802–10.

Copello, A., Orford, J., Velleman, R., Templeton, L. and Krishnan, M. (2000a) 'Methods for reducing alcohol and drug related family harm in non-specialist settings', *Journal of Mental Health*, 9, 329–43.

Copello, A., Templeton, L., Krishnan, M., Orford, J. and Velleman, R. (2000b) 'A treatment package to improve primary care services for relatives of people with alcohol and drug problems', *Addiction Research*, 8, 471–84.

Copello, A., Orford, J., Hodgson, R., Tober, G. and Barrett, C. on behalf of the UKATT Research Team (2002) 'Social behaviour and network therapy: basic principles and early experiences', *Addictive Behaviors*, 27 (2), 345–66.

Corbin, W.R., Vaughan, E.L. and Fromme, K. (2008) 'Ethnic differences and the closing of the sex gap in alcohol use among college-bound students', *Psychology of Addictive Behaviors*, 22 (2), 240–8.

Corbin, W.R., Bernat, J.A., Calhoun, K.S., McNair, L.D. and Seals, K.L. (2001) 'The role of alcohol expectancies and alcohol consumption among sexually victimized and nonvictimized college women', *Journal of Interpersonal Violence*, 16 (4), 297–311.

Corby, B. and Millar, M. (1998) 'Counselling women with alcohol problems – an outreach service with lessons for social work education', *Issues in Social Work Education*, 18 (1), 47–59.

Corrigan, J.D., Bogner, J., Lamb-Hart, G., Heinemann, A.W. and Moore, D. (2005) 'Increasing substance abuse treatment compliance for persons with traumatic brain injury', *Psychology of Addictive Behaviors*, 19 (2), 131–9.

Cosden, M. (2001) 'Risk and resilience for substance abuse among adolescents and adults with LD', *Journal of Learning Disabilities*, 34 (4), 352–8.

Costello, R.M. (1980) 'Alcoholism treatment effectiveness: slicing the outcome variance pie', in G. Edwards and M. Grant (eds) *Alcoholism treatment in transition*. London: Croom Helm.

Cousins, W. and Milner, S. (2006) 'Drug abuse and parenting: the impact on young children in the social care system in Northern Ireland', *Irish Journal of Applied Social Studies*, 7 (1), 95–108.

Crawford, V. and Crome, I. (2001) *Co-existing problems of mental health and substance misuse ('dual diagnosis'). A review of relevant literature*. London: College Research Unit, Royal College of Psychiatrists.

Crome, I., Chambers, P., Frisher, M., Bloor, R. and Roberts, D. (2009) *The relationship between dual diagnosis: Substance misuse and dealing with mental health issues.* SCIE briefing 30. Available online at: www.scie.org.uk/publications/briefings/briefing30/ [accessed 27 August 2011].

CSIP (Care Services Improvement Partnership) (2008a) *Themed review report 07. Dual diagnosis. National Service Framework for Mental Health.* Leeds: CSIP.

CSIP (2008b) *Dual diagnosis. Developing capable practitioners to improve services and increase positive service user experience.* Leeds: CSIP.

Cummings, S.M., Bride, B. and Rawlins-Shaw, A.M. (2006) 'Alcohol abuse treatment for older adults: a review of recent empirical research', *Journal of Evidence-Based Social Work*, 3 (1), 79–99.

Daddow, R. and Broome, S. (2010) *Whole person recovery: A user-centred systems approach to problem drug use.* Available online at: www.thersa.org/__data/assets/pdf_file/0011/362099/RSA-Whole-Person-Recovery-report.pdf [accessed 28 August 2011].

D'Agostino, C.S., Barry, K.L., Blow, F.C. and Podgorski, C. (2006) 'Community interventions for older adults with comorbid substance abuse: the geriatric addictions program (GAP)', *Journal of Dual Diagnosis*, 2 (3), 31–45.

Davidson, L., Andres-Hyman, R., Bedregal, L., Tondora, J., Fry, J. and Kirk, T.A. (2008) 'From "double trouble" to "dual recovery": integrating models of recovery in addiction and mental health', *Journal of Dual Diagnosis*, 4 (3), 273–90.

Davies, C., English, L., Lodwick, A., McVeigh, J. and Bellis, M.A. (eds) (2010) *United Kingdom drug situation: Annual report to the European Monitoring Centre for Drugs and Drug Addiction (EMCDDA).* Available online at: www.cph.org.uk/showPublication.aspx?pubid=707 [accessed 3 August 2011].

Davies, J.B., Duncan, K. and Coggans, N. (1995) *Community care plans for people with drug and alcohol problems: Assessment of impact.* Scotland: HMSO.

Davis, S.J., Koch, D.S., McKee, M.F. and Nelipovich, M. (2009) 'AODA training experiences of blindness and visual impairment professionals', *Journal of Teaching in the Addictions*, 8 (1), 42–50.

Dawson, D.A., Grant, B.F., Chou, P.S., Stinson, F.S. (2007) 'The impact of partner alcohol problems on women's physical and mental health', *Journal of Studies on Alcohol and Drugs*, 68 (1), 66–75.

DCSF (Department for Children, Schools and Families) (2003) *Every Child Matters.* London: The Stationery Office.

DCSF (2004) *Every Child Matters: Change for children.* London: DCSF.

DCSF (2007) *The Children's Plan: Building brighter futures.* London: The Stationery Office.

DCSF (2008) *Use of alcohol among children and young people.* Available online at: www.dcsf.gov.uk/research/ [accessed February 2009].

DCSF, Home Office and Department of Health (2008) *Youth Alcohol Action Plan*. London: The Stationery Office.

DCSF, National Treatment Agency and Department of Health (2009) *Joint guidance on development of local protocols between drug and alcohol treatment services and local safeguarding and family services*. Available online at: www.nta. nhs.uk/uploads/yp_drug_alcohol_treatment_protocol_1109.pdf [accessed 8 August 2011].

Delargy, A. (2009) 'Knowledge set 2: Parenting'. London: Alcohol Concern.

Denscombe, M. and Drucquer, N. (2000) 'Diversity within ethnic groups: alcohol and tobacco consumption by young people in the East Midlands', *Health Education Journal*, 59 (4), 340–50.

Department for Education (2011) *Professional Capabilities Framework for Social Work*. London: DfE. Available online at: www.education.gov.uk/ a0074240/professional-standards-for-social-workers-in-england [accessed 15 August 2011].

DfES (Department for Education and Skills), Home Office and Department of Health (2005) *Young people and drugs*. London: DfES.

DH (Department of Health) (1999) *A National Service Framework for Mental Health*. London: DH. Available online at: www.dh.gov.uk/prod_ consum_dh/groups/dh_digitalassets/@dh/@en/documents/digitalasset/ dh_4077209.pdf [accessed June 2010].

DH (2000) *No secrets: Guidance on developing and implementing multi-agency policies and procedures to protect vulnerable adults from abuse*. London: DH.

DH (2001a) *The National Service Framework for Older People*. Available online at: www.doh.gov.uk/nsf/olderpeople.htm [accessed 2 May 2010].

DH (2001b) *Valuing people: A new strategy for learning disability for the 21st century: A White Paper*. London: DH.

DH (2002) *Mental Health Policy Implementation Guide. Dual Diagnosis good practice guide*. London: Department of Health.

DH (2003) *Fair access to care services – guidance on eligibility criteria for adult social care*. Available online at: www.dh.gov.uk/prod_consum_dh/groups/ dh_digitalassets/@dh/@en/documents/digitalasset/dh_4019641.pdf [accessed 28 August 2011].

DH (2008a) *Code of Practice. Mental Health Act 1983*. London: The Stationery Office.

DH (2008b) *Refocusing the Care Programme Approach*. Available online at: http://cpaa.co.uk/files/DH_083649.pdf [accessed 29 August 2011].

DH (2009a) *Living well with dementia: A National Dementia Strategy*. Available online at: www.dh.gov.uk/prod_consum_dh/groups/dh_digitalassets/ @ dh/@en/documents/digitalasset/dh_094051.pdf [accessed 2 May 2010].

DH (2009b) *Valuing people now: A new three-year strategy for people with learning disabilities. 'Making it happen for everyone'*. London: DH.

DH (2010a) *Prioritising need in the context of Putting People First: A whole system approach to eligibility for social care. Guidance on Eligibility Criteria for Adult Social Care, England 2010.* London: DH.

DH (2010b) *A Vision for Adult Social Care: Capable communities and active citizens.* London: DH. Available online at: www.dh.gov.uk/en/ Publicationsandstatistics/Publications/PublicationsPolicyAndGuidance/ DH_121508.

DH (2011) 'Statement of government policy on adult safeguarding'. 16 May 2011. Available online at: www.dh.gov.uk/prod_consum_dh/groups/ dh_digitalassets/documents/digitalasset/dh_126770.pdf [accessed 19 December 2011].

DH and National Treatment Agency (2006) *Models of care for alcohol misusers (MOCAM).* London: Department of Health.

DH and National Treatment Agency (2010a) *Statistics from the National Alcohol Treatment Monitoring System (NATMS). 1st April 2008 – 31st March 2009.* Available online at: www.nta.nhs.uk/areas/alcohol/docs/NATMS_ Annual_Statistics_Report_2008_2009.pdf [accessed 2 May 2010].

DH and National Treatment Agency (2010b) *Statistics from the National Drug Treatment Monitoring System (NDTMS), 1st April 2008 – 31st March 2009.* Available online at: www.nta.nhs.uk/areas/facts_and_figures/0809/docs/ ndtms_annual_report_200809_final.pdf [accessed 3 May 2010].

DH and National Treatment Agency (2011) *Statistics from the National Alcohol Treatment Monitoring System (NATMS), 1st April 2009 – 31st March 2010.* Available online at: www.nta.nhs.uk/uploads/ natmsannualstatisticsreport2009-2010.pdf [accessed 3 August 2011].

DH, Department for Education and Employment and Home Office (2000) *Framework for the Assessment of Children in Need and their Families.* London: The Stationery Office.

DH, Home Office, Department for Education and Skills and Department for Culture, Media and Sport (2007) *Safe. Sensible. Social. The next steps in the National Alcohol Strategy.* London: Department of Health.

Dillon, L., Chivite-Matthews, N., Grewal, I., Brown, R., Webster, S., Weddell, E., Brown, G. and Smith, N. (2007) *Risk, protective factors and resilience to drug use: Identifying resilient young people and learning from their experiences.* Home Office Online Report 04/07. Available online at: www.homeoffice.gov. uk/rds [accessed 2007].

DirectGov (2010) 'Changes to the State Pension from 6 April 2010.' Available online at: www.direct.gov.uk/en/Pensionsandretirementplanning/ StatePension/DG_069498 [accessed 10 April 2010].

DirectGov (2011) *Drugs and crime.* www.direct.gov.uk/en/YoungPeople/ CrimeAndJustice/TypesOfCrime/DG_10027693 [accessed 25 July 2011].

Dobkin, P.L., De Civita, M., Paraherakis, A. and Gill, K. (2002) 'The role of functional social support in treatment retention and outcomes among outpatient adult substance abusers', *Addiction*, 97 (3), 347–56.

Donald, M., Dower, J. and Kavanagh, D. (2005) 'Integrated versus non-integrated management and care for clients with co-occuring mental health and substance use disorders: a qualitative systematic review of randomised controlled trials', *Social Science and Medicine*, 60 (6), 1371–83.

Downs, W.R. (1999) 'Violence against women: the need for improved medical screening, identification and service provision'. Paper presented at University of Hull, England, October 1999.

Downs, W.R. and Miller, B.A. (1994) 'Women's alcohol problems and experiences of partner violence: a longitudinal examination'. Paper presented at the Annual Meeting of the Research Society on Alcoholism, Maui, Hawaii.

Downs, W.R., Miller, B.A. and Panek, D.E. (1993) 'Differential patterns of partner-to-woman violence: a comparison of samples of community, alcohol-abusing, and battered women', *Journal of Family Violence*, 8 (2), 113–35.

Downs, W.R., Patterson, A., Barten, S., McCrory, M. and Rindels, B. (1998) 'Partner violence, mental health, and substance abuse among two samples of women'. Paper presented at the Annual Meeting of the American Society of Criminology, Washington, DC.

Drabble, L. (2007) 'Pathways to collaboration: exploring values and collaborative practice between child welfare and substance abuse treatment fields', *Child Maltreatment*, 12 (1), 31–42.

Drummond, C., Oyefeso, S., Phillips, T., Cheeta, S., Deluca, P., Perryman, K., Winfield, H., Jenner, J., Cobain, K., Galea, S., Saunders, V., Fuller, T., Pappalardo, D., Baker, O. and Christoupoulos, A. (2004) *Alcohol Needs Assessment Research Project (ANARP). The 2004 national alcohol needs assessment for England*. London: Department for Health.

Duff, L. and McNab, I. (2004) *Young people with, or at risk of developing, problematic substance misuse: A guide to assessment*. Edinburgh: Effective Interventions Unit.

Easton, C.J., Swan, S. and Sinha, R. (2000) 'Prevalence of family violence in clients entering substance abuse treatment', *Journal of Substance Abuse Treatment*, 18 (1), 23–8.

Elliott, L., Orr, L., Watson, L. and Jackson, A. (2002) *Drug treatment services for young people: A systematic review of effectiveness and the legal framework*. Edinburgh: Effective Interventions Unit.

Emlet, C.A., Hawks, H. and Callahan, J. (2001) 'Alcohol use and abuse in a population of community dwelling, frail older adults', *Journal of Gerontological Social Work*, 35 (4), 21–33.

Engstrom, M., El-Bassel, N., Go, H. and Gilbert, L. (2008) 'Childhood sexual abuse and intimate partner violence among women in methadone treatment: a direct or mediated relationship?' *Journal of Family Violence*, 23 (7), 605–17.

Fals-Stewart, W. (2003) 'The occurrence of partner physical aggression on days of alcohol consumption: a longitudinal diary study', in Caetano, R., Schafer, J., Fals-Stewart, W., O'Farrell, T. and Miller, B. 'Intimate partner violence and drinking: new research on methodological issues, stability and change, and treatment', *Alcoholism: Clinical and Experimental Research*, 27 (2), 292–300.

Field, C.A., Caetano, R., Harris, T.R., Frankowski, R. and Roudsari, B. (2010) 'Ethnic differences in drinking outcomes following a brief alcohol intervention in the trauma care setting', *Addiction*, 105 (1), 62–73.

Forrester, D. (2000) 'Parental substance misuse and child protection in a British sample', *Child Abuse Review*, 9, 235–46.

Forrester, D., Kershaw, S., Moss, H. and Hughes, L. (2008a) 'Communication skills in child protection: how do social workers talk to parents?' *Child and Family Social Work*, 13 (1), 41–51.

Forrester, D., McCambridge, J., Waissbein, C. and Rollnick, S. (2008b) 'How do child and family social workers talk to parents about child welfare concerns?' *Child Abuse Review*, 17, 23–35.

Foster, J.H., Marshall, E.J. and Peters, T.J. (2003) 'Non-NHS residential alcohol resources are allocated in an inconsistent manner: some preliminary data', *Drugs: Education, Prevention, Policy*, 10 (3), 271–9.

Fountain, J. (2006) *An overview of the nature and extent of illicit drug use amongst the traveler community: An exploratory study*. London: NACD. Available online at: www.nacd.ie/publications/prevalence_traveller.html [accessed 18 July 2011].

Fountain, J. (2009a) *Issues surrounding drug use and drug services among the South Asian communities in England*. Available online at: www.nta.nhs.uk/uploads/1_south_asian_final.pdf [accessed 7 July 2011].

Fountain, J. (2009b) *Issues surrounding drug use and drug services among the Black African communities in England*. Available online at: www.nta.nhs.uk/uploads/4_kurdish_turkish_cypriot_turkish_final.pdf [accessed 7 July 2011].

Fountain, J. (2009c) *Issues surrounding drug use and drug services among the Black Caribbean communities in England*. Available online at: www.nta.nhs.uk/uploads/3_black_caribbean_final.pdf [accessed 7 July 2011].

Fountain, J. (2009d) *Issues surrounding drug use and drug services among the Kurdish, Turkish Cypriot and Turkish communities in England*. Available online at: www.nta.nhs.uk/uploads/4_kurdish_turkish_cypriot_turkish_final.pdf [accessed 11 July 2011].

Fountain, J. (2009e) *Issues surrounding drug use and drug services among the Chinese and Vietnamese communities in England.* Available online at: www.nta. nhs.uk/uploads/5_chinese_vietnamese_final.pdf [accessed 11 July 2011].

Fox, C.L. and Forbing, S.E. (1991) 'Overlapping symptoms of substance abuse and learning handicaps: implications for educators', *Journal of Learning Disabilities*, 24 (1), 24–39.

Frontier Economics (2011) *Specialist drug and alcohol services for young people – a cost benefit analysis.* Report for Department for Education. Available online at: https://www.education.gov.uk/publications/eOrderingDownload/DFE-RR087.pdf [accessed 21 July 2011].

Fuller, E. (ed) (2011) *Smoking, drinking and drug use among young people in England in 2010. Summary.* London: National Centre for Social Research. Available online at: www.ic.nhs.uk/statistics-and-data-collections/health-and-lifestyles-related-surveys/smoking-drinking-and-drug-use-among-young-people-in-england/smoking-drinking-and-drug-use-among-young-people-in-england-in-2010 [accessed 19 August 2011].

Fuller, E., Jotangia, D. and Farrell, M. (2009) 'Drug misuse and dependence', in S. McManus, H. Meltzer, T. Brugha, P. Bebbington and R. Jenkins (eds) *Adult psychiatric morbidity in England, 2007. Results of a household survey.* Available online at: www.ic.nhs.uk/webfiles/publications/mental%20health/other%20mental%20health%20publications/Adult%20psychiatric%20morbidity%202007/APMS%2007%20%28FINAL%29%20Standard.pdf [accessed 24 August 2011].

Gallup Organization (2011) *Youth attitudes on drugs. Analytical report.* European Commission. Available online at: http://ec.europa.eu/public_opinion/flash/fl_330_en.pdf [accessed 20 July 2011].

Galvani, S. (2006) 'Alcohol and domestic violence: women's views', *Violence against Women*, 12 (7), 641–62.

Galvani, S. (2007) 'Refusing to listen: are we failing the needs of people with alcohol and drug problems?' *Social Work Education*, 27 (7), 697–707.

Galvani, S. (2010a) 'Grasping the nettle: alcohol and domestic violence'. *Acquire.* 2nd edn. London: Alcohol Concern.

Galvani, S. (2010b) *Supporting families affected by substance use and domestic violence. Research report.* London: Adfam.

Galvani, S. (2010c) *Women's perspectives: The role of alcohol in violence against women.* Saarbrucken, Germany: Lambert Academic Publishing.

Galvani, S. and Forrester, D. (2008) *What works in training social workers about drug and alcohol use? A survey of student learning and readiness to practice.* Final report for the Home Office.

Galvani, S. and Forrester, D. (2010) *Integrated and inter-professional working: A review of the evidence.* Final report. Submitted to the Welsh Assembly Government by Tilda Goldberg Centre for Social Work and Social Care, University of Bedfordshire.

Galvani, S. and Forrester, D. (2011a) 'How well prepared are newly qualified social workers for working with substance use issues? Findings from a national survey', *Social Work Education*, 30 (4), 422–39.

Galvani, S. and Forrester, D. (2011b) *Social work services and recovery from substance misuse: A review of the evidence.* Edinburgh: Scottish Government.

Galvani, S. and Hughes, N. (2010) 'Working with alcohol and drug use: exploring the knowledge and attitudes of social work students', *British Journal of Social Work*, 40, 946–62.

Galvani, S. and Thurnham, A. (2012) 'Social policy and substance use', in M. Davies (ed) *Social work's knowledge base.* London: Routledge (forthcoming).

Galvani, S., Dance, C. and Hutchinson, A. (2011) *Substance use and social work practice: findings from a national survey of social workers in England.* Final report. Available online at: www.beds.ac.uk/goldbergcentre.

Gentleman, A. (2010) 'Theresa May scraps legal requirement to reduce inequality', *Guardian*, 17 November.

Gilvarry, E. and Britton, J. (2009) *Guidance for the pharmacological management of substance misuse among young people.* London: NTA.

Godette, D., Edwards, E., Ford, C., Strunin, L., Heeren, T. and Kawachi, I. (2009) 'Social status, gender and alcohol-related problems: the black young adult experience', *Ethnicity and health*, 14 (5), 479–96.

Gomez, A., Conde, A., Santana, J.M., Jorrin, A., Serrano, I.M. and Medina, R. (2006) 'The diagnostic usefulness of AUDIT and AUDIT-C for detecting hazardous drinkers in the elderly', *Aging & Mental Health*, 10 (5), 558–61.

Goodman, C.C., Pasztor, E.M., Potts, M. and Scorzo, D. (2004) 'Grandmothers as *kinship* caregivers: private arrangements compared to public child welfare oversight', *Children and Youth Services Review*, 26 (3), 287–305.

Gorin, S. (2004) 'Understanding what children say about living with domestic violence, parental substance misuse or parental health problems', *Findings.* York: Joseph Rowntree Foundation.

Gorney, B. (1989) 'Domestic violence and chemical dependency: dual problems, dual interventions', *Journal of Psychoactive Drugs*, 21, 229–38.

Gossop, M. (2006) *Treating drug misuse problems: Evidence of effectiveness.* London: National Treatment Agency.

Gossop, M. (2008) *Substance use among older adults: A neglected problem.* Drugs in focus, 18. Briefing of the European Monitoring Centre for Drugs and Drug Addiction. Lisbon: EMCDDA.

Gossop, M., Darke, S., Griffiths, P., Hando, J., Powis, B., Hall, W. and Strang, J. (1995) 'The Severity of Dependence Scale (SDS): psychometric properties of the SDS in English and Australian samples of heroin, cocaine and amphetamine users', *Addiction*, 90, 607–14.

Graham, K., Plant, M. and Plant, M. (2004) 'Alcohol, gender and partner aggression: a general population study of British adults', *Addiction Research and Theory*, 12 (4), 385–401.

GSCC (General Social Care Council) (2010) *Code of practice for social care workers and code of practice for employers of social care workers.* London: General Social Care Council. Available online at: www.gscc.org.uk/page/91/Get+copies+of+our+codes.html [accessed 4 August 2011].

Gunning, N. and Nicholson, S. (2010) 'Drinking alcohol', in E. Fuller and M. Sanchez (eds) (2010) *Smoking, drinking and drug use among young people in England in 2009.* London: National Centre for Social Research. Available online at: www.natcen.ac.uk/media/492705/77cb8734-85f3-440d-9617-fb072f787bc4.pdf [accessed 26 July 2011].

Gurnack, A.M. and Johnson, W.A. (2002) 'Elderly drug use and racial/ethnic populations', *Journal of Ethnicity in Substance Abuse*, 1 (2), 55–71.

Gutierres, S.E. and Van Puymbroeck, C. (2006) 'Childhood and adult violence in the lives of women who misuse substances', *Aggression and Violent Behavior*, 11, 497–513.

Guy, P. and Harrison, L. (2003) 'Evidence-based social work with people who have substance problems', in J. Howarth and S.M. Shardlow (eds) *Making links across specialisms.* Lyme Regis, Dorset: Russell House Publishing.

Haase, T. and Pratschke, J. (2010) *Risk and protection factors for substance use among young people. A comparative study of early school-leavers and school-attending students.* Dublin: National Advisory Committee on Drugs.

Haddock, G., Barrowclough, C., Tarrier, N., Moring, J., O'Brien, R., Schofield, N., Quinn, J., Palmer, S., Davies, L., Lowens, I., McGovern, J. and Lewis, S. (2003) 'Cognitive behavioural therapy and motivational intervention for schizophrenia and substance misuse. 18-month outcomes of a randomised controlled trial', *British Journal of Psychiatry*, 183, 418–26.

Hall, P. (2011) 'Intimate violence: 2009/10 British Crime Survey', in K. Smith (ed), K. Coleman, S. Eder and P. Hall, *Homicides, firearm offences and intimate violence 2009/10. Supplementary Volume 2 to Crime in England and Wales 2009/10.* Available online at: www.homeoffice.gov.uk/publications/science-research-statistics/research-statistics/crime-research/hosb0111/ [accessed 22 August 2011].

Hallgren, M., Hogberg, P. and Andreasson, S. (2009) *Alcohol consumption among elderly European Union citizens. Health effects, consumption trends and related issues.* Report for the Expert Conference on Alcohol and Health 21–22 September, Stockholm, Sweden. Available online at: www.fhi.se/PageFiles/7938/alcohol-consumption-among-elderly-european-union-citizens-2009.pdf [accessed 21 April 2010].

Hamburger, M.E., Leeb, R.T. and Swahn, M.H. (2008) 'Childhood maltreatment and early alcohol use among high-risk adolescents', *Journal of Studies on Alcohol and Drugs*, 69 (2), 291–5.

Han, B., Gfroerer, J.C., Colliver, J.D. and Penne, M.A. (2009) 'Substance use disorder among older adults in the United States in 2020', *Addiction*, 104, 88–96.

Harding, J. (2009) *Older people and alcohol. Annual report – the first year of the pilot project.* Kensington and Chelsea. Project report for Foundation 66.

Harrell, Z.A.T. and Broman, C.L. (2009) 'Racial/ethnic differences in correlates of prescription drug misuse among young adults', *Drug and Alcohol Dependence*, 104 (3), 268–71.

Harrison, L. (1992) 'Substance misuse and social work qualifying training in the British Isles: a survey of CQSW courses', *British Journal of Addiction*, 87, 635–42.

Harwin, J. and Forrester, D. (2002) 'Parental substance misuse and child welfare: a study of social work with families in which parents misuse drugs or alcohol'. First stage report for the Nuffield Foundation (unpublished).

Harwin, J. and Forrester, D. (2006) 'Parental substance misuse and child care social work: findings from the first stage of a study of 100 families', *Child and Family Social Work*, 11 (4), 325–35.

Hassiotis, A., Strydom, A., Hall, I., Ali, A., Lawrence-Smith, G., Meltzer, H., Head, J. and Bebbington, P. (2008) 'Psychiatric morbidity and social functioning among adults with borderline intelligence living in private households', *Journal of Intellectual Disability Research*, 52 (2), 95–106.

Hayden, C. (2004) 'Parental substance misuse and child care social work: research in a city social work department in England', *Child Abuse Review*, 13 (1), 18–30.

Helwig, A.A. and Holicky, R. (1994) 'Substance abuse in persons with disabilities: treatment considerations', *Journal of Counseling and Development*, 72, 227–33.

Hester, M., Pearson, C. and Harwin, N. (2000) *Making an impact: Children and domestic violence – a reader.* London: Jessica Kingsley.

Hibell, B., Guttormsson,U., Ahlström, S., Balakireva, O., Bjarnason, T., Kokkevi, A. and Kraus, L. (2009) *The 2007 ESPAD report substance use among students in 35 European countries.* Available online at: www.espad.org/documents/Espad/ESPAD_reports/2007/The_2007_ESPAD_Report-FULL_091006.pdf [accessed 3 August 2011].

HM Government (2006a) *The Common Assessment Framework for children and young people: Supporting tools. Integrated working to improve outcomes for children and young people.* London: HMSO. Available online at: https://www.education.gov.uk/publications/standard/publicationDetail/Page1/CAF-SUPPORT-TOOLS [accessed 17 August 2011].

HM Government (2006b) *Working Together to Safeguard Children: A guide to interagency working to safeguard and promote the welfare of children.* London: The Stationery Office.

HM Government (2007) *Putting People First: A shared vision and commitment to the transformation of adult social care.* Available online at: www.dh.gov.uk/en/Publicationsandstatistics/Publications/PublicationsPolicyAndGuidance/DH_081118 [accessed 28 August 2011].

HM Government (2008a) *Carers at the heart of 21st-century families and communities.* Available online at: www.dh.gov.uk/prod_consum_dh/groups/dh_digitalassets/@dh/@en/documents/digitalasset/dh_085338.pdf [accessed 29 August 2011].

HM Government (2008b) *Drugs: Protecting families and communities. The 2008 Drug Strategy.* London: Home Office.

HM Government (2009) *New Horizons: A shared vision for mental health.* London: DH. Available online at: www.dh.gov.uk/prod_consum_dh/groups/dh_digitalassets/@dh/@en/documents/digitalasset/dh_109708.pdf [accessed June 2010].

HM Government (2010a) *Drugs Strategy 2010. Reducing demand, restricting supply, building recovery: Supporting people to live a drug free life.* London: Home Office.

HM Government (2010b) *The Equality Act 2010.* Available online at: www.legislation.gov.uk/ukpga/2010/15/pdfs/ukpga_20100015_en.pdf [accessed 21 June 2011].

HM Government (2010c) *Healthy Lives, Healthy People. White Paper: Our strategy for public health in England.* Available online at: www.dh.gov.uk/en/Publichealth/Healthyliveshealthypeople/index.htm [accessed 19 August 2011].

HM Government (2010d) *Recognised, valued and supported: Next steps for the Carers Strategy.* Available online at: www.dh.gov.uk/prod_consum_dh/groups/dh_digitalassets/@dh/@en/documents/digitalasset/dh_085338.pdf [accessed 29 August 2011].

HM Government (2011a) *Call to end violence against women and girls: An action plan.* London: Home Office. Available online at: www.homeoffice.gov.uk/publications/crime/call-end-violence-women-girls/vawg-action-plan?view=Binary [accessed 22 August 2011].

HM Government (2011b) *Equality Act 2010. Guidance on matters to be taken into account in determining questions relating to the definition of disability.* Available online at: http://odi.dwp.gov.uk/docs/law/ea/ea-guide-2.pdf [accessed 28 June 2011].

HM Government (2011c) *No health without mental health. A cross-government mental health outcomes strategy for people of all ages.* Available online at: www.dh.gov.uk/prod_consum_dh/groups/dh_digitalassets/documents/digitalasset/dh_124058.pdf [accessed 29 August 2011].

Hoare, J. (2009) *Drug misuse declared: Findings from the 2008/09 British Crime Survey England and Wales.* London: Home Office.

Hoare, J. and Moon, D. (eds) (2010) *Drug misuse declared: Findings from the 2009/10 British Crime Survey England and Wales.* London: Home Office.

Hodges, C., Paterson, S., Taikato, M., McGarrol, S., Crome, I. and Baldacchino, A. (2006) *Co-morbid mental health and substance misuse in Scotland.* Edinburgh: Scottish Executive.

Hollar, D. and Moore, D. (2004) 'Relationship of substance use by students with disabilities to long-term educational, employment, and social outcomes', *Substance Use and Misuse*, 39 (6), 931–62.

Holley, L.C., Kulis, S., Marsiglia, F.F. and Keith, V.M. (2006) 'Ethnicity versus ethnic identity: what predicts substance use norms and behaviors?', *Journal of Social Work Practice in the Addictions*, 6 (3), 53–79.

Home Office (1995) *Tackling drugs together. A strategy for England 1995–1998.* London: HMSO.

Home Office (2002a) *Updated Drugs Strategy 2002.* London: Home Office.

Home Office (2002b) *Tackling Crack: a national plan.* London: Home Office.

Home Office, Department of Health and Department for Children, Schools and Families (2008) *Safe. Sensible. Social. Alcohol strategy local implementation toolkit.* London: DH/Home Office.

Howard, D.E. and Wang, M.Q. (2003) 'Risk profiles of adolescent girls who were victims of dating violence', *Adolescence*, 38 (149), 1–14.

Hughes, L. (2006) *Closing the gap. A capability framework for working effectively with people with combined mental health and substance use problems (dual diagnosis).* Mansfield, Nottinghamshire: University of Lincoln.

Humphreys, C., River, D. and Thiara, R.K. (2004) *Domestic violence and substance misuse. 'Mind the gap.'* Interim report for the Drug Strategy Directorate and the Greater London Authority.

Humphreys, C., Thiara, R.K. and Regan, L. (2005) *Domestic violence and substance use: Overlapping issues in separate services?* Briefing report. London: Greater London Authority.

Hurcombe, R., Bayley, M. and Goodman, A. (2010) *Ethnicity and alcohol: A review of the UK literature. Summary report.* York: Joseph Rowntree Foundation. Available at www.jrf.org.uk.

Huxley, A., Copello, A. and Day, E. (2005) 'Substance misuse and the need for integrated services', *Learning Disability Practice*, 8 (6), 14–17.

IAS (Institute of Alcohol Studies) (2010) *Alcohol and the elderly.* Cambridgeshire: IAS.

Jack, G. and Jack, D. (2000) 'Ecological social work: the application of a systems model of development in context', in P. Stepney and D. Ford (eds) *Social work models, methods and theories.* Lyme Regis, Dorset: Russell House.

Jobling, A. and Cuskelly, M. (2006) 'Young people with Down syndrome: a preliminary investigation of health knowledge and associated behaviours', *Journal of Intellectual and Developmental Disability*, 31 (4), 210–18.

Johnson, M.R.D., Menzies Banton, P., Dhillon, H., Subhra, G. and Hough, J. (2006) *Alcohol issues and the South Asian and African Caribbean communities. Improving education, research and service development.* Available online at: www.aerc.org.uk/documents/pdfs/finalReports/AERC_FinalReport_0028.pdf [accessed 11 July 2011].

Jonas, S., Bebbington, P., McManus, S., Meltzer, H., Jenkins, R., Kuipers, E., Cooper, C., King, M. and Brugha, T. (2011) 'Sexual abuse and psychiatric disorder in England: results from the 2007 Adult Psychiatric Morbidity Survey', *Psychological Medicine*, 41 (4), 709–19.

Jones, A., Donmall, M., Millar, T., Moody, A., Weston, S., Anderson, T., Gittins, M., Abeywardana, V. and D'Souza, J. (2009) *The Drug Treatment Outcomes Research Study (DTORS): Final outcomes report.* London: Home Office.

Jotangia, D., Ogunbadejo, T. and Simmonds, N. (2010) 'Drug use', in E. Fuller and M. Sanchez (eds) *Smoking, drinking and drug use among young people in England in 2009.* London: National Centre for Social Research. Available online at: www.natcen.ac.uk/media/492705/77cb8734-85f3-440d-9617-fb072f787bc4.pdf [accessed 26 July 2011].

Kalunta-Crumpton, A. (2004) A community without a drug problem? Black drug use in Britain', *Social Justice*, 31 (1/2), 200–16. Available online at: http://findarticles.com/p/articles/mi_hb3427/is_1-2_31/ai_n29150707/ [accessed 6 July 2011].

Kalunta-Crumpton, A. (2007) 'Black problem drug users: drug treatment service provisions and delivery', *Prison Service Journal*, 172, 32–7.

Kent, R. (1995) *Alcohol interventions: Education and training for CCETSW's post qualifying and advanced awards in social work. Guidelines for social workers, employers and training programmes.* London: CCETSW.

Kershaw, C., Nicholas, S. and Walker, A. (eds) (2008) *Crime in England and Wales 2007/08. Findings from the British Crime Survey and police recorded crime.* London: HMSO.

Klein, C.W. and Jess, C. (2002) 'One last pleasure? Alcohol use among elderly people in nursing homes', *Health and Social Work*, 27 (3), 193–20.

Krahn, G., Deck, D., Gabriel, R. and Farrell, N. (2007) 'A population-based study on substance abuse treatment for adults with disabilities: access, utilization, and treatment outcomes', *The American Journal of Drug and Alcohol Abuse*, 33, 791–8.

Krahn, G., Farrell, N., Gabriel, R. and Deck, D. (2006) 'Access barriers to substance abuse treatment for persons with disabilities: an exploratory study', *Journal of Substance Abuse Treatment*, 31, 375–84.

Kroll, B. and Taylor, A. (2003) *Parental substance use and child welfare.* London: Jessica Kingsley.

Kuntsche, E. and Kuendig, H. (2006) 'What is worse? A hierarchy of family-related risk factors predicting alcohol use in adolescence', *Substance Use and Misuse*, 41 (1), 71–86.

Kvaternik, I. and Grebenc, V. (2009) 'The role of social work in the field of mental health: dual diagnoses as a challenge for social workers', *European Journal of Social Work*, 12 (4), 509–21.

Lader, D. and Steel, M. (2010) *Drinking: Adults' behaviour and knowledge in 2009*. Opinions Survey Report No. 42. Available online at: www.statistics. gov.uk/downloads/theme_health/drink2009.pdf [accessed 25 August 2011].

Laing, I., Wallace, R.B., Huppert, F.A. and Melzer, D. (2007) 'Moderate alcohol consumption in older adults is associated with better cognition and well-being than abstinence', *Age and Ageing*, 36, 256–61.

Laming, Lord (2009) *The protection of children in England: A progress report*. London: The Stationery Office.

Law Commission (2011) *Adult social care* (Law Com No. 326) HC 941. London: The Stationery Office. Available online at: www.justice.gov.uk/ lawcommission/ docs/lc326_adult_social_care.pdf [accessed 21 June 2011].

Lawrence-Jones, J. (2010) 'Dual diagnosis (drug/alcohol and mental health): service user experiences', *Practice: Social Work in Action*, 22 (2), 115–31.

Lawson, A. (1994) 'Identification of and responses to problem drinking amongst social services users', *British Journal of Social Work*, 24, 325–42.

Leonard, K.E. and Quigley, B.M. (1999) 'Drinking and marital aggression in newlyweds: an event-based analysis of drinking and the occurrence of husband marital aggression', *Journal of Studies on Alcohol*, 60 (4), 537–45.

Leonard, K.E. and Senchak, M. (1996) 'Prospective prediction of husband marital aggression within newlywed couples', *Journal of Abnormal Psychology*, 105 (3), 369–80.

Levy, J.A. and Anderson, T. (2005) 'The drug career of the older injector', *Addiction Research and Theory*, 13 (3), 245–58.

Li, L., Ford, J. and Moore, D. (2000) 'An exploratory study of violence, substance abuse, disability and gender', *Social Behavior and Personality*, 28 (1), 61–72.

Loughran, H., Hohman, M., and Finnegan, D. (2010) 'Predictors of role legitimacy and role adaquacy of social workers working with substance-using clients', *British Journal of Social Work*, 40 (1), 239–56.

Luger, L. and Sookhoo, D. (2005) 'Rapid needs assessment of the provision of drug and alcohol services for people from minority ethnic groups with drug and alcohol problems', *Diversity in Health and Social Care*, 2 (3), 167–76.

Maag, J.W., Irvin, D.M., Reid, R. and Vasa, S.F. (1994) 'Prevalence and predictors of substance use: a comparison between adolescents with and without learning disabilities', *Journal of Learning Disabilities*, 27 (4), 223–34.

McAlpine, C., Courts Marshall, C. and Harper Doran, N. (2001) 'Combining child welfare and substance abuse services: a blended model of intervention', *Child Welfare*, 80 (2), 129–49.

MacAndrew, C. and Edgerton, R.B. (1969) *Drunken comportment: A social explanation*. New York: Aldine.

McAuley, C. and Young, C. (2006) 'The mental health of looked after children: challenges for CAMHS provision', *Journal of Social Work Practice*, 20 (1), 91–103.

McCabe, S.E., Morales, M., Cranford, J.A., Delva, J., McPherson, M.D. and Boyd, C.J. (2007) 'Race/ethnicity and gender differences in drug use and abuse among college students', *Journal of Ethnicity in Substance Abuse*, 6 (2), 75–95.

McCambridge, J. and Strang, J. (2005) 'Can it really be this black and white? An analysis of the relative importance of ethnic group and other sociodemographic factors to patterns of drug use and related risk among young Londoners', *Drugs: Education, Prevention and Policy*, 12 (2), 149–59.

McCarthy, T. and Galvani, S. (2004) 'SCARS: a new model for social work with substance users', *Practice*, 16 (2), 85–97.

McCarthy, T. and Galvani, S. (2010) *Alcohol and other drugs: Essential information for social workers. A BASW pocket guide*. Luton: University of Bedfordshire.

McCaul, K.A., Almeida, O.P., Hankey, G.J., Jamrozik, K., Byles, J.E. and Flicker, L. (2010) 'Alcohol use and mortality in older men and women', *Addiction*, 105 (8), 1391–400.

McCusker, C.G., Clare, I.C.H., Cullen, C. and Reep, J. (1993) 'Alcohol-related knowledge and attitudes in people with a mild learning disability – the effects of a "sensible drinking" group', *Journal of Community and Applied Social Psychology*, 3 (1), 29–40.

MacDonald, E.M., Luxmoore, M., Pica, S., Tanti, C., Blackman, J.M., Catford, N. and Stockton, P. (2004) 'Social networks of people with dual diagnosis: the quantity and quality of relationships at different stages of substance use treatment', *Community Mental Health Journal*, 40 (5), 451–64.

McGillicuddy, N.B. and Blane, H.T. (1999) 'Substance use in individuals with mental retardation', *Addictive Behaviors*, 24 (6), 869–78.

McGillivray, J.A. and Moore, M.R. (2001) 'Substance use by offenders with mild intellectual disability', *Journal of Intellectual and Developmental Disability*, 26 (4), 297–310.

McGuire, B.E., Daly, P. and Smyth, F. (2007) 'Lifestyle and health behaviours of adults with an intellectual disability', *Journal of Intellectual Disability Research*, 51 (7), 497–510.

McKeganey, N., Neale, J. and Robertson, M. (2005) 'Physical and sexual abuse among drug users contacting drug treatment services in Scotland', *Drugs: Education, Prevention and Policy*, 12 (3), 223–32.

McLaughlin, D.F., Taggart, L., Quinn, B. and Milligan, V. (2007) 'The experiences of professionals who care for people with intellectual disability who have substance-related problems', *Journal of Substance Use*, 12 (2), 133–43.

McManus, S., Meltzer, H., Brugha, T., Bebbington, P. and Jenkins, R. (eds) (2009) *Adult psychiatric morbidity in England, 2007. Results of a household survey.* Available online at: www.ic.nhs.uk/webfiles/publications/mental%20health/other%20mental%20health%20publications/Adult%20psychiatric%20morbidity%202007/APMS%202007%20%28FINAL%29%20Standard.pdf [accessed 24 August 2011].

Mahoney, C. and MacKechnie, S. (eds) (2001) *In a different world. Parental drug and alcohol use: A consultation into its effects on children and families in Liverpool.* Liverpool: Liverpool Health Authority.

Mallett, C.A. (2009) 'Disparate juvenile court outcomes for disabled delinquent youth: a social work call to action', *Journal of Child and Adolescent Social Work*, 26, 197–207.

Manning, V., Best, D.W., Faulkner, N. and Titherington, E. (2009) *New estimates of the number of children living with substance misusing parents: Results from UK national household surveys.* Available online at: www.biomedcentral.com/content/pdf/1471-2458-9-377.pdf [accessed 15 May 2011].

Manning, V.C., Strathdee, G., Best, D., Keaney, F. and McGillivray, L. (2002) 'Dual diagnosis screening: preliminary findings on the comparison of 50 clients attending community mental health services and 50 clients attending community substance misuse services', *Journal of Substance Use*, 7 (4), 221–8.

Manthorpe, J., Walsh, M., Alaszewski, A. and Harrison, L. (1997) 'Issues of risk practice and welfare in learning disability services', *Disability and Society*, 12 (1), 69–82.

Mariathasan, J. and Hutchinson, D. (2010) *Children talking to ChildLine about parental alcohol and drug misuse.* ChildLine Casenotes series. London: NSPCC.

Marlatt, G.A. and Gordon, J.R. (1985) *Relapse prevention: Maintenance strategies in the treatment of addictive behaviors.* New York: Guilford Press.

Mattson, M.E. (1995) 'Preface', *Twelve step facilitation therapy manual*, vol 1. Available online at: http://pubs.niaaa.nih.gov/publications/MATCHSeries3/preface.htm [accessed 29 July 2009].

Mencap (2000) *Am I making myself clear? Mencap's guidelines for accessible writing.* Available online at: www.mencap.org.uk/sites/default/files/documents/2009-07/Am%20%20I%20%20making%20%20myself%20%20clear%20%5B1%5D.pdf [accessed 8 June 2011].

Mencap (2011) 'Hate crime: real life stories'. Available online at: www.mencap.org.uk/campaigns/what-we-campaign-about/equal-rights/hate-crime-real-life-stories [accessed 8 June 2011].

Menezes, P.R., Johnson, S., Thornicroft, G., Marshall, J., Prosser, D., Bebbington, P. and Kuipers, E. (1996) 'Drug and alcohol problems among individuals with severe mental illness in South London', *British Journal of Psychiatry*, 168, 612–19.

Messman-Moore, T.L., Ward, R.M. and Brown, A.L. (2009) 'Substance use and PTSD symptoms impact the likelihood of rape and revictimization in college women', *Journal of Interpersonal Violence*, 24, 499–521.

Millard, B. (2011) 'Extent and trends in illicit drug use', in K. Smith and J. Flatley (eds) *Drug misuse declared: Findings from the 2010/11 British Crime Survey England and Wales*. London: HMSO.

Miller, B.A., Wilsnack, S.C. and Cunradi, C.B. (2000) 'Family violence and victimization: treatment issues for women with alcohol problems', *Alcoholism: Clinical & Experimental Research*, 24 (8), 1287–97.

Miller, W.R. and Rollnick, S. (eds) (2002) *Motivational interviewing: Preparing people to change addictive behaviour*. 2nd edn. London: Guilford Press.

Miller, W.R. and Rollnick, S. (eds) (in press) *Motivational interviewing*. 3rd edn. London: Guilford Press.

Miller, W.R., Zweben, A., Di Clemente, C.C., Richtaryk, R.C. (1995) *Motivational enhancement therapy manual: A clinical research guide for therapists treating individuals with alcohol abuse and dependence*. Rockville, MD: National Institute on Alcohol Abuse and Alcoholism /DIANE Publishing.

Miller-Day, M. and Barnett, J. (2004) '"I'm not a druggie": adolescents' ethnicity and (erroneous) beliefs about drug use norms', *Health Communication*, 16 (2), 207–28.

Mirrlees-Black, C. (1999) *Domestic violence: Findings from a new British Crime Survey self-completion questionnaire*. London: HMSO.

Misca, G. (2009) 'Perspectives on the life course: childhood and adolescence', in R. Adams, L. Dominelli and M. Payne (eds) *Social work: Themes, issues and critical debates*. 3rd edn. Basingstoke: Palgrave Macmillan.

Mitchell, A.J., Malone, D. and Doebbeling, C.C. (2009) 'Quality of medical care for people with and without comorbid mental illness and substance misuse: systematic review of comparative studies', *British Journal of Psychiatry*, 194 (6), 491–9.

Molina, B.S.G. and Pelham, W.E. (2001) 'Substance use, substance abuse, and LD among adolescents with a childhood history of ADHD', *Journal of Learning Disabilities*, 34, 333–52.

Moore, A., Whiteman, E.J. and Ward, K.T. (2007) 'Risks of combined alcohol/medication use in older adults', *The American Journal of Geriatric Pharmacotherapy*, 5 (1), 64–74.

Moore, D. (1998) *Substance use disorder treatment for people with physical and cognitive disabilities*. Treatment Improvement Protocol (TIP) Series 29. DHHS Publication No. (SMA) 98–3249. Rockville, MD: Substance Abuse and Mental Health Services Administration.

Moore, D., Guthmann, D., Rogers, N., Fraker, S. and Embree, J. (2009) 'E-therapy as a means for addressing barriers to substance use disorder treatment for persons who are deaf', *Journal of Sociology & Social Welfare*, 36 (4), 75–92.

Morley, R. and Mullender, A. (1994) 'Domestic violence and children: what do we know from research?' in A. Mullender and R. Morley (eds) *Children living with domestic violence: Putting men's abuse of women on the child care agenda*. London: Whiting and Birch.

Moselhy, H.F. (2009) 'Co-morbid post-traumatic stress disorder and opioid dependence syndrome', *Journal of Dual Diagnosis*, 5 (1), 30–40.

Mueser, K.T., Drake, R.E., Sigmon, S.C. and Brunette, M.F. (2005) 'Psychosocial interventions for adults with severe mental illnesses and co-occurring substance use disorders: a review of specific interventions', *Journal of Dual Diagnosis*, 1 (2), 57–82.

Mullender, A., Hague, G., Imam, U., Kelly, L., Malos, E. and Regan, L. (2002) *Children's perspectives on domestic violence*. London: Sage.

Munro, E. (2011) *The Munro Review of Child Protection: Final Report: A child-centred system*. London: DfE.

National Institute of Neurological Disorders and Stroke (2007) 'Wernicke-Korsakoff Syndrome information page'. Available online at: www.ninds. nih.gov/disorders/wernicke_korsakoff/wernicke-korsakoff.htm [accessed 1 May 2010].

Needham, M. (2007) *Changing habits. North West dual diagnosis intelligence report. Informing the commissioning, management and provision of integrated service provision for dual diagnosis treatment populations. Emerging findings – access to mental health treatment for adults with substance and/or alcohol misuse problems. Part of the CSIP national dual diagnosis programme*. Hyde, Cheshire: North West CSIP.

Newman, T. and Blackburn, S. (2002) *Transitions in the lives of children and young people: Resilience factors*. Edinburgh: Scottish Executive.

NHS Health Advisory Service (1996) *The substance of young needs: Children and young people substance misuse services*. London: HMSO.

NHS Choices (2011) 'Alcohol units'. Available online at: www.nhs.uk/ Livewell/alcohol/Pages/alcohol-units.aspx [accessed 3 August 2011].

NIAAA (National Institute on Alcohol Abuse and Alcoholism) (2005) 'Module 10I disabilities and alcohol use disorders'. Available online at: http://pubs.niaaa.nih.gov/publications/social/Module10IDisabilities/ Module10I.html [accessed October 2010].

NICE (National Institute for Health and Clinical Excellence) (2007) *Drug misuse psychosocial interventions*. London: NICE.

NICE (2010) *Alcohol-use disorders: Preventing the development of hazardous and harmful drinking*. NICE Public Health Guidance 24. Available online at: www.nice.org.uk/guidance/PH24 [accessed 25 July 2011].

NICE (2011a) *Alcohol-use disorders. Diagnosis, assessment and management of harmful drinking and alcohol dependence*. London: NICE.

NICE (2011b) *Psychosis with coexisting substance misuse. Assessment and management in adults and young people.* Available online at: www.nice.org.uk/nicemedia/live/13414/53729/53729.pdf [accessed 29 August 2011].

NSPCC (2008) *Seeing and hearing the child: Rising to the challenge of parental substance misuse.* London: NSPCC Available online at: www.nspcc.org.uk/inform/trainingandconsultancy/learningresources/seeingandhearing_wda56195.html [accessed 17 August 2011].

NTA (National Treatment Agency) (2006) *Models of care for the treatment of adult drug misusers: Update 2006.* London: NTA.

NTA (2007) *Good practice in care planning.* London: NTA.

NTA (2009) *Diversity: Learning from good practice in the field.* Available online at: www.nta.nhs.uk [accessed 18 July 2011].

NTA (2010a) *A long-term study of the outcomes of drug users leaving treatment.* London: NTA.

NTA (2010b) 'Equality analysis: audit tool'. Available online at: www.nta.nhs.uk/equality-analysis-checklist.aspx [accessed 15 August 2011].

NTA (2010c) *Substance misuse among young people: The data for 2009–10.* London: NTA.

NTA (2011) *Supporting information for the development of joint local protocols between drug and alcohol partnerships, children and family services.* London: NTA.

O'Connell, H., Chin, A., Cunningham, C. and Lawlor, B. (2003) 'Alcohol use disorders in elderly people – redefining an age old problem in old age', *British Medical Journal*, 327 (20), 664–7.

O'Farrell, T.J., Fals-Stewart, W., Murphy, C.M., Stephan, S.H. and Murphy, M. (2004) 'Partner violence before and after couples-based alcoholism treatment for male alcoholic patients: the role of treatment involvement and abstinence', *Journal of Consulting and Clinical Psychology*, 72 (2), 202–17.

Ofsted (2008) *Learning lessons, taking action: Ofsted's evaluations of serious case reviews 1 April 2007 to 31 March 2008.* Available online at: www.ofsted.gov.uk [accessed 29 March 2010].

O'Hare, T., Sherrer, M.V., LaButti, A. and Emrick, K. (2004) 'Validating the Alcohol Use Disorders Identification Test with persons who have a serious mental illness', *Research on Social Work Practice*, 14 (1), 36–42.

Okiishi, J., Lambert, M.J., Nielsen, S.L. and Ogles, B.M. (2003) 'Waiting for supershrink: an empirical analysis of therapist effects', *Clinical Psychology & Psychotherapy*, 10 (6), 361–73.

ONS (Office for National Statistics) (2009a) 'Ageing'. Available online at: www.statistics.gov.uk/cci/nugget.asp?ID=949 [accessed 27 April 2010].

ONS (2009b) 'Healthy life expectancy'. Available on line at: www.statistics.gov.uk/cci/nugget.asp?id=2159 [accessed 27 April 2010].

ONS (2010) *Population by country of birth and nationality Oct 2009 to Sep 2010. Table 2.3. Estimated population resident in the United Kingdom, by foreign nationality. 60 most common nationalities.* Available online at: www.statistics. gov.uk/statbase/Product.asp?vlnk=15147 [accessed 4 July 2011].

Orford, J., Templeton, L., Patel, A., Copello, A. and Velleman, R. (2007) 'The 5-step family intervention in primary care: I. Strengths and limitations according to family members', *Drugs: Education, Prevention and Policy*, 14 (1), 29–47.

Ouimette, P.C., Finney, J.W. and Moos, R.H. (1997) 'Twelve-step and cognitive-behavioral treatment for substance abuse: a comparison of treatment effectiveness', *Journal of Consulting and Clinical Psychology*, 65 (2), 230–40.

Parfrement-Hopkins, J. (2011) 'Extent and trends', in R. Chaplin, J. Flatley and K. Smith (eds) *Crime in England and Wales 2010/11. Findings from the British Crime Survey and police recorded crime.* 1st edn. London: Home Office. Available online at: www.homeoffice.gov.uk/publications/science-research-statistics/research-statistics/crime-research/hosb1011/ [accessed 22 August 2011].

Pavee Point (2007) *Spring 2007 e-bulletin.* Available online at: www. paveepoint.ie/pdf/DrugsInitiativeNews07.pdf [accessed 16 August 2011].

Peele, S. and Alexander, B. (1998) 'Theories of addiction', in S. Peele (ed) *The meaning of addiction. Compulsive experience and its interpretation.* Available online at: http://peele.net/lib/moa.html [accessed 6 August 2011].

Philp, I. (2006) *A new ambition for old age. Next steps in implementing the National Service Framework for Older People.* London: Department of Health.

Powell, B.J., Landon, J.F., Cantrell, P.J., Penick, E.C., Nickel, E.J., Liskow, B.I., Coddington, T.M., Campbell, J.L., Dale, T.M., Vance, M.D. and Rice, A.S. (1998) 'Prediction of drinking outcomes for male alcoholics after 10 to 14 years', *Alcoholism: Clinical and Experimental Research*, 22 (3), 559–66.

Preston-Shoot, M. (2012) 'The legal foundations of social work in the field of drug and alcohol abuse', in M. Davies (ed) (2012) *Social work with adults: From policy to practice.* Basingstoke: Palgrave Macmillan (forthcoming).

Prochaska, J.O., DiClemente, C.C. and Norcross, J.C. (1992) 'In search of how people change: applications to addictive behaviors', *American Psychologist*, 4 (9), 1102–14.

Project MATCH Research Group (1998) 'Therapist effects in three treatments for alcohol problems', *Psychotherapy Research*, 8 (4), 455–74.

Raistrick, D., Heather, N. and Godfrey, C. (2006) *Review of the effectiveness of treatment for alcohol problems.* London: NTA.

Rao, R. (2006) 'Alcohol misuse and ethnicity', *British Medical Journal*, 332 (7543), 682.

Rapuri, P.B., Gallagher, J.C., Balhorn, K.E. and Ryschon, K.L. (2000) 'Alcohol intake and bone metabolism in elderly women', *American Journal of Clinical Nutrition*, 72, 1206–13.

RCP (Royal College of Psychiatrists) (2011) *Our invisible addicts*. London: RCP. Available online at: www.rcpsych.ac.uk/files/pdfversion/CR165. pdf [accessed 25 August 2011].

Redelinghuys, J. and Dar, K. (2008) 'A survey of parents receiving treatment for substance dependence: the impact on their children', *Journal of Substance Use*, 13 (1), 37–48.

Reid, G., Aitken, C., Beyer, L. and Crofts, N. (2001) 'Ethnic communities' vulnerability to involvement with illicit drugs', *Drugs: Education, Prevention and Policy*, 8 (4), 359–74.

Respect and Relate (2008) *Indicators for referral to couples counselling following domestic violence prevention programme attendance*. Available online at: www. respect.uk.net/data/files/indicators_for_referral_to_couples_work_final. pdf [accessed 23 August 2011].

Rethink Dual Diagnosis Research Group (2004) *Living with severe mental health and substance use problems*. Research report. London: Adfam and Rethink.

Richards, M., Doyle, M. and Cook, P. (2009) 'A literature review of family interventions for dual diagnosis: implications for forensic mental health services', *British Journal of Forensic Practice*, 11 (4), 39–49.

Richter, K.P. and Bammer, G. (2000) 'A hierarchy of strategies heroin-using mothers employ to reduce harm to their children', *Journal of Substance Abuse Treatment*, 19, 403–13.

Rivaux, S.L., Sohn, S., Peterson Armour, M. and Bell, H. (2008) 'Women's early recovery: managing the dilemma of substance abuse and intimate partner relationships', *Journal of Drug Issues*, 38 (4), 957–79.

Robinson, S. and Harris, H. (2011) *Smoking and drinking among adults, 2009. A report on the 2009 General Lifestyle Survey*. London: Office for National Statistics.

Rodham, K., Hawton, K., Evans, E. and Weatherall, R. (2005) 'Ethnic and gender differences in drinking, smoking and drug taking among adolescents in England: a self-report school-based survey of 15 and 16 year olds', *Journal of Adolescence*, 28 (1), 63–73.

Rollnick, S. and Miller, W.R. (1995) 'What is motivational interviewing?' *Behavioural and Cognitive Psychotherapy*, 23 (4), 325–34.

Room, R., Bondy, S.J. and Ferris, J. (1995) 'The risk of harm to oneself from drinking, Canada 1989', *Addiction*, 90, 499–513.

Rossow, I. (1996) 'Alcohol-related violence: the impact of drinking pattern and drinking context', *Addiction*, 91 (11), 1651–61.

Roxburgh, M., Donmall, M., White, M. and Jones, A. (2010) *Statistics from the National Drug Treatment Monitoring System (NDTMS) 1 April 2009 – 31 March 2010.* London: DH/NTA.

Sample, E.B., Li, L. and Moore, D. (1997) 'Alcohol use, ethnicity and disability. A comparison of African-American and Caucasian groups', *Social Behavior and Personality,* 25 (3), 265–76.

Sangster, D., Shiner, M., Patel, K. and Sheikh, N. (2002) 'Delivering drug services to black and ethnic-minority communities'. DPAS paper 16. Available online at: www.emcdda.europe.eu [accessed 18 July 2011].

Satre, D.D., Mertens, J.F., Areán, P.A. and Weisner, C. (2004) 'Five-year alcohol and drug treatment outcomes of older adults versus middle-aged and younger adults in a managed care program', *Addiction,* 99, 1286–97.

Schumacher, J.A., Fals-Stewart, W. and Leonard, K.E. (2003) 'Domestic violence treatment referrals for men seeking alcohol treatment', *Journal of Substance Abuse Treatment,* 24, 279–83.

Schütt, N. (2006) *Domestic violence in adolescent relationships. Young people in Southwark and their experiences with unhealthy relationships.* London: Safer Southwark Partnership.

Scottish Education Department Social Work Services Group (1988) *Practice guidance: Towards effective practise with problem drinkers.* Scotland: SWSG.

Scottish Executive (2001) *Getting Our Priorities Right. Policy and practice guidelines for working with children and families affected by problem drug use. A consultation paper.* Edinburgh: Scottish Executive.

Shaw, C. and Palattiyil, G. (2008) 'Issues of alcohol misuse among older people: attitudes and experiences of social work practitioners', *Practice,* 20 (3), 181–93.

Silverman, J.G., Raj, A., Mucci, L.A. and Hathaway, J.E. (2001) 'Dating violence against adolescent girls and associated substance use, unhealthy weight control, sexual risk behavior, pregnancy, and suicidality', *Journal of the American Medical Association,* 286, 572–9.

Simeons, S., Matheson, C., Inkster, K., Ludbrook, A. and Bond, C. (2004) *The effectiveness of treatment for opiate dependent drug users: An international systematic review of the evidence.* Edinburgh: Effective Interventions Unit, Scottish Executive.

Simpson, M.K. (1998) 'Just say "no"? Alcohol and people with learning difficulties', *Disability and Society,* 13 (4), 541–55.

Simpson, T.L. and Miller, W.R. (2002) 'Concomitance between childhood sexual and physical abuse and substance use problems: a review', *Clinical Psychology Review,* 22 (1), 27–77.

Slayter, E.M. (2007) 'Substance abuse and mental retardation: balancing risk management with the "dignity of risk"', *Families in Society,* 88 (4), 651–9.

Slayter, E.M. (2008) 'Understanding and overcoming barriers to substance abuse treatment access for people with mental retardation', *Journal of Social Work in Disability and Rehabilitation*, 7 (2), 63–80.

Slayter, E.M. and Steenrod, S.A. (2009) 'Addressing alcohol and drug addiction among people with mental retardation in nonaddiction settings: a need for cross-system collaboration', *Journal of Social Work Practice in the Addictions*, 9 (1), 71–90.

Smale, G., Tuson, G. and Statham, D. (2000) *Social work and social problems: Working towards social inclusion and social change*. Basingstoke: Macmillan.

Snow, P.C., Wallace, S.D. and Munro, G.D. (2001) 'Drug education with special needs populations: identifying and understanding the challenges', *Drugs: Education, Prevention and Policy*, 8 (3), 261–73.

Social Work Task Force (2009) *Building a safe, confident future. The final report of the Social Work Task Force*. Available online at: https://www.education.gov.uk/publications/eOrderingDownload/01114-2009DOM-EN.pdf [accessed 17 May 2011].

Sociology Guide (2011) 'Acculturation.' Available online at: www.sociologyguide.com/basic-concepts/Acculturation.php [accessed 8 July 2011].

Stanley, N., Miller, P., Richardson Foster, H. and Thomson, G. (2010) *Children and families experiencing domestic violence: Police and children's social services' responses*. Available online at: www.nspcc.org.uk/Inform/research/findings/children_experiencing_domestic_violence_wda68549.html [accessed 23 August 2011].

Stella Project (2007) *Domestic violence, drugs and alcohol: Good practice guidelines*. 2nd edn. London: The Stella Project.

Stillwell, G., Boys, A. and Marsden, J. (2004) 'Alcohol use by young people from different ethnic groups: consumption, intoxication and negative consequences', *Ethnicity & Health*, 9 (2), 171–87.

Strada, M.J., Donohue, B. and Lefforge, N.L. (2006) 'Examination of ethnicity in controlled treatment outcome studies involving adolescent substance abusers: a comprehensive literature review', *Psychology of Addictive Behaviors*, 20 (1), 11–27.

Stuart, G.L., O'Farrell, T.J. and Temple, J.F. (2009) 'Review of the association between treatment for substance misuse and reductions in intimate partner violence', *Substance Use & Misuse*, 44, 1298–317.

Suchman, N.E. and Luther, S. (2000) 'Maternal addiction, child maladjustment and socio-demographic risks: implications for parent's behaviors', *Addiction*, 95, 1417–28.

Swan, S., Farber, S. and Campbell, D. (2001) *Violence in the lives of women in substance abuse treatment: Service and policy implications*. Report to the New York State Office for the Prevention of Domestic Violence, Rensselear, New York.

Taggart, L., Huxley, A. and Baker, G. (2008) 'Alcohol and illicit drug misuse in people with learning disabilities: implications for research and service development', *Advances in Mental Health and Learning Disabilities*, 2 (1), 11–21.

Taggart, L., McLaughlin, D., Quinn, B. and McFarlane, C. (2007) 'Listening to people with intellectual disabilities who misuse alcohol and drugs', *Health and Social Care in the Community*, 15 (4), 360–8.

Talbot, S. and Crabbe, T. (2008) *Binge drinking: Young people's attitudes and behaviour.* London: Positive Futures/Crime Concern.

Taylor, L.A., Kreutzer, J.S., Demm, S.R. and Meade, M.A. (2003) 'Traumatic brain injury and substance abuse: a review and analysis of the literature', *Neuropsychological Rehabilitation*, 13 (1), 165–88.

Templeton, L.J., Zohhadi, S.E. and Velleman, R.D.B. (2007) 'Working with family members in specialist drug and alcohol services: findings from a feasibility study', *Drugs: Education, Prevention and Policy*, 14 (2), 137–50.

Templeton, L., Zohhadi, S., Galvani, S. and Velleman, R. (2006) *Looking beyond risk: Parental substance misuse: Scoping study.* Research report to Scottish Executive. Available at: www.scotland.gov.uk/Publications/2006/07/05120121/0.

Titus, J.C. and White, W.L. (2008) 'Substance use among youths who are deaf and hard of hearing: a primer for student assistance professionals', *Student Assistance Journal*, late fall, 14–18.

TOPSS (2002) *The National Occupational Standards for Social Work.* London: TOPSS.

Tracy, E.M. and Martin, T.C. (2007) 'Children's roles in the social networks of women in substance abuse treatment', *Journal of Substance Abuse Treatment*, 32, 81–8.

Tracy, S.W., Kelly, J.F. and Moos, R.H. (2005) 'The influence of partner status, relationship quality and relationship stability on outcomes following intensive substance-use disorder treatment', *Journal of Studies on Alcohol*, 66, 497–505.

Trippier, J. and Parker, S. (2008) 'Reflections on the role of the specialist dual diagnosis clinician', *Advances in Dual Diagnosis*, 1 (1), 14–19.

Tunnard, J. (2002) *Parental drug misuse – a review of impact and intervention studies.* Available online at: www.rip.org.uk.

Turner, R.J., Lloyd, D.A. and Taylor, J. (2006) 'Physical disability and mental health: an epidemiology of psychiatric and substance disorders', *Rehabilitation Psychology*, 51 (3), 214–23.

UKATT Research Team (2005) 'Effectiveness of treatment for alcohol problems: findings of the randomised UK alcohol treatment trial (UKATT)', *British Medical Journal*, 351, 541–4.

UKDPC (UK Drug Policy Commission) (2008) *Recovery consensus statement.* Available online at: www.ukdpc.org.uk/ Recovery_Consensus_Statement. shtml [accessed May 2011].

UKDPC (2010) *Drugs and diversity: Disabled people. Learning from the evidence.* Available online at: www.ukdpc.org.uk/resources/disabled_policy_briefing.pdf [accessed 31 August 2011].

Van Cleemput, P. (2010) 'Social exclusion of Gypsies and Travellers: health impact', *Journal of Research in Nursing*, 15, 315–27.

Van Hout, M.C. (2010a) 'Alcohol use and the Traveller community in the west of Ireland', *Drug and Alcohol Review*, 29, 59–63.

Van Hout, M.C. (2010b) 'The Irish Traveller community: social capital and drug use', *Journal of Ethnicity in Substance Abuse*, 9, 186–205.

Van Tubergen, F. and Poortman, A.-R. (2010) 'Adolescent alcohol use in the Netherlands: the role of ethnicity, ethnic intermarriage, and ethnic school composition', *Ethnicity and Health*, 15 (1), 1–13.

Vandevelde, S., Vanderplasschen, W. and Broekaert, E. (2003) 'Cultural responsiveness in substance-abuse treatment: a qualitative study using professionals' and clients' perspectives', *International Journal of Social Welfare*, 12, 221–8.

Velleman, R. and Baker, A. (2008) 'Moving away from medicalised and partisan terminology: a contribution to the debate', *Mental Health and Substance Use: Dual Diagnosis*, 1 (1), 2–9.

Velleman, R. and Orford, J. (1999) *Risk and resilience: Adults who were the children of problem drinkers.* London: Martin Dunitz.

Vogt Yuan, A. (2011) 'Black–white differences in aging out of substance use and abuse', *Sociological Spectrum*, 31 (1), 3–31.

Volk, R.J., Steinbauer, J.R., Cantor, S.B. and Holzer, C.E. (1997) 'The alcohol use disorders identification test (AUDIT) as a screen for at-risk drinking in primary care patients of different racial/ethnic backgrounds', *Addiction*, 92 (2), 197–206.

Waern, M. (2003) 'Alcohol dependence and misuse in elderly suicides', *Alcohol and Alcoholism*, 38 (3), 249–54.

Wales, A. and Gillan, E. (2009) *Untold damage: Children's accounts of living with harmful parental drinking.* London: NSPCC.

Wanigaratne, S., Dar, K., Abdulrahim, D. and Strang, J. (2003) 'Ethnicity and drug use: exploring the nature of particular relationships among diverse populations in the United Kingdom', *Drugs: Education, Prevention and Policy*, 10 (1), 39–55.

Ward, L. (2008) *Cheers!? A project about older people and alcohol. Research findings.* Available at: www.brighton.ac.uk/sass/research/publications/Cheers_Findings.pdf [accessed 21 April 2010].

Ware, M.A., Adams, H. and Guy, G.W. (2005) 'The medicinal use of cannabis in the UK: results of a nationwide survey', *International Journal of Clinical Practice*, 59 (3), 291–5.

Warfa, N., Bhui, K., Phillips, K., Nandy, K. and Griffiths, S. (2006) 'Comparison of life events, substance misuse, service use and mental illness among African-Caribbean, black African and white British men in east London: a qualitative study', *Diversity in Health and Social Care*, 3 (2), 111–21.

Watson, S., Hawkings, C. and Aram, L. (2007) *Dual diagnosis: Good practice handbook*. London: Turning Point.

Welsh Assembly Government (2010) *Children and Families (Wales) Measure 2010*. Available online at: www.legislation.gov.uk/mwa/2010/1/part/3 [accessed 17 August 2011].

West, S.L. (2007) 'The accessibility of substance abuse treatment facilities in the United States for persons with disabilities', *Journal of Substance Abuse Treatment*, 33 (1), 1–5.

West, S.L., Graham, C.W. and Cifu, D.X. (2009a) 'Prevalence of persons with disabilities in alcohol/other drug treatment in the United States', *Alcoholism Treatment Quarterly*, 27 (3), 242–52.

West, S.L., Graham, C.W. and Cifu, D.X. (2009b) 'Physical and programmatic accessibility of British alcohol/other drug treatment centers', *Alcoholism Treatment Quarterly*, 27 (3), 294–304.

White, R. (2001) 'Heroin use, ethnicity and the environment: the case of the London Bangladeshi community', *Addiction*, 96, 1815–24.

WHO (World Health Organisation) (2006) *International statistical classification of diseases and related health problems. 10th revision. Version for 2007*. Available online at: http://apps.who.int/classifications/apps/icd/icd10online/ [accessed 24 May 2010].

Wilkinson, C., Allsop, S. and Chikritzhs, T. (2011) 'Alcohol pouring practices among 65- to 74-year-olds in Western Australia', *Drug and Alcohol Review*, 30 (2), 200–6.

Witkiewitz, K. and Marlatt, G.A. (2004) 'Relapse prevention for alcohol and drug problems. That was Zen, this is Tao', *American Psychologist*, 59 (4), 224–35.

Wolf-Branigin, M. (2007) 'Disability and abuse in relation to substance abuse: a descriptive analysis', *Journal of Social Work in Disability & Rehabilitation*, 6 (3), 65–74.

Women's Aid (2007) 'What is domestic violence?' Available online at: www.womensaid.org.uk/domestic-violence-articles.asp?section=000100010 02200410001&itemid=1272&itemTitle=What+is+domestic+violence [accessed 22 August 2011].

Woolfall, K., Sumnall, H. and McVeigh, J. (2008) 'Addressing the needs of children of substance using parents: an evaluation of Families First's intensive intervention. Final report for the Department of Health'. Liverpool: John Moores University.

Wu, H.Z., Temple, J.R., Shokar, N.K., Nguyen-Oghalai, T.U. and Grady, J.J. (2010) 'Differential racial/ethnic patterns in substance use initiation among young, low-income women', *The American Journal of Drug and Alcohol Abuse*, 36 (2), 123–9.

Youth Justice Board (2010) *The Youth Rehabilitation Order and other Youth Justice Provisions of the Criminal Justice and Immigration Act 2008. Practice guidance for Youth Offending Teams.* Available online at: www.yjb.gov.uk/publications/ Scripts/prodView.asp?idproduct=467&eP [accessed 19 August 2011].

Index

Note: The following abbreviations have been used – *f* = figure; *n* = note; *t* = table